Database Reliability Engineering
Designing and Operating Resilient Database Systems

Laine Campbell and Charity Majors

Beijing · Boston · Farnham · Sebastopol · Tokyo

Database Reliability Engineering

by Laine Campbell and Charity Majors

Printed in the United States of America.

Published by O'Reilly Media, Inc., 1005 Gravenstein Highway North, Sebastopol, CA 95472.

O'Reilly books may be purchased for educational, business, or sales promotional use. Online editions are also available for most titles (*http://oreilly.com/safari*). For more information, contact our corporate/institutional sales department: 800-998-9938 or *corporate@oreilly.com*.

Editors: Courtney Allen and Virginia Wilson
Production Editor: Melanie Yarbrough
Copyeditor: Bob Russell, Octal Publishing, Inc.
Proofreader: Matthew Burgoyne

Indexer: Ellen Troutman-Zaig
Interior Designer: David Futato
Cover Designer: Karen Montgomery
Illustrator: Rebecca Demarest

November 2017:   First Edition

Revision History for the First Edition
2017-10-26:   First Release

See *http://oreilly.com/catalog/errata.csp?isbn=9781491925942* for release details.

978-1-491-92594-2

[LSI]

Table of Contents

Foreword. xi

Preface. xiii

1. Introducing Database Reliability Engineering. 1
    Guiding Principles of the DBRE   2
        Protect the Data   2
        Self-Service for Scale   3
        Elimination of Toil   4
        Databases Are Not Special Snowflakes   5
        Eliminate the Barriers Between Software and Operations   5
    Operations Core Overview   6
    Hierarchy of Needs   7
        Survival and Safety   7
        Love and Belonging   8
        Esteem   9
        Self-actualization   10
    Wrapping Up   11

2. Service-Level Management. 13
    Why Do I Need Service-Level Objectives?   13
    Service-Level Indicators   15
        Latency   15
        Availability   16
        Throughput   16
        Durability   16
        Cost or Efficiency   16
    Defining Service Objectives   17

Latency Indicators   17
Availability Indicators   20
Throughput Indicators   23
Monitoring and Reporting on SLOs   25
Monitoring Availability   25
Monitoring Latency   28
Monitoring Throughput   28
Monitoring Cost and Efficiency   28
Wrapping Up   29

3. Risk Management. **31**
Risk Considerations   32
Unknown Factors and Complexity   32
Availability of Resources   33
Human Factors   33
Group Factors   34
What Do We Do?   35
What Not to Do   35
A Working Process: Bootstrapping   37
Service Risk Evaluation   38
Architectural Inventory   40
Prioritization   41
Control and Decision Making   43
Ongoing Iterations   46
Wrapping Up   48

4. Operational Visibility. **49**
The New Rules of Operational Visibility   51
Treat OpViz Systems Like BI Systems   52
Distributed Ephemeral Environments Trending to the Norm   52
Store at High Resolutions for Key Metrics   54
Keep Your Architecture Simple   55
An OpViz Framework   56
Data In   57
Telemetry/Metrics   59
Events   60
Logs   60
Data Out   60
Bootstrapping Your Monitoring   61
Is the Data Safe?   63
Is the Service Up?   64
Are the Consumers in Pain?   65

Instrumenting the Application   66
    Distributed Tracing   66
    Events and Logs   68
Instrumenting the Server or Instance   68
    Events and Logs   70
Instrumenting the Datastore   71
Datastore Connection Layer   71
    Utilization   71
    Saturation   72
    Errors   73
Internal Database Visibility   74
    Throughput and Latency Metrics   74
    Commits, Redo, and Journaling   75
    Replication State   75
    Memory Structures   76
    Locking and Concurrency   77
Database Objects   78
Database Queries   79
Database Asserts and Events   79
Wrapping Up   80

5. Infrastructure Engineering. 81
Hosts   81
    Physical Servers   81
    Operating a System and Kernel   82
    Storage Area Networks   92
    Benefits of Physical Servers   92
    Cons of Physical Servers   92
Virtualization   93
    Hypervisor   93
    Concurrency   94
    Storage   94
    Use Cases   94
Containers   95
Database as a Service   95
    Challenges of DBaaS   96
    The DBRE and the DBaaS   96
Wrapping Up   97

6. Infrastructure Management. 99
Version Control   100
Configuration Definition   101

Building from Configuration   103
Maintaining Configuration   104
   Enforcement of Configuration Definitions   105
Infrastructure Definition and Orchestration   105
   Monolithic Infrastructure Definitions   106
   Separating Vertically   107
   Separated Tiers (Horizontal Definitions)   108
Acceptance Testing and Compliance   109
Service Catalog   109
Bringing It All Together   110
Development Environments   111
Wrapping Up   112

7. **Backup and Recovery**. **113**
Core Concepts   114
   Physical versus Logical   114
   Online versus Offline   114
   Full, Incremental, and Differential   115
Considerations for Recovery   115
Recovery Scenarios   116
   Planned Recovery Scenarios   116
   Unplanned Scenarios   118
   Scenario scope   121
   Scenario Impact   121
Anatomy of a Recovery Strategy   122
   Building Block 1: Detection   122
   Building Block 2: Tiered Storage   124
   Building Block 3: A Varied Toolbox   125
   Building Block 4: Testing   127
A Recovery Strategy Defined   128
   Online, Fast Storage with Full and Incremental Backups   128
   Online, Slow Storage with Full and Incremental Backups   129
   Offline Storage   130
   Object Storage   131
Wrapping Up   132

8. **Release Management**. **133**
Education and Collaboration   133
   Become a Funnel   134
   Foster Conversations   134
   Domain-Specific Knowledge   135
   Collaboration   137

Integration   138
  Prerequisites   139
Testing   141
  Test-Friendly Development Practices   142
  Post-Commit Testing   143
  Full Dataset Testing   144
  Downstream Tests   145
  Operational Tests   145
Deployment   146
  Migrations and Versioning   146
  Impact Analysis   147
  Migration Patterns   148
  Manual or Automated   151
Wrapping Up   151

9. Security.. 153
The Purpose of Security   153
  Protecting Data from Theft   154
  Protecting from Purposeful Damage   154
  Protecting from Accidental Damage   154
  Protecting Data from Exposure   155
  Compliance and Auditing Standards   155
Database Security as a Function   155
  Education and Collaboration   155
  Self-Service   156
  Integration and Testing   157
  Operational Visibility   158
Vulnerabilities and Exploits   160
  STRIDE   160
  DREAD   161
  Basic Precautions   162
  Denial of Service   163
  SQL Injection   166
  Network and Authentication Protocols   168
Encryption of Data   168
  Financial Data   169
  Personal Health Data   169
  Private Individual Data   170
  Military or Government Data   170
  Confidential/Sensitive Business Data   170
  Data in Transit   171
  Data in the Database   174

       Data in the Filesystem   177
       Wrapping Up   179

10. Data Storage, Indexing, and Replication. **181**
       Data Structure Storage   181
         Database Row Storage   182
         Sorted-String Tables and Log-Structured Merge Trees   185
         Indexing   188
         Logs and Databases   189
       Data Replication   189
         Single-Leader   190
         Multi-Leader Replication   203
       Wrapping Up   209

11. Datastore Field Guide. **211**
       Conceptual Attributes of a Datastore   212
         The Data Model   212
         Transactions   216
         BASE   221
       Internal Attributes of a Datastore   222
         Storage   222
         The Ubiquitous CAP Theorem Section   223
         Consistency Latency Trade-offs   225
         Availability   226
       Wrapping Up   228

12. A Data Architecture Sampler. **229**
       Architectural Components   229
         Frontend Datastores   229
         Data Access Layer   230
         Database Proxies   231
         Event and Message Systems   233
         Caches and Memory Stores   235
       Data Architectures   238
         Lambda and Kappa   238
         Event Sourcing   241
         CQRS   242
       Wrapping Up   243

13. Making the Case For DBRE. **245**
       A Culture of Database Reliability   246
         Breaking-Down Barriers   246

Data-Driven Decision Making   251
Data Integrity and Recoverability   252
Wrapping Up   252

Index. **253**

Foreword

Collectively, we are witnessing a time of unprecedented change and disruption in the database industry. Technology adoption life cycles have accelerated to the point where all of our heads are spinning—with both challenge and opportunity.

Architectures are evolving so quickly that the tasks we became accustomed to performing are no longer required, and the related skills we invested in so heavily are barely relevant. Emerging innovations and pressures in security, Infrastructure as Code, and cloud capabilities (such as Infrastructure and Database as a Service), have allowed us—and required us, actually—to rethink how we build.

By necessity, we have moved away from our traditional, administrative workloads to a process emphasizing architecture, automation, software engineering, continuous integration and delivery, and systems instrumentation skills, above all. Meanwhile, the value and importance of the data we've been protecting and caring for all along has increased by an order of magnitude or more, and we see no chance of a future in which it doesn't continue to increase in value. We find ourselves in the fortunate position of being able to make a meaningful, important difference in the world.

Without a doubt, many of us who once considered ourselves outstanding database administrators are at risk of being overwhelmed or even left behind. Simultaneously, newcomers into our field are thirsty for an organizing paradigm. The answer to both circumstances is the same: a commitment to the delight of learning, to self-improvement, to the optimism, enthusiasm, and confidence it takes to take on a task and see it through to conclusion, despite the inevitable travails and pitfalls. This book is a remarkable achievement. It is an introduction to a new way of thinking about database infrastructure engineering and operations, a guidebook, and a playbook taking all of what we used to do and reimagining it into a new way forward: Database Reliability Engineering.

— Paul Vallée, President and CEO,
Pythian

Preface

In this book, we hope to show you a framework for the next iteration of the database professional: the *database reliability engineer*, or DBRE. Consider any preconceived notions of what the profession of database administration looks like. Any software or systems engineer who has interacted with these mysterious creatures probably has a lot of these preconceived notions.

Traditionally, database administrators (DBAs) understood database (DB) internals thoroughly; they ate, lived, and breathed the optimizer, the query engine, and the tuning and crafting of highly performant, specialized systems. When they needed to pick up other skill sets to make their databases run better, they did. They learned how to distribute load across computer processing units (CPUs) or disk spindles, how to configure their DB to use CPU affinity, and how to evaluate storage subsystems.

When the DBA ran into visibility problems, they learned how to build graphs for the things they identified as key metrics. When they ran into architectural limitations, they learned about caching tiers. When they ran into the limits of individual nodes, they learned (and helped drive the development of) new design patterns like sharding. Throughout this, they were mastering new operational techniques, such as cache invalidation, data rebalancing, and rolling DB changes.

But for a long long time, DBAs were in the business of crafting silos and snowflakes. Their tools were different, their hardware was different, and their languages were different. DBAs were writing SQL, systems engineers were writing perl, software engineers were writing C++, web developers were writing PHP, and network engineers were crafting their own perfect appliances. Only half of the teams were using version control in any kind of way, and they certainly didn't talk or step on each other's turf. How could they? It was like entering a foreign land.

The days in which this model can prove itself to be effective and sustainable are numbered. This book is a view of *reliability engineering* as seen through a pair of database engineering glasses. We do not plan on covering everything possible in this book. Instead, we are describing what we do see as important, through the lens of your experience. This framework can then be applied to multiple datastores, architectures, and organizations.

Why We Wrote This Book

This book has been an evolving dream of ours for about five years. Laine came to the DBA role without any formal technical training. She was neither a software engineer nor a sysadmin; rather, she chose to develop a technical career after leaving music and theater. With this kind of background, the ideas of structure, harmony, counterpoint, and orchestration found in databases called to her.

Since that time, she's hired, taught, mentored, and worked with probably a hundred different DBAs. Us database folks are a varied bunch. Some came from software backgrounds, others from systems. Some even came from data analyst and business backgrounds. The thing that consistently shone through from the best, however, was a passion and a sense of ownership for the safety and availability of the company's data. We fulfilled our roles of stewards of data with a fierceness that bordered on unhealthy. But we also functioned as a lynchpin between the software engineers and the systems engineers. Some might say we were the original DevOps, with a foot in each world.

Charity's background is firmly in operations and startup culture. She has a gloriously sloppy history of bootstrapping infrastructures fast, making quick decisions that can make or break a startup, taking risks, and making difficult choices based on severely limited resources. Mostly successfully, give or take. She is an accidental DBA who loves data. She has always worked on ops teams for which there were no specialized DBAs, so the software engineering and operations engineering teams ended up sharing that work.

Doing this for so long and with varied pasts, we've recognized and embraced the trends of the past decade. The life of the DBA has often been one of toil and invisibility. Now we have the tools and the collective buy-in to transform the role to that of first-class citizen and to focus on the highest areas of value that the DBA can bring.

With this book, we wanted to help the next generation of engineers have truly happy, productive careers and to continue the impact previous generations had.

Who This Book Is For

This book is written for anyone with an interest in the design, building, and operations of reliable data stores. Perhaps you are a software engineer, looking to broaden your knowledge of databases. You might also be a systems engineer looking to do the same. If you're a database professional looking to develop your skill set, you will also find value here. If you are newer to the industry, this should also be able to give you a solid understanding. This book, after all, is a framework.

We assume that you already have a baseline of technical proficiency in Linux/Unix systems administration as well as web and/or cloud architectures. We also assume that you are an engineer on one of two paths. On one path, you have existing depth in another discipline, such as systems administration or software engineering, and are interested in developing your technical breadth to include the database engineering discipline. On the other path, you are early- to mid-career and looking to build your technical depth as a specialist in database engineering.

If you are management, or even project management, you can use this book to understand the needs of the datastores that will be underpinning your services. We believe firmly that management needs to understand operational and database principles to increase the likelihood of success of their teams and their projects.

You might also be someone without a traditional technical background. Perhaps you are an "accidental DBA" who was a business analyst and learned to run databases by jumping into the deep end of the pool. There are many database professionals who have come to the database world via Excel rather than a development or systems job.

How This Book Is Organized

As we go into this book, we present the information in two sections. The first section is operations core curriculum. This is a foundation of operations that anyone—database engineer, software engineer, even product owner—should know. After this, we dig into data: modeling, storing, replicating, accessing, and much more. This is also where we discuss architectural choices and data pipelines. It should be thrilling!

There is a reason there is an ops-heavy approach to this narrative: you can't be a good "DBRE" without being a good "RE." Which you can't be without being a plain old good "E." The modern DBRE specializes in understanding data-specific domain problems on top of the fundamentals of systems engineering.

But the point of this is that *any engineer can run data services*. We now speak the same languages. We use the same repos and the same code review processes. Caring for databases is an extension of operations engineering—a creamy frosting of special knowledge and awareness atop the cupcake of running systems at scale—just as being an exceptional network engineer also means knowing how to be an engineer first, and then knowing extra things about how to handle traffic, what to be scared of, what the current best practices are, how to evaluate network topology, and so on.

Here is a breakdown of what you can expect in each chapter:

Chapter 1 is an introduction to the concept of database reliability engineering. We start with guiding principals, move on to the operations centric core, and finally give a framework for building a vision for DBRE based on Maslow's hierarchy of needs.

In Chapter 2, we start with service level requirements. This is as important as feature requirements for a product. In this chapter we discuss what service level requirements are and how to define them, which is not as easy as it sounds. We then discuss how to measure and work with these requirements over time.

In Chapter 3, we discuss risk assessment and management. After a foundational discussion on risk, we discuss a practical process for incorporating risk assessment into systems and database engineering. Pitfalls and complexities are also brought to attention.

In Chapter 4, we discuss operational visibility. This is where we discuss metrics and events, and how build a plan for what to start measuring, and what to iterate on over time. We dig into the components of monitoring systems, the clients that use them.

We then dive into infrastructure engineering and infrastructure management in Chapters 5 and 6. This is the section where we discuss the principles of building hosts for datastores. We will dive into virtualization and containerization, configuration management, automation and orchestration in an attempt to help you understand all the moving parts required to build these systems that store and access data.

Chapter 7 is backup and recovery. This is, perhaps, the most critical things for the DBE to master. Losing data is simply game over. Starting from service level requirements, we evaluate appropriate backup and restore methods, how to scale and how to test this critical and oft overlooked aspect of operations.

Chapter 8 is a discussion on release management. How do we test, build and deploy changes to data stores? What about changes to data access code and SQL? Deployment, integration and delivery are the meat of this section.

Chapter 9 is on security. Data security is critical to a company's survival. Strategies on how to do plan for and manage security in ever evolving data infrastructures are in this chapter.

Chapter 10 is on data storage, indexing, and replication. We will discuss how relational data is stored, and then compare this to sorted strings and log structured merge trees. After reviewing indexing variants, we will explore data replication topologies.

Chapter 11 is our datastore field guide. Here we will discuss a myriad of various properties to look for in datastores you will be evaluating or operating. This includes conceptual attributes of great importance to application developers and architects, as well as the internal attributes focused on the physical implementation of the datastores.

In Chapter 12, we look at some of the more common architectural patterns used for distributed databases and the pipelines they are involved with. We start with a look at the architectural components that typically reside in a database ecosystem, along with their benefits, complexities and general usage. We then explore architectures and pipelines, or at least few examples.

Finally, in Chapter 13 we discuss how to build a culture of database reliability engineering in your organization. We explore the different ways in which you can transform the role of DBRE from one of administrator to that of engineer in today's organizations.

Conventions Used in This Book

The following typographical conventions are used in this book:

Italic
: Indicates new terms, URLs, email addresses, filenames, and file extensions.

`Constant width`
: Used for program listings, as well as within paragraphs to refer to program elements such as variable or function names, databases, data types, environment variables, statements, and keywords.

`Constant width bold`
: Shows commands or other text that should be typed literally by the user.

`Constant width italic`
: Shows text that should be replaced with user-supplied values or by values determined by context.

O'Reilly Safari

 *Safari* (formerly Safari Books Online) is a membership-based training and reference platform for enterprise, government, educators, and individuals.

Members have access to thousands of books, training videos, Learning Paths, interactive tutorials, and curated playlists from over 250 publishers, including O'Reilly Media, Harvard Business Review, Prentice Hall Professional, Addison-Wesley Professional, Microsoft Press, Sams, Que, Peachpit Press, Adobe, Focal Press, Cisco Press, John Wiley & Sons, Syngress, Morgan Kaufmann, IBM Redbooks, Packt, Adobe Press, FT Press, Apress, Manning, New Riders, McGraw-Hill, Jones & Bartlett, and Course Technology, among others.

For more information, please visit *http://oreilly.com/safari*.

How to Contact Us

Please address comments and questions concerning this book to the publisher:

O'Reilly Media, Inc.
1005 Gravenstein Highway North
Sebastopol, CA 95472
800-998-9938 (in the United States or Canada)

707-829-0515 (international or local)
707-829-0104 (fax)

We have a web page for this book, where we list errata, examples, and any additional information. You can access this page at *http://bit.ly/database-reliability-engineering*.

To comment or ask technical questions about this book, send email to *bookquestions@oreilly.com*.

For more information about our books, courses, conferences, and news, see our website at *http://www.oreilly.com*.

Find us on Facebook: *http://facebook.com/oreilly*

Follow us on Twitter: *http://twitter.com/oreillymedia*

Watch us on YouTube: *http://www.youtube.com/oreillymedia*

CHAPTER 1

Introducing Database Reliability Engineering

Our goal with this book is to provide the guidance and framework for you, the reader, to grow on the path to being a truly excellent database reliability engineer (DBRE). When naming the book we chose to use the words *reliability engineer*, rather than administrator.

Ben Treynor, VP of Engineering at Google, says the following about reliability engineering:

> fundamentally doing work that has historically been done by an operations team, but using engineers with software expertise, and banking on the fact that these engineers are inherently both predisposed to, and have the ability to, substitute automation for human labor.

Today's database professionals must be engineers, not administrators. We build things. We create things. As engineers practicing devops, we are all in this together, and nothing is someone else's problem. As engineers, we apply repeatable processes, established knowledge, and expert judgment to design, build, and operate production data stores and the data structures within. As database reliability engineers, we must take the operational principles and the depth of database expertise that we possess one step further.

If you look at the non-storage components of today's infrastructures, you will see systems that are easily built, run, and destroyed via programmatic and often automatic means. The lifetimes of these components can be measured in days, and sometimes even hours or minutes. When one goes away, there is any number of others to step in and keep the quality of service at expected levels.

Our next goal is that you gain a framework of principles and practices for the design, building, and operating of data stores within the paradigms of reliability engineering and devops cultures. You can take this knowledge and apply it to any database technology or environment that you are asked to work in at any stage in your organization's growth.

Guiding Principles of the DBRE

As we sat down to write this book, one of the first questions we asked ourselves was what the principles underlying this new iteration of the database profession were. If we were redefining the way people approached data store design and management, we needed to define the foundations for the behaviors we were espousing.

Protect the Data

Traditionally, protecting data always has been a foundational principle of the database professional and still is. The generally accepted approach has been attempted via:

- A strict separation of duties between the software and the database engineer
- Rigorous backup and recovery processes, regularly tested
- Well-regulated security procedures, regularly audited
- Expensive database software with strong durability guarantees
- Underlying expensive storage with redundancy of all components
- Extensive controls on changes and administrative tasks

In teams with collaborative cultures, the strict separation of duties can become not only burdensome, but also restrictive of innovation and velocity. In Chapter 8, *Release Management*, we will discuss ways to create safety nets and reduce the need for separation of duties. Additionally, these environments focus more on testing, automation, and impact mitigation than extensive change controls.

More often than ever, architects and engineers are choosing open source datastores that cannot guarantee durability the way that something like Oracle might have in the past. Sometimes, that relaxed durability gives needed performance benefits to a team looking to scale quickly. Choosing the right datastore, and understanding the impacts of those choices, is something we look at Chapter 11. Recognizing that there are multiple tools based on the data you are managing and choosing effectively is rapidly becoming the norm.

Underlying storage has also undergone a significant change as well. In a world where systems are often virtualized, network and ephemeral storage is finding a place in database design. We will discuss this further in Chapter 5.

Production Datastores on Ephemeral Storage

In 2013, Pinterest moved their MySQL database instances to run on ephemeral storage in Amazon Web Services (AWS). Ephemeral storage effectively means that if the compute instance fails or is shut down, anything stored on disk is lost. Pinterest chose the ephemeral storage option because of consistent throughput and low latency.

Doing this required substantial investment in automated and rock-solid backup and recovery, as well as application engineering to tolerate the disappearance of a cluster while rebuilding nodes. Ephemeral storage did not allow snapshots, which meant that the restore approach was full database copies over the network rather than attaching a snapshot in preparation for rolling forward of the transaction logs.

This shows that you can maintain data safety in ephemeral environments with the right processes and the right tools!

The new approach to data protection might look more like this:

- Responsibility of the data shared by cross-functional teams.
- Standardized and automated backup and recovery processes blessed by DBRE.
- Standardized security policies and procedures blessed by DBRE and Security teams.
- All policies enforced via automated provisioning and deployment.
- Data requirements dictate the datastore, with evaluation of durability needs becoming part of the decision making process.
- Reliance on automated processes, redundancy, and well-practiced procedures rather than expensive, complicated hardware.
- Changes incorporated into deployment and infrastructure automation, with focus on testing, fallback, and impact mitigation.

Self-Service for Scale

A talented DBRE is a rarer commodity than a site reliability engineer (SRE) by far. Most companies cannot afford and retain more than one or two. So, we must create the most value possible, which comes from creating self-service platforms for teams to use. By setting standards and providing tools, teams are able to deploy new services and make appropriate changes at the required pace without serializing on an overworked database engineer. Examples of these kinds of self-service methods include:

- Ensure the appropriate metrics are being collected from data stores by providing the correct plug-ins.
- Building backup and recovery utilities that can be deployed for new data stores.
- Defining reference architectures and configurations for data stores that are approved for operations, and can be deployed by teams.
- Working with Security to define standards for data store deployments.
- Building safe deployment methods and test scripts for database changesets to be applied.

In other words, the effective DBRE functions by empowering others and guiding them, not functioning as a gatekeeper.

Elimination of Toil

The Google SRE teams often use the phrase "Elimination of Toil," which is discussed in Chapter 5 of the Google SRE book. In the book, "toil" is defined as:

> Toil is the kind of work tied to running a production service that tends to be manual, repetitive, automatable, tactical, devoid of enduring value, and that scales linearly as a service grows.

Effective use of automation and standardization is necessary to ensure that DBREs are not overburdened by toil. Throughout this book, we will be bringing up examples of DBRE-specific toil and the approaches to mitigation of this. That being said, the word "toil" is still vague, with lots of preconceptions that vary from person to person. When we discuss toil in this book, we are specifically talking about manual work that is repetitive, non-creative, and non-challenging.

Manual Database Changes

In many customer environments, database engineers are asked to review and apply DB changes, which can include modifications to tables or indexes, the addition, modification, or removal of data, or any other number of tasks. Everyone feels reassured that the DBA is applying these changes and monitoring the impact of the changes in real time.

At one customer site, the rate of change was quite high, and those changes were often impactful. We ended up spending about 20 hours a week applying rolling changes throughout the environment. Needless to say, the poor DBA who ended up spending half of their week running these repetitive tasks became jaded and ended up quitting.

Faced with a lack of resources, management finally allowed the DB team to build a rolling schema change automation utility that software engineers could use once the changeset had been reviewed and approved by one of the database engineers. Soon, everyone trusted the tool and monitoring to introduce change, paving the way for the DBRE team to focus more time on integrating these processes with the deployment stack.

Databases Are Not Special Snowflakes

Our systems are no more or less important than any other components serving the needs of the business. We must strive for standardization, automation, and resilience. Critical to this is the idea that the components of database clusters are not sacred. We should be able to lose any component and efficiently replace it without worry. Fragile data stores in glass rooms are a thing of the past.

The metaphor of pets versus cattle is often used to show the difference between a special snowflake and a commodity service component. Original attribution goes to Bill Baker, Microsoft Distinguished Engineer. A pet server, is one that you feed, care for, and nurture back to health when it is sick. It also has a name. At Travelocity in 2000, our servers were Simpsons characters, and our two SGI servers running Oracle were named Patty and Selma. I spent so many hours with those gals on late nights. They were high maintenance!

Cattle servers have numbers, not names. You don't spend time customizing servers, much less logging on to individual hosts. When they show signs of sickness, you cull them from the herd. You should, of course, keep those culled cattle around for forensics, if you are seeing unusual amounts of sickness. But, we'll refrain from mangling this metaphor any further.

Data stores are some of the last hold outs of "pethood." After all, they hold "The Data," and simply cannot be treated as replaceable cattle with short lifespans and complete standardizations. What about the special replication rules for our reporting replica? What about the different config for the primary's redundant standby?

Eliminate the Barriers Between Software and Operations

Your infrastructure, configurations, data models, and scripts are all part of software. Study and participate in the software development lifecycle as any engineer would. Code, test, integrate, build, test, and deploy. Did we mention test?

This might be the hardest paradigm shift for someone coming from an operations and scripting background. There can be an organizational impedance mismatch in the way software engineers navigate an organization and the systems and services built to meet that organization's needs. Software engineering organizations have very defined approaches to developing, testing, and deploying features and applications.

In a traditional environment, the underlying process of designing, building, testing, and pushing infrastructure and related services to production was separate among software engineering (SWE), system engineering (SE), and DBA. The paradigm shifts discussed previously are pushing for removal of this impedance mismatch, which means DBREs and Systems Engineers find themselves needing to use similar methodologies to do their jobs.

Software Engineers Must Learn Operations!

Too often, operations folks are told to learn to "code or to go home." While I do agree with this, the reverse must be true as well. Software engineers who are not being pushed and led to learn operations and infrastructure principles and practices will create fragile, non-performant, and potentially insecure code. The impedance mismatch only goes away if all teams are brought to the same table!

DBREs might also find themselves embedded directly in a software engineering team, working in the same code base, examining how code is interacting with the data stores, and modifying code for performance, functionality, and reliability. The removal of this organizational impedance creates an improvement in reliability, performance, and velocity an order of magnitude greater than traditional models, and DBREs must adapt to these new processes, cultures, and tooling.

Operations Core Overview

One of the core competencies of the DBRE is operations. These are the building blocks for designing, testing, building, and operating any system with scale and reliability requirements that are not trivial. This means that if you want to be a database engineer, you need to know these things.

Operations at a macro level is not a role. Operations is the combined sum of all of the skills, knowledge, and values that your company has built up around the practice of shipping and maintaining quality systems and software. It's your implicit values as well as your explicit values, habits, tribal knowledge, and reward systems. Everybody, from tech support to product people to the CEO participates in your operational outcomes.

Too often, this is not done well. So many companies have an abysmal ops culture that burns out whoever gets close to it. This can give the discipline a bad reputation, which many folks think of when they think of operations jobs, whether in systems, database, or network. Despite this, your ops culture is an emergent property of how your org executes on its technical mission. So if you go and tell us that your company doesn't do any ops, we just won't buy it.

Perhaps you are a software engineer or a proponent of infrastructure and platforms as a service. Perhaps you are dubious that operations is a necessity for the intrepid database engineer. The idea that serverless computing models will liberate software engineers from needing to think or care about operational impact is flat out wrong. It is actually the exact opposite. It's a brave new world where you have no embedded operations teams—where the people doing operations engineering for you are Google SREs and AWS systems engineers and PagerDuty and DataDog and so on. This is a world where application engineers need to be much better at operations, architecture, and performance than they currently are.

Hierarchy of Needs

Some of you will be coming at this book with experience in enterprises and some in startups. As we approach and consider systems, it is worth thinking about what you would do on day one of taking on the responsibility of operating a database system. *Do you have backups? Do they work? Are you sure? Is there a replica you can fail over to? Do you know how to do that? Is it on the same power strip, router, hardware, or availability zone as the primary? Will you know if the backups start failing somehow? How?*

In other words, we need to talk about a hierarchy of database needs.

For humans, Maslow's hierarchy of needs is a pyramid of desire that must be satisfied for us to flourish: physiological survival, safety, love and belonging, esteem, and self-actualization. At the base of the pyramid are the most fundamental needs, like survival. Each level roughly proceeds to the next—survival before safety, safety before love and belonging, and so forth. Once the first four levels are satisfied, we reach self-actualization, which is where we can safely explore and play and create and reach the fullest expression of our unique potential. So that's what it means for humans. Let's apply this as a metaphor for what databases need.

Survival and Safety

Your database's most essential needs are backups, replication, and failover. *Do you have a database? Is it alive? Can you ping it? Is your application responding? Does it get backed up? Will restores work? How will you know if this stops being true?*

Is your data safe? Are there multiple live copies of your data? Do you know how to do a failover? Are your copies distributed across multiple physical availability zones or multiple power strips and racks? Are your backups consistent? Can you restore to a point in time? Will you know if your data gets corrupted? How? Plan on exploring this much more in the backup and recovery section.

This is also the time when you start preparing for scale. Scaling prematurely is a fool's errand, but you should consider *sharding*, growth, and scale now as you determine ids for key data objects, storage systems, and architecture.

Scaling Patterns

We will discuss scale quite frequently. Scalability is the capability of a system or service to handle increasing amounts of work. This might be *actual* ability, because everything has been deployed to support the growth, or it might be *potential* ability, in that the building blocks are in place to handle the addition of components and resources required to scale. There is a general consensus that scale has four pathways that will be approached.

- Scale vertically, via resource allocation. *aka scale up*
- Scale horizontally, by duplication of the system or service. *aka scale out*
- Separate workloads to smaller sets of functionality, to allow for each to scale independently, also known as *functional partitioning*
- Split specific workloads into partitions that are identical, other than the specific set of data that is being worked on also known as *sharding*

The specific aspects of these patterns will be reviewed in Chapter 5, *Infrastructure Engineering*.

Love and Belonging

Love and belonging is about making your data a first-class citizen of your software engineering processes. It's about breaking down silos between your databases and the rest of your systems. This is both technical and cultural, which is why you could also just call this the "devops needs." At a high level, it means that managing your databases should look and feel (as much as possible) like managing the rest of your systems. It also means that you culturally encourage fluidity and cross-functionality. The love and belonging phase is where you slowly stop logging in and performing cowboy commands as root.

It is here where you begin to use the same code review and deployment practices. Database infrastructure and provisioning should be part of the same process as all other architectural components. Working with data should feel consistent to all other parts of the application, which should encourage anyone to feel they can engage with and support the database environment.

Resist the urge to instill fear in your developers. It's quite easy to do and quite tempting because it feels better to feel like you have control. It's not—and you don't. It's much better for everyone if you invest that energy into building guard rails so that it's

---

harder for anyone to accidentally destroy things. Educate and empower everyone to own their own changes. Don't even talk about preventing failure, as such is impossible. In other words, create resilient systems and encourage everyone to work with the datastore as much as possible.

Guardrails at Etsy

Etsy introduced a tool called *Schemanator* to apply database changes, otherwise known as change-sets, safely to their production environments. Multiple guardrails were put in place to empower software engineers to apply these changes. These guardrails included:

- Change-set heuristic reviews to validate standards had been followed in schema definitions.
- Change-set testing to validate the scripts run successfully.
- Preflight checks to show the engineer the current cluster status.
- Rolling changes to run impactful changes on "out of service" databases.
- Breaking workflows into subtasks to allow for cancelling out when problems occur that can not be predicted.

You can read more about this at Etsy's blog (*http://bit.ly/2zy74uz*).

Esteem

Esteem is the highest of the needs in the pyramid. For humans, this means respect and mastery. For databases, this means things like observability, debuggability, introspection, and instrumentation. It's about being able to understand your storage systems themselves, but also being able to correlate events across the stack. Again, there are two aspects to this stage: one of them is about how your production services evolve through this phase, and the other is about your humans.

Your services should tell you if they're up or down or experiencing error rates. You should never have to look at a graph to find this out. As your services mature, the pace of change slows down a bit as your trajectory becomes more predictable. You're running in production so you're learning more every day about your storage system's weaknesses, behaviors, and failure conditions. This can be compared to teenager years for data infrastructure. What you need more than anything is visibility into what is going on. The more complex your product is, the more moving pieces there are and the more engineering cycles you need to allocate into developing the tools you need to figure out what's happening.

You also need knobs. You need the ability to selectively degrade quality of service instead of going completely down, e.g.:

- Flags where you can set the site into read-only mode
- Disabling certain features
- Queueing writes to be applied later
- The ability to blacklist bad actors or certain endpoints

Your humans have similar but not completely overlapping needs. A common pattern here is that teams will overreact once they get into production. They don't have enough visibility, so they compensate by monitoring everything and paging themselves too often. It is easy to go from zero graphs to literally hundreds of thousands of graphs—99% of which are completely meaningless. This is not better. It can actually be worse. If it generates so much noise that your humans can't find the signal and are reduced to tailing log files and guessing again, it's as bad or worse than not having the graphs.

This is where you can start to burn out your humans by interrupting them, waking them up, and training them not to care or act on alerts they do receive. In the early stages, if you're expecting everyone to be on call, you need to document things. When you're bootstrapping, you have shared on call, and you're pushing people outside of their comfort zones, give them a little help. Write minimally effective documentation and procedures.

Self-actualization

Just like every person's best possible self is unique, every organization's self-actualized storage layer is unique. The platonic ideal of a storage system for Facebook doesn't look like the perfect system for Pinterest or Github, let alone a tiny startup. But just like there are patterns for healthy, self-actualized humans (doesn't throw tantrums in the grocery store, they eat well and exercise), there are patterns for what we can think of as healthy, self-actualized storage systems.

In this context, self-actualization means that your data infrastructure helps you get where you're trying to go and that your database workflows are not obstacles to progress. Rather, they empower your developers to get work done and help save them from making unnecessary mistakes. Common operational pains and boring failures should remediate themselves and keep the system in a healthy state without needing humans to help. It means you have a scaling story that works for your needs. Whether that means 10x'ing every few months or just being rock solid, stable, and dumb for three years before you need to worry about capacity. Frankly, you have a mature data infrastructure when you can spend most of your time thinking about other things. Fun things. Like building new products or anticipating future problems instead of reacting to current ones.

It's okay to float back and forth between levels over time. The levels are mostly there as a framework to help you think about relative priorities, like making sure you have working backups is *way* more important than writing a script to dynamically re-shard and add more capacity. Or if you're still at the point where you have one copy of your data online, or you don't know how to fail over when your primary dies, you should probably stop whatever you're doing and figure that out first.

Wrapping Up

The DBRE role is a paradigm shift from an existing, well-known role. More than anything, the framework gives us a new way to approach the functions of managing datastores in a continually changing world. In the upcoming section, we will begin exploring these functions in detail, prioritizing operational functions due to their importance in day-to-day database engineering. With that being said, let's move bravely forward, intrepid engineer!

CHAPTER 2

Service-Level Management

One of the first steps required to successfully design, build, and deploy a service is to understand the expectations of that service. In this chapter, we define what service-level management is and discuss the components of it. We then discuss how to define the expectations of a service and how to monitor and report to ensure we are meeting those expectations. Throughout the chapter, we also build a robust set of service-level requirements to explain this process.

Why Do I Need Service-Level Objectives?

Services that we design and build must have a set of requirements about their runtime characteristics. This is often referred to as a *Service-Level Agreement* (SLA). An SLA is more than just an enumerated list of requirements, however. SLAs include remedies, impacts, and much more that is beyond the scope of this book. So, we will focus on the term *Service-Level Objective* (SLO). SLOs are commitments by the architects and operators that guide the design and operations of the system to meet those commitments.

Service-level management is difficult! Condensing it to a chapter is reductive, and it is important to understand the nuances. Let's take a few examples to illustrate why this problem is difficult:

- Maybe you say, I'll just report on the percentage of requests that are successfully served by my API. Okay...as reported by whom? By the API? That's obviously a problem, because what if your load balancers are down? Or, what if it returned a 200 error from the database because your service discovery system knew that particular database was unavailable?

- Or, what if you say, "Ok, we'll use a third-party end-to-end checker and calculate how many of those read and write the correct data?" That's a great thing to do—

end-to-end checks are the best high-level reliability alerts. But is it exercising *every* backend?

- Do you factor less-important services into your SLO? Your customers would probably rather have a 99.95% availability rate from your API and a 97% availability from your batch processing product than 99.8% from both your API and and batch processing.

- How much control do you have over clients? If your API has a 98% availability, but your mobile clients automatically retry and have a 99.99% reliability response rate within three tries, they might never notice. Which is the accurate number?

- Maybe you say, "I'll just count error percentages," but what about the errors that are caused by users sending invalid or malformed requests? You can't actually do anything about that.

- Maybe you return a correct result 99.999% of the time, but 15% of the time the latency is more than 5 seconds. Is that acceptable? Depending on the client behavior, that might actually mean your website is unresponsive for some people. You might technically have five 9's by your own accounting, and yet your users can be incredibly and justifiably unhappy with you.

- What if the site is 99.999% up for 98% of your users but only 30% to 70% available for the other 2% of your users? How do you calculate that?

- What if one shard or one backend is down or slow? What if you experience 2% data loss due to a bug in an upgrade? What if you experience an entire day of data loss but only for certain tables? What if your users never noticed that data was lost due to the nature of it, but you reported a 2% data loss, alarming everyone and encouraging them to migrate off your stack? What if that 2% data loss actually included rewriting pointers to assets so that even though the data wasn't "lost" it "could not be found?"

- What if some users are experiencing 95% availability because they have bad WiFi, old cable internet, or bad router tables between their client and your server? Can they hold you responsible?

- What if it's from entire countries? Well, then it probably is something that they can blame you for (e.g., packet overruns for DNS UDP packets by some providers—you can fix this).

- What if your number is 99.97%, but every error causes your entire website to fail to load? What if your number is 99.92%, but each page has 1,500 components and users almost never notice when a tiny widget has failed to load. Which experience is better?

- Is it better to count actual error rate or by time slices? By the number of minutes (or seconds) when errors or timeouts exceeded a threshold?

Five 9's?

Many people use a number of 9's as shorthand to describe availability. For instance, a system is designed to have "five 9's" of availability. This means that it is built to be available 99.999% of the time, whereas "three 9's" would be 99.9%.

This is why the practice of designing, curating, and adapting SLO and availability metrics over time is less of a computation problem and more of a social science problem. How do you calculate an availability percentage that accurately reflects the experience of your users, builds trust, and incentivizes in the right direction?

From the perspective of your team, whatever availability metrics you all agree are important to deliver become numbers to be gamed to some extent, even if only subconsciously. Those are the numbers you pay attention to when you're determining whether your reliability is getting better or worse or whether you need to switch resources from feature development to reliability, or vice versa.

From the perspective of your customers, the most important thing about the metric is that it *reflects their experience* as much as possible. If you have the ability to calculate metrics per customer or slice and dice the data along arbitrary dimensions—even high-cardinality ones like UUID—this is incredibly powerful. Facebook's Scuba does this and so does Honeycomb.io.

Service-Level Indicators

When evaluating requirements for SLOs, we will generally consider a finite set of *indicators*, or *metrics*, against which we will set requirements. In these objectives, we will consider ideal parameters as well as working parameters. An SLO can be considered a set of one or more indicators that define the expectations of a service, often, because these indicators can be intrinsically linked.

For instance, latency past a certain point will become an availability issue because the system is effectively unusable. Latency without throughput is easy to game and not necessarily an accurate view of the system at load. Typical indicators are enumerated and explained in the subsections that follow.

Latency

Latency, also known as response time, is a time-based measurement indicating how long it takes to receive a response from a request. It is best to measure this for end-to-end response from the customer rather than breaking it down component by component. This is customer-centric design and is crucial for any system that has customers, which is any system!

Latency versus Response Time

Vast wars of ink and blood have been spilled on the topic of latency versus response time. There are some factions that consider latency to be the time it takes to get to the service, whereas response time is the time it takes to service the request. In this book, we use "latency" to refer to the total round-trip time of a request, from initiation to payload delivery.

Availability

This is generally expressed as a percentage of overall time the system is expected to be available. Availability is defined as the ability to return an expected response to the requesting client. Note that time is not considered here, which is why most SLOs include both response time and availability. After a certain latency point, the system can be considered unavailable even if the request is still completing. Availability is often denoted in percentages, such as 99.9% over a certain window. All samples within that window will be aggregated.

Throughput

Another common SLI is throughput, or the rate of successful requests in a specific period of time, typically measured on a per-second basis. Throughput actually becomes quite useful as a companion to latency. When a team is preparing for launch and measuring latency, it must do it at the top throughput goals; otherwise, its tests will be useless. Latency tends to be steady until a certain tipping point, and we must know that tipping point in reference to throughput goals.

Durability

Durability is specific to storage systems and datastores. It indicates the successful persistence of a write operation to storage so that it can be retrieved at another time. This can be expressed in a time window, such as: in the event of a system failure, no more than the past two seconds of data can be lost.

Cost or Efficiency

"Cost or Efficiency" is often overlooked, or not considered in service-level discussions. Instead, you will find it relegated to budget and often not tracked effectively. Still, the overall cost of a service is a critical component to most businesses. Ideally, this should be expressed in cost per action, such as a page view, a subscription, or a purchase.

An organization should expect to have the following actions as part of the operations of their services:

New service

SLOs Defined. In more traditional models, this might be called operating-level agreements.

New SLOs

Set up appropriate monitoring to evaluate actual versus target metrics.

Existing service

Regular reviews of SLOs should be scheduled to validate that current service criticality is taken into account for defined SLOs.

SLO fulfillment

Regular reports to indicate historical and current status of the achievement or violation of SLOs.

Service issues

A portfolio of issues that have affected service-levels, and their current status in terms of workarounds and fixes.

Defining Service Objectives

SLOs should be built from the same set of requirements toward which product features are built. We call this customer-centric design because we should be defining requirements based on the needs of our customers. We generally only want up to three indicators. More than three indicators rarely add significant value. Often, excessive numbers of indicators could mean you are including symptoms of primary indicators.

Latency Indicators

A latency SLO can be expressed as a range based on a certain indicator. For instance, we might say that request latency must be less than 100 ms (which is actually a range between 100 ms and 0s when we make assumptions explicit). Latency is absolutely critical to the user experience.

Why Is Latency Critical?

Slow or inconsistently performing services can lose more customers than a system that is down. In fact, speed matters enough that Google Research found that introducing a delay of 100 to 400 ms caused a reduction in searches by 0.2% to 0.6% over 4 to 6 weeks. You can find more details at Speed Matters (*http://googlere search.blogspot.com/2009/06/speed-matters.html*). Here are some other startling metrics:

- Amazon: for each 100 ms, it loses 1% of sales
- Google: if it increases page load by 500 ms, it results in 25% fewer searches
- Facebook: pages that are 500 ms slower cause a 3% dropoff in traffic
- A one-second delay in page response decreases customer satisfaction by 16%

We can express an availability SLO like this: *Request latency must be less than 100 ms.*

If we leave the lower bound at 0, we might drive certain dysfunctions. A performance engineer might spend a week of time getting the response time down to 10 ms, but the mobile devices using the application will rarely have networks that can deliver the results fast enough to utilize this optimization. In other words, your performance engineer just wasted a week of work. We can iterate on the SLO like this: *request latency must be between 25 ms and 100 ms.*

Let's next consider how we collect this data. If we are reviewing logs, we might take one minute's worth of requests and average them. There is a problem with this, however. Most distributed, networked systems create distributions with small percentages of outliers that can be fairly significant. This will skew an average and also hide the complete workload characteristics from the engineers monitoring it. In other words, aggregating response times is a *lossyprocess.*

In fact, thinking about latency must be done by thinking of latency distributions. Latency almost never follows normal, gaussian or poisson distributions, so averages, medians, and standard deviations are useless at best and lies at worst. More details of this can be considered at "Everything you know about latency is wrong." (*http://brave newgeek.com/everything-you-know-about-latency-is-wrong/*)

To better understand, take a look at Figures 2-1 and 2-2 provided by Circonus, a high scale monitoring product. In the blog (*http://www.circonus.com/spike-erosion/*), these graphs are being used to show *spike erosion,* which is the phenomenon we're discussing. In Figure 2-1, we have averages graphed with a larger time window in each average to accommodate for a month's worth of data.

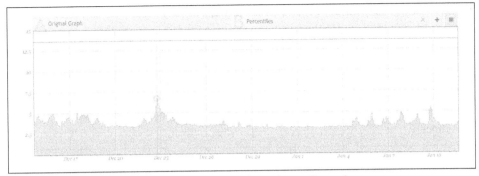

Figure 2-1. Latency averages with larger window of time for each average

In Figure 2-2, we are averaging on much shorter time windows because we are displaying only four hours.

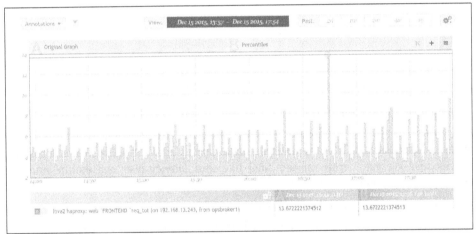

Figure 2-2. Latency averages with a smaller window of time for each average

Even though this is the exact same dataset, the averages in Figure 2-1 indicate a peak of around 9.3, while Figure 2-2 shows 14!

Be Careful Storing Averages!

Remember to store the actual values rather than averages! If you have a monitoring application that is averaging values every minute and not retaining the actual full history of values, you will find a time when you want to average at five minutes, using the one-minute averages. This will absolutely give you incorrect data because the original averaging was lossy!

If you think of the minute of data as a full dataset rather than an average, you will want to be able to visualize the impact of outliers (in fact, you might be more interested in the outliers). You can do this in multiple ways. First, you can visualize the minimum and maximum values over the average. You can also remove outliers by averaging a certain percentage of values in that minute, such as the fastest 99.9%, 99%, and 95%. If you overlay those three averages with the 100% average, as demonstrated in Figure 2-3, and a minimum/maximum, you get a very good feel for the outlier impacts.

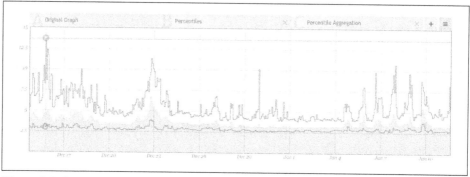

Figure 2-3. Latency average (100% sample size) overlaid with minimum and maximum

Now, with that segue, let's think of our SLO regarding latency. If we are averaging every minute, no matter what our SLO is, we cannot prove we hit it because we are measuring averages only! Why don't we make our objective more relevant to real life workloads? We can iterate on this SLO like this: *latency over one minute must be between 25 and 100 ms for 99% of requests.*

Why do we choose something like 99% instead of 100%? Latency distributions tend to be very multimodal. There are normal times, and there are edge cases, which are due to any number of possibilities in a complex distributed system, such as Java Virtual Machine (JVM) garbage collection, database flushing, cache invalidations, and more. So, we expect a certain percentage of outliers, and our goal in setting an SLO is to recognize the percentage of outliers we are willing to tolerate.

Now, let's consider the workload. Are we talking about simple response such as you might see in an API? Or, are we measuring a page rendering, which is an aggregation of many calls that happen over a period of time. If we are measuring a page render, we might want to specify initial response as one requirement and final rendering as a second because there can be quite a period of time between them.

Availability Indicators

As mentioned earlier, availability is the amount of time, generally expressed as a percentage, that a service is able to respond to requests with system-defined responses.

For instance, we might say that a system should be available 99.9% of the time. This can be expressed like this: *service must be available 99.9% of the time.*

This gives us about 526 minutes of downtime per year to work with. Almost 9 hours! A king's feast of downtime. You might ask why we don't just say 100%? If you are a product owner, or a salesperson, you probably will. It is generally accepted that the differences from 99%, to 99.9%, to 99.99% are each an order of magnitude more complex to manage, more expensive, and more distracting for engineers. Additionally, if this is an application that relies on delivery over the internet or large geographical distances, you can expect that the transport mediums will create their own disruptions, which would not allow you to utilize more than 99% to 99.9% of the uptime your system has.

That being said, there is a big difference between 526 one-minute outages in a year and one 526 minute outage. The shorter the downtime, the greater the chance that most users will not even notice the disruption. In contrast, an eight-hour outage for some services generates news articles, thousands of tweets, and erodes trust from users. It makes sense to consider two data points around your service. The first is Mean Time Between Failures (MBTF). Traditionally, avoidance of failure has been the priority, which means increasing MTBF. The second data point is Mean Time To Recover (MTTR). This is how long it takes to resume service after a failure has occurred. Shorter is better!

Resiliency versus robustness in availability

There has been much discussion over the past decade about building resilient systems that have three specific traits:

- Low MTTR due to automated remediation to well-monitored failure scenarios.
- Low impact during failures due to distributed and redundant environments.
- The ability to treat failure as a normal scenario in the system, ensuring that automated and manual remediation is well documented, solidly engineered, practiced, and integrated into normal day-to-day operations.

Note that there is not a focus on eliminating failures. Systems without failures, although robust, become brittle and fragile. When failures occur, it is more likely that the teams responding will be unprepared, and this could dramatically increase the impact of the incident. Additionally, reliable but fragile systems can lead users to expect greater reliability than the SLO indicates and for which the service has been engineered. This means that even if an SLO has not been violated, customers might be quite upset when an outage does occur.

Armed with this knowledge, as you evaluate an SLO for availability, you should ask yourself some key questions:

- Are there workarounds during downtime? Can you function in a degraded mode, such as read only? Can you use caches to provide data even if it is stale?

- Is there a different tolerance for downtime if it is limited to a small percentage of users?

- What experience does a user have during downtimes of increasing lengths?
  — One failed request

  — 30 seconds

  — One minute

  — Five minutes

  — An hour or more

After considering this, you might want to reevaluate the naive availability SLO by doing the following:

- Defining the time interval
- Defining a maximum incident duration
- Defining a percentage of the user population affected before calling availability down

With that in mind, you can express the SLO as follows:

- 99.9% availability averaged over one week
- No single incident greater than 10.08 minutes
- Call for downtime if more than 5% of users are affected

Designing for downtime allowed

This new iteration allows us to engineer processes such as failovers, database locks, and restarts that can fit within the parameters provided. We can do rolling upgrades that affect fewer than one percent of users. We can lock tables to build indexes if it takes less than 10 minutes and no downtime has occurred that week. By designing for the downtime allowed, rather than trying to achieve zero downtime, we can be more efficient with our design and allow for some risks in the name of innovation and velocity.

It is worth noting that even in today's world in which 99.9% uptime is considered ubiquitous, there are times when services truly can tolerate planned and managed downtime safely. Being willing to take four hours of downtime that is communicated, mitigated with read-only options, and broken up into smaller percentages of users can eliminate hours of carefully orchestrated migrations that introduce risk of data corruption, privacy issues, and more.

After considering this, you might want to reevaluate the availability SLO by adding planned downtime options to guide the operations team in their maintenance efforts.

Sample availability SLO, iteration 2:

- 99.9% availability averaged over one week
- No single incident greater than 10.08 minutes
- Downtime is called if more than 5% of users are affected
- One annual four-hour downtime allowed, if:
  — Communicated to usersat least two weeks ahead of time
  — Affects no more than 10% of users at a time

Throughput Indicators

Throughput, as a service-level indicator, should list a peak value that the service must be able to support while maintaining the latency and availability SLOs provided in conjunction with it. You might say, "Laine and Charity, why do we have it? Shouldn't latency and availability be enough?" To which one of us would respond, "Intrepid Ops Scout, excellent question!" She would then puff thoughtfully on a pipe...

There might be times when there is a bottleneck that puts an upper boundary on throughput without necessarily tipping over performance or availability. Perhaps there is locking in your system that constrains you to 50 queries per second (qps). Those might be incredibly snappy and tight responses, but if you have 1,000 people waiting to run this query, you have a problem. Because there are times when you cannot measure end-to-end latency, throughput indicators can often be an extra layer of validation that a system is living up to the needs of the business.

Throughput can suffer from similar visibility issues as latency when it comes to using averages and less granular sampling, so please do keep this in mind while monitoring.

Cost/efficiency indicators

As you consider effective indicators for the cost of a system, the biggest variable is what you will use to reference cost against. This is really a business decision, but you should choose the action in the service that drives value. If you are a content provider such as an online magazine, pages being delivered is critical. If you are a Software as a Service (SaaS) provider, subscriptions to your service makes sense. For retailers, transaction counts will be appropriate.

Considerations

Why do you, as a database engineer, need to know this? You are managing one component of the service, so why must you concern yourself with the overall requirements? In the dark days of dysfunction, you might have been given a target for your datastore and graded based on your ability to maintain that. But, as part of a larger team, you have great opportunities to affect the service's velocity and availability.

By knowing the holistic SLO, you can prioritize your own focus. If you have a latency SLO of 200 ms, you can assume that this 200 ms is being shared by the following:

- DNS resolution
- Load balancers
- Redirection to an http server
- Application code
- Applications querying the database
- TCP/IP transport times across oceans and worlds
- Retrieval from memory, both solid-state devices (SSD) and spinning disks

So, if your datastores are doing well and contributing minimally, you know to focus elsewhere. On the other hand, if you see that the SLO is at risk and you see low-hanging fruit, you can devote some time in your sprint to plucking that ripe, delicious performance fruit.

While assembling an SLO for your new and exciting service, there are some additional things to consider:

Don't go overboard
> We're metrics hoarders, and we understand the urge. But please try to keep your list simple and concise enough that the SLO status can be reviewed on a single page dashboard.

Stay user-centric
> Think about what your users would find critical and build from there. Remember that most application services focus on latency, throughput, and availability, whereas storage services add data durability to this list.

Defining SLOs is an iterative process
> If you have an SLO review process, you can modify and add on to this over time. While you are in early stages, you might not need to be as aggressive with SLOs. This will allow your engineers to focus on features and improvements.

Use your SLOs to determine how you want to design your services, processes, and infrastructure.

Monitoring and Reporting on SLOs

Now that you have well-defined SLOs, it is critical to monitor how you are doing in real-life in comparison to your ideal objectives. We have not gone into operational visibility in this book yet, but there are crucial things to discuss before moving on to the next topic.

Our top goal in monitoring for service-level management is to preemptively identify and remediate any potential impacts that could cause us to miss our SLOs. In other words, we don't want to ever have to rely on monitoring to tell us that we are currently *in violation*. Think of it like canoeing. We don't want to know rapids are present *after we are in them*. We want to know what is happening that could indicate rapids there are downstream *while we are still in calm waters*. We then want to be able to take appropriate action to ensure that we stay within the SLOs to which we have committed ourselves and our systems.

When monitoring, we will always rely on automated collecting and analysis of metrics. This analysis will then be fed into automated decision-making software for remediation, for alerting of human operators (aka, you), or for ticket creation for later work. Additionally, you will want to visualize this data for real-time analysis by humans, and potentially you will want to create a dashboard for a high-level view of current state. We'll want to consider all three of these scenarios when we discuss the various indicators we will be monitoring.

In other words, suppose that you have 10.08 minutes of downtime for the week, and by Tuesday, you've had three minutes of downtime over three days due to "Stop the World" Cassandra Garbage Collection events and one minute from a load balancer failover. You've used up 40% of the SLO already, and you still have four days left to go. Now is the time to tune that garbage collection! By having an alert after a certain threshold (i.e., 30%) create an email in the ticketing system, the database reliability engineer (DBRE) can jump right on this issue.

Monitoring Availability

Let's use the availability SLO that we defined in the previous section. How do we monitor for this? We will need to monitor system availability as well as user-level errors to get an appropriate picture. As a reminder, our current sample availability SLO is as follows:

- 99.9% availability averaged over one week
- No single incident greater than 10.08 minutes
- Downtime is called if more than 5% of users are affected
- One annual four-hour downtime allowed, if:
  — Communicated to users at least two weeks ahead of time

— Affects no more than 10% of users at a time

Traditionally, Ops staff would tend to focus on fairly low-level monitoring to inform them whether a system was available. For instance, they might measure to see whether a host was up, whether it was reachable, and whether the expected services that were hosted by that system were running and connectable. In a distributed system, this rapidly proves to be unsustainable and not a good predictor of service availability. If we have 1,000 JVMs, 20 database instances, and 50 web servers in place, how can we learn if any one of these components is affecting the service and to what degree that impact exists?

With this in mind, the first thing we want to focus on is error rates from user requests. This is also known as *Real User Monitoring* (RUM). For instance, when a user submits an HTTP call from her browser, does she receive a well-formed response from the service? If your service is popular, this can potentially be a lot of data. Consider a major global news event that is generating in excess of 70,000 hits per second on a web service. Any modern CPU can calculate errors rates for this amount of data fairly efficiently. This data is logged from the application (such as Apache HTTP) to a logging daemon (such as a Linux syslog).

At this point, the way in which a system would get the data from these logs into appropriate tools for monitoring and analysis varies wildly. We're going to gloss over this for now and assume that we've stored the success/error rates of the service to a production datastore without any aggregation or averaging at the base level. We discussed this in the previous section, but it is worth repeating that storing averages alone loses the valuable data.

With our data stored, it is relatively trivial to evaluate whether one percent or more of our calls failed, and if so, mark that second as downtime. This regular tally of downtime can be summed and compared to our budget of 604.8 seconds for the week and reported in a dashboard that is displayed in browsers, on monitors in a network operations center or office, or any other number of places to help all stakeholders see how the team is performing.

Ideally, we want to be able to use this data to predict whether the current downtime amounts will lead to violation of the budget by the end of the week. The largest challenge in most environments is workload shifts due to product development. In a system for which releases are happening weekly, and sometimes daily, any previous datasets become relatively useless. This is particularly true of the older datasets compared to the ones in the recent past. This is called a *decaying function*.

Exploring predictive data science is beyond the scope of this book. But, there are numerous approaches that you can take here to predict whether you will violate your SLO in the current week or potentially in future weeks. It is worthwhile to take the previous N weeks' value (N could be larger in stable environments or as small as one in continuous deployment models of downtimes) and see how many SLO violations occurred during those periods for which downtime was equal to or less than the current period.

For instance, your script might take the current downtime, which could be 10 seconds for the week, and the current time in the week in seconds. That downtime could be defined as a downtime of 10 seconds and a time of 369,126 seconds into the week.

You would then evaluate the previous 13 weeks, and for each week for which downtime was 10 seconds or less at the same point in the week (between 1 and 369,126 seconds), evaluate whether an SLO violation occurred that week. You would then give a weight based on the nearness of the previous period. For instance, in 13 weeks, the previous week is assigned 13 points, the one before it, 12, and so on. Adding up the weights for weeks for which the SLO violations occurred, you might issue a high-priority ticket to your Ops team and notify them in chat if the combined values are 13 or above. This is just one example of a way to ensure that you have some level of data-driven monitoring in place if you do not have a crack team of data scientists with the time and inclination to review service-level data. The goals here are to get proactive eyes on a potential problem before it is an emergency, which means fewer pages to humans and fewer availability impacts.

In addition to real user monitoring, it is useful to create a second data-set of artificial tests. This is called *synthetic* monitoring. Just because these are artificial, does not mean that they are not identical in activity to a real user. For instance, a transactional email company might trigger email requests from QA accounts just as any other customer would do.

The case for synthetic monitoring is to provide coverage that is consistent and thorough. Users might come from different regions and be active at different times. This can cause blind spots if we are not monitoring all possible regions and code paths into our service. With synthetic monitoring, we are able to identify areas where availability or latency is proving to be unstable or degraded, and prepare or mitigate appropriately. Examples of such preparation/mitigation include adding extra capacity, performance tuning queries, or even moving traffic away from unstable regions.

With synthetic and RUM, you can identify when availability is affected and even predict when you might have an SLO violation. But, this does not help us when it comes to larger impacts due to system failures or capacity limitations. One of the key reasons to implement robust monitoring is to capture enough data to predict failures and overloads before they occur.

Monitoring Latency

Monitoring latency is quite similar to monitoring for errors in requests. Although availability is Boolean, latency is a value of time that we must measure to validate whether it fits within the constraints given in our SLO.

Latency SLO

Ninety-nine percent request latency over one minute must be between 25 and 100 ms.

As with our error telemetry, we assume that our HTTP request logs have gone through syslog and into a time–series datastore. With that in place, we can take an interval of time, order all data points by latency, and eliminate the top one percent of requests. In this case, we are averaging values in each one-second time window. If any of the remaining 99% of calls are longer than 100 ms, we have a violation that counts toward downtime.

This kind of data can also lend itself to predictive analytics via any multitude of tools or scripts. By measuring previous latencies during similar time or traffic patterns, you can look for anomalies that indicate a climbing response time that could lead to an SLO violation.

Monitoring Throughput

Throughput is easy to assess with the data we've assembled and reviewed for availability and latency SLOs. If you are storing every record, you will be able to measure transactions per second quite easily. If you are exceeding the minimum transaction count in your SLO, you are good. If you are not generating enough traffic to exceed your SLO, you will need to rely on periodic load tests to ensure that your system can support the demands of the SLO. Load testing is covered in more detail later.

Monitoring Cost and Efficiency

Cost and efficiency can be a challenging SLO to monitor because there are some costs that are not as quantifiable as others. You must consider the overall cost for a window of time. If you are working in a cloud environment, for which resources are billed like utilities, you can fairly easily quantify costs for resources such as storage, processing, memory, and interinstance bandwidth. If you are using your own bare metal, you will need to get hardware costs for all machines dedicated to the services, estimating when shared resources are in play. Often, the period of time for the cost is not very granular, however, so it can prove challenging to understand costs for specific periods of time, such as by hour, if you are getting monthly reports from the provider.

For fixed-cost items such as instances and storage, you can keep an uploaded cost matrix from your provider or from your own internal databases. This data can be referenced as resources are deployed and decommissioned, creating an estimated spend. For usage costs such as bandwidth, IOPS, and similar items, you can reference other gathered metrics on a scheduled interval to also estimate costs.

You also need to consider the costs of staff who are maintaining the service. This can include operations, database and network engineers, anyone on-call, and coordinating project managers. These can be shared resources, and again, you will find yourself estimating percentage of time devoted to the specific service you are monitoring. If you are in an environment in which time tracking is in use, you can potentially reference that data to build a somewhat real-time human spend metric. Otherwise, you will need to estimate on a regular basis, taking into account factors such as terminations, new hires, and team changes.

This is manual work, and some of it we can not automate easily, but nonetheless it provides incredibly valuable data in terms of the cost of operating services. Comparing this to the value being generated by services gives reliability engineers a target for efficiency improvements.

Wrapping Up

Service-level management is the cornerstone of infrastructure design and operations. We cannot emphasize enough that all actions must be a result of planning to avoid violations of our SLOs. The SLOs create the rules of the game that we are playing. We use the SLOs to decide what risks we can take, what architectural choices to make, and how to design the processes needed to support those architectures.

Having completed this chapter, you should now understand the core concepts of service-level management, including SLAs, SLOs, and SLIs. You should know the common indicators that are used, including availability, latency, durability, and efficiency. You should also understand the approaches to monitoring these indicators effectively to catch problems before your SLOs are violated. This should give you a good foundation to effectively communicate what is expected of the services you manage and to contribute to meeting those goals.

In Chapter 3, we cover risk management. This is where we begin to evaluate what might affect the service-levels we've committed to meeting. Using these service-level requirements and recognizing the potential risks, we can effectively design services and processes to ensure that we fulfill the promises we've made to the business.

CHAPTER 3

Risk Management

Operations is a set of promises and the work it takes to fulfill it. In Chapter 2, we discussed how to create, monitor, and report on them. Risk management is what we do to identify, assess, and prioritize the uncertainties that could cause us to violate these promises we've made. It is also the application of resources (technology, tools, people, and processes) to monitor, mitigate, and reduce the probability of these uncertainties coming to pass.

This is not a perfect science! The goal of this is not to eliminate all risks. That is a quixotic goal that will waste resources. The goal is to bake the assessment and mitigation of risk into all of our processes and to iteratively reduce the impact of risks through mitigation and prevention techniques. This process should be continually performed with inputs from observation of incidents, introduction of new architectural components, and the increased or decreased impact as an organization evolves. The cycle of this process can be broken down into seven categories:

- Identify possible hazards/threats that create operational risk to the service
- Conduct assessment of each risk, looking at likelihood and impacts
- Categorize the likelihood and outcome of the risks
- Identify controls for mitigating consequences or reducing likelihood of the risk
- Prioritize which risks to tackle first
- Implement controls and monitor effectiveness
- Repeat process

By repeating this process, you are exercising *Kaizen*, or continuous improvement. And no where is this more important than in risk assessment, where you must evolve a strategy incrementally.

Risk Considerations

There are multiple variables that can affect the quality of our risk assessment processes (*http://www.au.af.mil/au/awc/awcgate/usmc/orm.pdf*). These can be broken down into the following categories:

- Unknown factors and complexity
- Availability of resources
- Human factors
- Group factors

Each of these need to be taken into consideration to help define a realistic process for your team, and so we'd like to briefly touch on them in this section.

Unknown Factors and Complexity

Compounding the challenge of a risk assessment process is the sheer amount of complexity involved in today's systems. The more complex and convoluted the domain, the greater the difficulty people have in transferring their knowledge to situations they have not experienced. The tendency to oversimplify concepts so that they can be dealt with easily is called *reductive bias*. What works in initial learning no longer works in advanced knowledge acquisition. There are numerous risks that are unknown, and many that are out of our control. Here are some examples:

- Impacts from other customers in hosted environments such as Amazon or Google
- Impacts from vendors integrated into the infrastructure
- Software engineers pushing code
- Marketing efforts creating workload spikes
- Upstream and downstream services
- Patches, repository changes, and other incremental software changes

To assess risk in such environments, problem-solving in these domains help with the assessment process. The operations team must utilize its collective experience and continually grow knowledge to continue to build richer models for planning. The teams must also acknowledge that they will not be able to consider all possibilities and that they must plan for unknown possibilities by creating resilient systems.

Availability of Resources

If any of you have worked in a resource-starved department or a scrappy startup, you know that trying to acquire resources for ongoing, proactive processes like this can be...well, challenging (aka Sisyphean)? So, you might find yourself with 4 hours or perhaps only 30 minutes a month to visit risk-management processes. Therefore, you must create value. The cost of your time and the resources you apply to mitigation must be less than the cost of inaction. In other words, be relentless in prioritizing against the most probable and highest impacting risks with the time available. Create resilient systems and learn from the incidents that occur.

Human Factors

There are numerous potential issues (*http://bit.ly/2zyoBmm*) when humans begin doing things. We're brilliant, but we have a lot of fine print in our owner's manuals. Here are some things that can damage these processes:

Inaction syndrome
> Many Ops folks will find themselves working under a manager or surrounded by peers who are risk averse. Characterized by inertia, these people choose inaction because they consider risk of change greater than risk of inaction. It is important to do the math rather than falling back on inaction in the face of the unknown.

Ignoring familiar hazards
> Experienced engineers will often ignore common risks, focusing more on exotic and rare events. For instance, someone who is quite used to dealing with disks filling up might focus more on datacenter-wide events and not plan adequately for disk space controls.

Fear
> Fear can be considered a positive as well as a negative stressor depending on the individual. Some individuals thrive within high-stress, high-stakes environments and will bring great value to your planning, mitigation, and production work. It is not uncommon for those who have fear reactions to ignore worst-case scenarios because of their fear. This could lead to lack of preparation on key, high-risk components and systems. It is important to recognize these reactions in your team.

Overoptimism
> Another human tendency in response to risk assessment is that of overoptimism. We often believe the best of ourselves and the others in our teams. This can lead us to consider things in ideal situations (nonfatigued, no other incidents distracting us, junior staff being available). This applies not only to people, but to events. Have you ever thought, *"There's no way three disks can fail in the same day,"* only to experience the pain of a bad batch of disks causing exactly that?

We must also consider physical factors, such as fatigue, in creating risk, and as a hindrance in manual remediation (aka firefighting). Any time we consider human effort and the risks inherent to that effort, such as manual changes and forensics, we must assume that the Ops staff digging into the meaty problem has been woken up after a long day of work. Perhaps this won't be the case, but we must consider it. Additionally, while designing controls for mitigating or eliminating risk, we must consider that the person doing manual remediation could be just as fatigued and perhaps even fighting multiple fires at the same time.

Pager Fatigue

Pager fatigue (http://bit.ly/2zyfqCv) is when unnecessary or excessive paging creates fatigue and overwhelm. You should consider this when deciding how much alerting (manual response and remediation) is built into the monitoring processes. It is often caused by false positives (alerts for issues that aren't issues, often due to poorly tuned thresholds), or using alerts instead of warnings for trends that might become dangerous in the near future.

Group Factors

Just as individuals have their blind spots, groups have their own dynamics that can skew a process of risk management. Here are some factors to keep in mind:

Group polarization

Also known as risky shift, group polarization occurs because groups tend to make decisions that are more extreme than their individual members hold. This will tend toward contrary shifts from initial views. For instance, if individuals feel cautious, they will tend towards being much more risk tolerant after consensus has been met. Similarly, risk-tolerance will shift toward risk-avoidance. Individuals often will not want to appear the most conservative in a group environment. This can cause a team to be more risk-tolerant than is necessarily appropriate.

Risk transfer

Groups will also tend towards greater risk tolerance when they have other groups to which they can assign risk. For instance, if I am planning for the Ops team, I might take greater risks if I know I have a database team to fall back on. Building a sense of ownership and working in cross-functional teams that cannot shift risk to others will help this.

Decision transfer

Decision transfer can occur when teams overestimate risk, so that they can transfer responsibility for specific decisions to others. For example, if high-risk changes require CTO approval, and thus responsibility, people will tend to measure risks higher so as to push decision making up the chain. This can also be mitigated through more autonomous teams that rely on the expertise and experience of individuals and teams rather than hierarchical approval processes.

What Do We Do?

We face a reality that a risk-management process can easily become overly burdensome. Even with significant resources, teams will still not be able to capture all potential risks that can affect availability, performance, stability, and security. It makes sense for us to create a process that iterates and improves over time. Striving for resilience in handling risks versus elimination of all risks also allows for intelligent risk taking in the name of innovation and improvements.

We would argue that the goal of eliminating all risks is actually a poor one. Systems without stressors do not tend to strengthen and improve over time. They end up being brittle against unknown stressors that have not been planned for. Systems that experience stressors regularly, and thus have been designed for resiliency, will tend to handle unknown risks more gracefully.

It is arguable that systems should use their downtime budgets, as Google coined, to use risk for opportunities that provide great benefit while incurring a manageable amount of risk. At Google, if it has a budget of 30 minutes of downtime for a quarter and has not used that time, it is willing to take greater risks for the sake of new feature releases, improvements, and enhancements. This is an excellent use of the full budget for innovation rather than a completely risk-averse approach.

So how does this translate into a real-world approach to risk assessment as a process? Let's begin with what *not* to do!

What Not to Do

OK, so that's a lot to keep in mind! Here are some last-minute tips to consider as we actually dig into the process of risk management:

- Don't allow subjective biases to damage your process
- Don't allow anecdotes and word of mouth to be the primary source of risk assessment
- Don't focus only on previous incidents and issues; look ahead
- Don't stagnate; keep reviewing previous work
- Don't ignore human factors
- Don't ignore evolution in architecture and workflow
- Don't assume that your environment is the same as previous environments

- Don't create brittle controls or ignore worst-case contingencies

We're sure you'll add to this list over time, but this is a good list to keep in mind to avoid the pitfalls awaiting you as you consider your systems.

A Working Process: Bootstrapping

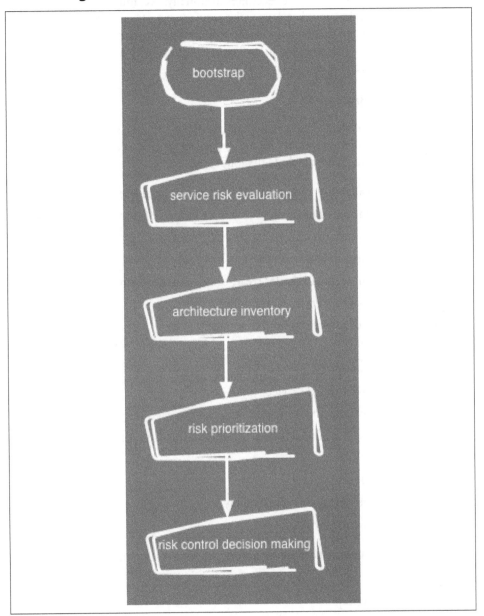

Figure 3-1. Initial bootstrapping of a risk management process

Whether for a new service or for inheritance of an existing one, our process begins with an initial bootstrapping. In a bootstrapping (see Figure 3-1), the goal is to recognize the major risks that would endanger the Service Level Objective (SLO) for the service or that are most likely to occur. Additionally, we must take into account worst-case scenarios that could endanger the service's long-term viability. Remember, brave database engineer, that trying to build a comprehensive risk portfolio is not the goal here. The goal is a starting list to mitigate, eliminate, or plan how, operationally, to drive the most value for existing resources available.

Service Risk Evaluation

Armed with a list of the services and microservices that you are supporting, you should sit down with the product owners and evaluate risk tolerance for each. The questions you want to answer include the following:

- What are the availability and latency SLOs defined for this service?
- What does downtime or unacceptable latency look like for this service when:
  — All customers are affected?
  — A subset of customers are affected?
  — The service in degraded mode? (read-only, some functions turned off, etc.)
  — Performance of the service is degraded?
- What is the cost of downtime for this service?
  — Revenue lost?
  — Customer retention?
    — Is this a free or paid service?
    — Are there competitors the customer can easily go to?
  — Are there downtime impacts that can undermine the entire company?
    — Data loss?
    — Privacy breach?
    — Downtime during an event/holiday?
    — Extended downtime?

Let's look at an example. UberPony is a pony-on-demand company comprising six services:

1. New customer signup
2. Pony-on-demand, order/fulfillment
3. Pony handler signup
4. Pony handler logistics

5. Pony handler payments

6. Internal analytics

Let's look at two services, New Customer Signup, and Order/Fulfillment:

UberPony sustomer signup

Availability SLO	99.90%
Latency SLO	1 second
New customers per day	5,000
SLO allowed errors	5
Infrastructure cost per day	$13,698
Infrastructure cost per dollar of revenue	$0.003
Customer lifetime value	$1,000
Lifetime value per day	$5,000,000
Peak customers per minute	100
Customer dropout after error	60%
Peak value loss per minute	$60,000

UberPony ordering and fulfillment

Availability SLO	99.90%
Latency SLO	1 second
Current Orders per day	500,000
SLO allowed errors	500
Infrastructure cost per day	$30,000
Infrastructure cost per dollar of revenue	$0.006
Revenue per order	$10
Daily revenue	$5,000,000
Peak orders per minute	1,000
Order dropout after error	25%
Customer loss after error	1%
Peak revenue loss per minute	$2,500
Customer value loss per minute	$10,000
Total loss per minute	$12,500

So, it appears that our customer signup service can cost us up to 4.8 times as much revenue per minute as ordering and fulfillment service. Seventy-five percent of customers will retry an order, but only 40% of customers will come back if they can't sign up. Apparently they are happy to go to UberDonkey, instead. Notice that we tried to consider variables such as customer loss after an order error and how many customers or orders were retried after an error. This can be difficult without good business intelligence, but guesses can suffice if you do not have data available. It is better than nothing!

This data will change and evolve, so be sure to keep it up to date as your go through the process. For instance, if UberDonkey becomes more competitive and UberPony loses 5% of its customers after an order error, suddenly our loss per minute of downtime for the order/fulfillment service becomes $52,500. This has increased in priority significantly. Thus, it makes much more sense for us to focus on the customer signup service as a priority.

Architectural Inventory

Now that we've defined our scope, we take inventory of the systems and environments for which we are responsible:

- Datacenters
- Architectural components/tiers (i.e., MySQL, Nginx load balancers, J2EE application instances, network, firewall, Hadoop/HDFS, Content Delivery Network [CDN])
- Roles within those component (i.e., Writer/Primary, Replica)
- Interactions/Communication pathways between services (queries from app to mysql, Load balancer to app, app post to Redis)
- Jobs (Extract, Transform, and Load [ETL] process, CDN loading, cache refresh, configuration management, orchestration, backup and recovery, log aggregation)

Here is a simplistic inventory for our top priority service:

UberPony customer signup

Component	Datacenter 1 count	Datacenter 2 count
Front end load balancers	2	2
Web servers	20	20
Java load balancers	2	2
Java servers	10	10
Database proxies	2	2
Cloudfront CDN	Service	Service
Redis cache servers	4	4
MySQL cluster write servers	1	0
MySQL cluster read servers	2	2
MySQL replication	Service	Service
CDN refresh	Job	Job
Redis cache refresh	Job	Job
MySQL backups	Job	n/a
ETL process	Job	n/a
RedShift data warehouse	Service	n/a

Our next step is to assess the risks in this architecture that could affect the service.

Prioritization

How do we identify and prioritize the risks that could potentially cause us to violate our SLO targets? The field of risk management defines risk in terms of the likelihood of a hazard leading to an adverse outcome multiplied by the consequence of that outcome. For instance, this grid shows an assessment spectrum:

Likelihood/Impact	Severe	Major	Moderate	Minor	Negligible
Almost Certain	Unacceptable	Unacceptable	High	Moderate	Acceptable
Likely	Unacceptable	High	High	Moderate	Acceptable
Possible	Unacceptable	High	Moderate	Moderate	Acceptable
Unlikely	High	Moderate	Moderate	Acceptable	Acceptable
Rare	High	Moderate	Acceptable	Acceptable	Acceptable

With the goal of removing ambiguity, it is important to quantify what the values for likelihood and outcome are. Outcomes will vary based on your specific domain problem. In terms of the issue of ambiguity in likelihood/probability, we would suggest reviewing "Describing probability: The limitations of natural language" (*http://www.risk-doctor.com/pdf-files/emeamay05.pdf*).

Let's break up probabilities as follows:

Scale	Range
Almost certain	>50%
Likely	26–50%
Possible	11–25%
Unlikely	5–10%
Rare	<5%

We will consider this the percentage that we will violate SLOs during a specific period, such as, for example, a week. In terms of impact, we will consider our SLO when defining impact categories as well as other issues that could destroy a business, including data corruption, privacy exposures, and security incidents. Most of those will go into severe or major categorizations. Again, these are only examples.

Severe impact (immediate SLO violation)

A severe impact's potential are as follows:

- The entire service will be unavailable or degraded past 100 ms for 10 minutes or more for 5% or more of users. (In a 7 day week, there are 10,080 minutes. 10 minutes of downtime violates a 99.9% SLO).

- Imminent or current exposing of customer data to other customers.
- Letting nonauthorized person access production systems and/or data.
- Data corruption of transactional data.

Any of the preceding would trigger a severe classification.

Major (imminent SLO violation)

A major impact's potential are as follows:

- The entire service will be unavailable or degraded past 100 ms for 3 to 5 minutes for 5% or more of users (up to 50% of availability budget).
- System capacity degraded to 100% of needed capacity instead of 200% target.

Any of the above would trigger a major classification.

Moderate (could contribute to SLO violation with other incidents in the same period)

A moderate impact's potential characteristics are as follows:

- The entire service will be unavailable or degraded past 100 ms for 1 to 3 minutes for 5% or more of users (up to 33% of availability budget).
- System capacity degraded to 125% of needed capacity instead of 200% target.

Any of the preceding would trigger a moderate classification.

Minor

A minor impact's potential characteristics are as follows:

- The entire service will be unavailable or degraded past 100ms for up to one minute for 5% or more of users (up to 10% of availability budget).
- System capacity degraded to 150% of needed capacity instead of 200% target.

Any of the preceding would trigger a minor classification.

As a reminder, we will not try to capture every potential risk. You will add more to this portfolio day to day as part of the ongoing incident management and risk-management processes. What we are doing is called *framing*, which means that we are creating a limited scope to bound our work in a pragmatic way. In this case, we are framing based on the *most likely* and *most impactful* scenarios.

For instance, we know that component failures and instance failures are common events in public cloud environments, such as the one UberPony uses as a host. In other words, there is a low mean time between failures (MTBF). We will classify these failures as "Likely" for the web and Java instance groups because we have a moderate amount of them in play at any time (20 or 10, respectively). That being said, failure of one web instance means 5% of customers are affected. Failure of a Java instance means 10% of customers are affected. That is a violation of SLO, and because it might take three to five minutes to launch a new copy of this, we would have a *major* impact. With a *likely* probability and a *major* impact, risk is *high*. After we put in automated remediation (take the instance out of service and launch a new one in its place), we test, and this process takes five seconds on average. This puts the new impact to *minor*, and thus the risk moves to *moderate*.

If we consider failure at the service or instance level for our inventory, we might come up with something like this:

UberPony customer signup service

Component	Likelihood	Impact	Risk
Frontend load balancers	Possible	Severe	Unacceptable
Web servers	Likely	Major	High
Java load balancers	Possible	Major	High
Java servers	Likely	Major	High
Database proxies	Possible	Major	High
Cloudfront CDN	Rare	Major	Moderate
Redis cache servers	Possible	Major	Moderate
MySQL write servers	Unlikely	Severe	High
MySQL read servers	Possible	Major	High
MySQL replication	Possible	Major	High
CDN refresh	Unlikely	Minor	Acceptable
Redis cache refresh	Unlikely	Minor	Acceptable
MySQL backups	Unlikely	Major	Acceptable
ETL process	Unlikely	Minor	Acceptable
RedShift data warehouse	Rare	Minor	Acceptable

Based on framing, we want to dive deeper into anything with an *unacceptable* or *high* risk first, and then we can dig deeper into the *moderate* cases, and so on. In the database section after operations core, we will do risk assessment for databases in greater detail. Our goal here is to help you understand the process. The other caveat is that we do need to consider full datacenter-level risks. Although these are rare, they go in the same category as privacy violation, data loss, and other risks that require consideration due to the potentially business-ending impacts.

Control and Decision Making

Now that we have a prioritized list of risks to evaluate, let's look at the techniques for deciding on controls to mitigate and potentially eliminate those risks. We started this in the previous section with our web and Java servers by putting in automated replacements to reduce the mean time to recover (MTTR) of the failure. Remember, our goal is to focus on rapid recovery and reduction of MTTR over elimination of failures. Resiliency over brittle high availability!

Why MTTR Over MTBF?

When you create a system that rarely breaks, you create a system that is inherently fragile. Will your team be ready to do repairs when the system does fail? Will it even know what to do? Systems that have frequent failures that are controlled and mitigated such that their impact is negligible have teams that know what to do when things go sideways. Processes are well documented and honed, and automated remediation becomes actually useful rather than hiding in the dark corners of your system.

For each potential risk, there are three approaches the team can choose from:

- Avoidance (find a way to eliminate the risk)
- Reduction (find a way to lessen the impact of the risk when it occurs)
- Acceptance (label the risk tolerable and plan for it to happen accordingly)

Technically, in risk management circles, there is a fourth approach, called risk sharing, in which you use outsourcing, insurance, and other risk transfer approaches. None of those apply to risk in IT, however, so it will not be analyzed.

For each component, we will look at the types of failure, the impacts of those failures and a few controls to automate recovery, improve recovery times, and reduce frequency. Associated with these controls will be a cost and effort. By comparing this cost with the costs of downtime, we can make decisions on the proper choice in mitigation.

Identification

In our UberPony risk evaluation, we identified multiple tiers of our MySQL storage service as high risk. This is very typical of the database tier. So, let's look at what we can do to reduce this risk. We've identified four key failure points in this service:

- Write instance failure
- Read instance failure
- Replication failure
- Backup failures

Each of these are common failure points for a datastore.

Evaluation

For write failures, the UberPony ops team sits down and evaluates its options for automating MySQL writer failure recovery. If a write instance failure occurs, our customer signup service cannot create or change any data. This means no new customers and no ability for customers, or UberPony, to change customer data. We've identified that if the signup service is down at peak, we can potentially lose $60,000 of lifetime customer value per minute. So, it is pretty critical that we figure this one out! This means that *risk acceptance* is not an option.

Mitigation and controls

There are some *risk elimination* items already in place. We have a RAID 10-disk system that provides disk redundancy so that disk failure does not create database failure. There are similar redundancies across the environment. Another *elimination* approach that is brought up is replacing the base MySQL database engine with Galera, an architecture that allows us to write to any node in the MySQL cluster. This would require a significant architectural change, and no one on the team has much experience with this engine. After consideration, the risks introduced by a new system seem to outweigh the gains from the approach.

If the application is designed correctly, customers could still log in to the service and view their data from the read instances. This is *risk mitigation*. Speaking to the software engineering team, we find out that this is on its roadmap. But, new customers still can't sign up in degraded mode, so we do not get much value for the cost of this feature (other features not being developed is a high cost in a competitive marketplace).

Ultimately, the team decides to do an automated remediation—in this case, an automated failover to another master. They choose automated over manual because the 10 minutes of downtime allowed in the SLO simply doesn't allow for the time it takes to get a human online and ready to take action. That being said, with managing writes, we have a potential for data loss, so the process must be rock solid.

Implementation

The team decides on MySQL MHA as the technology it will use to do automated failover. MySQL MHA, or MySQL High Availability, is software to manage the failover and ensuing replication topology changes required in such a failover. The team creates a plan for vigorous testing before implementing such a critical process. Such tests are phased, starting with a test environment with no traffic, followed by a test environment with simulated traffic, and finally on production, closely monitored. These tests are done numerous times to ensure they aren't looking at an outlier. The tests include the following:

- Cleanly shutting down the master database in a test environment
- Killing the MySQL process in a test environment
- Killing the server instance running MySQL in a test environment
- Simulating a network partition

After each test, the team does the following:

- Record the amount of time the failover took
- Record the latency of simulated and production traffic to evaluate impacts to performance
- Validate that tables are not corrupt
- Validate the data was not lost
- Look at error logs from the clients to see what the impact was during this time

When the team is satisfied that the system works and will meet its SLOs, it considers how to incorporate this process into other daily processes to ensure that it is well exercised, documented, and free of bugs. The team initially chooses to incorporate it into its deployment process, using the failover process to do rolling changes to database objects so as to not affect MySQL single-threaded replication processes. By the time the team finishes, failover is down to a 30-second or less impact.

As the software engineering team practices the failover processes, it also realizes that there could be a potential for data loss during that 30-second interval. So, the team enacts double write for its applications, sending all of its inserts, updates, and deletes to an event broker in case data must be recovered. This is a further mitigation of the impacts of the write-master failover.

These controls are for the initial bootstrapping. It is important to remember that this doesn't need to be perfect. This is an initial set of controls only, focused on the highest priorities and the greatest value.

With the bootstrapping process complete, you've gone a long way toward covering the most common cases of risk. From this point on, it is a process of iterating.

Ongoing Iterations

With a bootstrapped process in place, our priorities for risk elimination and mitigation are pushed into the architectural pipeline for design, build, and ongoing operations. We have mentioned previously that risk management is a continual process; thus, there is no need to be comprehensive in the beginning because continued processes will add to the risk portfolio, providing deeper coverage, as depicted in Figure 3-2. So, what are those processes?

- Service delivery reviews
- Incident management
- Architectural pipeline

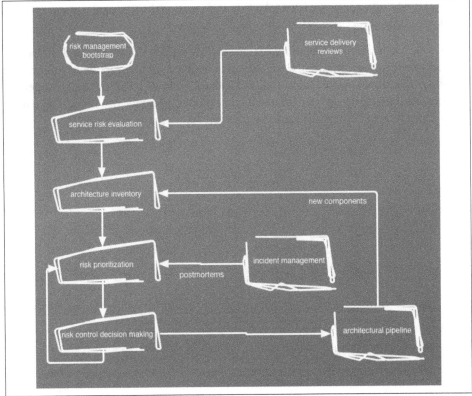

Figure 3-2. The ongoing life cycle and inputs to the risk-management process

Service delivery reviews are periodic revisiting of the service's evolution with an eye toward shifts in risk tolerance, revenue, cost of impacts, and user base. As these values shift significantly, previous risk acceptances, mitigations, and eliminations must be revisited to ensure that they are still acceptable.

Incident management processes will also create inputs for risk prioritization. As postmortems reveal new vulnerabilities, we must analyze those vulnerabilities and add them into the priority list. Finally, as the architectural pipeline is built, we must bring new components through the risk-management process to identify any risks that might have been missed in the design phase.

Wrapping Up

By now you've learned the importance of incorporating risk management into the daily processes of IT. You've gone over some of the considerations and factors that can affect the process and broken out a realistic bootstrapping process in addition to the day-to-day processes that can keep an incremental risk-management process developing over time.

Even armed with an understanding of our service-level commitments and the potential risks to those commitments, we still are missing a vital component: operational visibility. Situational awareness as well as historical knowledge of our systems performance and characteristics over time will be needed to preempt issues and make decisions about how to continually improve the systems we manage.

CHAPTER 4

Operational Visibility

Visibility (often referred to as monitoring) is the cornerstone of the craft of database reliability engineering. Operational visibility means that we have awareness of the working characteristics of a database service due to the regular measuring and collection of data points about the various components. Why is this important? Why do we need operational visibility? Here are just some of the reasons:

Break/fix and alerting
> We need to know when things break, or are about to break, so that we can fix them to avoid violating our Service-Level Objectives (SLOs).

Performance and behavior analysis
> It's important to understand the latency distribution in our applications, including outliers, and we need to know the trends over time. This data is critical to understanding the impact of new features, experiments, and optimization.

Capacity planning
> Being able to correlate user behavior and application efficiency to real resources (CPU, network, storage, throughput, memory) is critical to ensuring that you never encounter a lack of capacity at a critical business moment.

Debugging and postmortems
> Moving fast means things do break. Good operational visibility gives you the ability to rapidly identify failure points and optimization points to mitigate future risk. Human error is never a root cause, but systems can always be improved upon and made to be more resilient.

Did We Mean to Say Human Error Is Never a Root Cause?

When analyzing an incident or problem, it can be tempting to use human error as a root cause. If we dig in deeper, though, what appears to be human error is caused by an underlying failure of process or environment. How can that be? Here are some possibilities:

- A fragile, poorly instrumented, or overly complex system can cause humans to make mistakes.

- A process that doesn't take into account human needs, such as sleep, context, or skill can also cause humans to make mistakes.

- A process of hiring and training operators may be broken, allowing the wrong operators into the environment.

Furthermore, "root cause" itself is a problematic statement, as there is rarely a single issue that leads to errors and incidents. Complex systems lead to complex failures, and adding humans into the mix complicates things further. Instead of thinking in terms of root cause, we suggest you consider a *list* of contributing factors, prioritized by risk and impact.

Business analysis
> Understanding how your business functionality is being utilized can be a leading indicator of issues, but it is also critical for everyone to see how people are using your features and how much value versus cost is being driven.

Correlation and causation
> By having events in the infrastructure and application register themselves in your operational visibility stack, you can rapidly correlate changes in workload, behavior, and availability. Examples of these events are application deployments, infrastructure changes, and database schema changes.

Pretty much every facet of your organization requires true operational visibility—*OpViz*. Our goal in this chapter is to help you to understand observability in the architectures with which you will be working. Although there is no one set of tools we espouse, there are principles, a general taxonomy, and usage patterns to learn. We present this via numerous case studies and example approaches. First, let's consider the evolution of OpViz from traditional approaches to those utilized today.

Operational visibility is a big deal! We need some rules on how we design, build, and utilize this critical process.

The New Rules of Operational Visibility

Modern operational visibility assumes that data stores are distributed, often massively. It recognizes that collection, and even presentation of data, are not as crucial as the analysis. It always asks—and hopefully elicits rapid answering of—two questions: "How is this impacting my SLOs?" and "How is this broken, and why?" In other words, rather than treating your OpViz stack as a set of utilities to be relegated to the Ops team, you must design, build, and maintain it as a business intelligence (BI) platform. This that you must treat it the same way you would a data warehouse or big data platform. The rules of the game have changed to reflect this.

Treat OpViz Systems Like BI Systems

When designing a BI system, you begin by thinking about the kinds of questions your users will be asking and building out from there. Consider your users needs for data latency ("How quickly is data available?"), data resolution ("How deep down can the user drill?"), and data availability. In other words, you are defining SLOs for your OpViz service. (Refer to Chapter 2.)

The hallmark of a mature OpViz platform is that it can provide not only the state of the infrastructure running the application, but also the behavior of the applications running on that infrastructure. Ultimately, this should also be able to show anyone how the business is doing and how that is being affected by the infrastructure and applications on which the business is relying. With that in mind, the OpViz platform must support operations and database engineers, software engineers, business analysts, and executives.

Distributed Ephemeral Environments Trending to the Norm

We've already discussed the fact that our database instance life cycles are trending down with the adoption of virtual infrastructures. Even though they are still much longer lived than other infrastructure components, we still must be able to gather metrics for services consisting of short-lived components that are aggregated rather than individual database hosts.

Figure 4-1 demonstrates a fairly stable master/replica setup for a relational datastore in which numerous activities can occur in one day. By the end of the day, we can see a completely new setup, as illustrated in Figure 4-2.

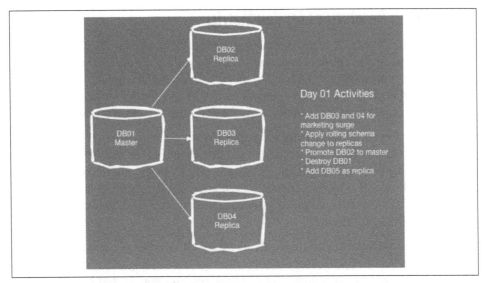

Figure 4-1. Typical master/replica setup

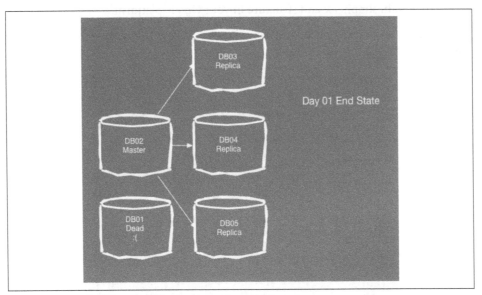

Figure 4-2. End of day 1

This kind of dynamic infrastructure requires us to store metrics based on roles rather than hostnames or IPs. So, instead of storing a set of metrics as DB01, we would add metrics to the "master" role, allowing us to see all master behavior even after switching to a new master. Service discovery systems do a great job of maintaining abstraction above the dynamic portions of infrastructure to facilitate this.

Store at High Resolutions for Key Metrics

As reviewed in Chapter 2, high resolution is critical for understanding busy application workloads. At a minimum, anything related to your SLOs should be kept at one-second or lower sampling rates to ensure that you understand what is going on in the system. A good rule of thumb is to consider whether the metric has enough variability to affect your SLOs in the span of 1 to 10 seconds and to base granularity on that.

For instance, if you are monitoring a constrained resource, such as CPU, you would want to collect this data at a one-second or smaller sample given that CPU queues can build up and die down quite quickly. With latency SLOs in the milliseconds, this data must be good enough to see if CPU saturation is the reason your application latency is being affected. Database connection queues are another area that can be missed without very frequent sampling.

Conversely, for infrequently changing items such as disk space or service availability, you can measure these in the one-minute or higher sampling rates without losing data. High sample rates consume a lot of resources, and you should be judicious in using them. Similarly, you should probably keep less than five different sampling rates to maintain simplicity and structure in your OpViz platform.

For an example of the impacts of a sampling rate that is too long, let's consider the graph in Figure 4-3.

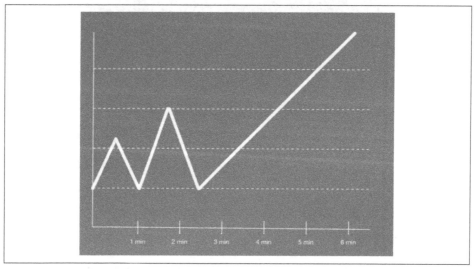

Figure 4-3. Real workload showing spikes

Figure 4-3 shows two spikes followed by a long ascension. Now, if we are sampling this metric at one-minute intervals, the graph would look like Figure 4-4.

Notice now that we don't see even a single spike, and the second graph looks much more benign. In fact, our alerting threshold is not even exceeded until minute three. Assuming a one-minute schedule for storage and for alert rules checking, we wouldn't even send an alert to an operator until 7.5 minutes after the rule was violated!

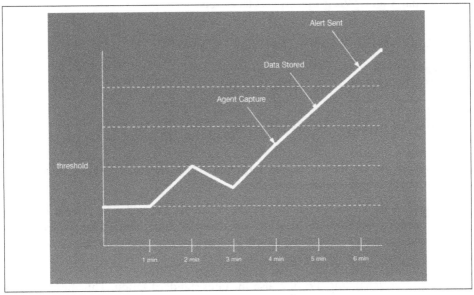

Figure 4-4. Workload visualized via one-minute sampling.

Keep Your Architecture Simple

It is not unusual for a growing platform to have 10,000 or more metrics being checked at various levels of granularity for any number of instances/servers that are going in and out of service in the infrastructure at any time. Your goal is to be able to rapidly answer the aforementioned questions, which means that you must continually push for reducing the signal-to-noise ratio. This means being ruthless in the amount of data you allow into your system, particularly at the human interaction points, such as presentation and alerting.

"Monitor everything" has been the watch-cry for quite a while and was a reaction to environments in which monitoring was sparse and ad hoc. The truth, though, is that distributed systems and multiservice applications create too many metrics. Early stage organizations have neither the money nor the time to manage this amount of monitoring data. Larger organizations should have the knowledge to focus on what is critical to their systems.

Focusing Your Metrics

Focus initially on metrics directly related to your SLOs. This can also be called the critical path. Based on Chapter 2, what are the metrics that should be a priority for getting into your OpViz platform? Let's take a look:

Latency
>   Client calls to your service. How long do they take?

Availability
>   How many of your calls result in errors?

Call Rates
>   How often are calls sent to your service?

Utilization
>   Looking at a service, you should know how critical resources are being utilized to ensure quality of service and capacity.

Of course, as the database reliability engineer (DBRE), you will want to immediately begin breaking out these metrics into the datastore subsystems. That only makes sense, and its a natural evolution that will be discussed later in this chapter.

Simplicity and signal amplification also includes standardization. This means standardizing templates, resolutions, retentions, and any other knobs and features presented to engineers. By doing so, you ensure that your system is easy to understand and thus user friendly for answering questions and identifying issues.

Remembering these four rules will help keep you on track with designing and building incredibly valuable and useful monitoring systems. If you find yourself violating them, ask yourself why. Unless you have a really good answer, consider going back to the foundation.

An OpViz Framework

We could write an entire book on this stuff. As you begin to gather and prepare the appropriate data to go into the OpViz platform for you to do your job, you should be able to recognize a good platform and advocate for a better platform. This is our goal for this section.

Let's think of our OpViz platform as a great big distributed I/O device. Data is sent in, routed, structured, and eventually comes out the other side in useful ways that help you to understand your systems better, to identify behaviors caused by broken or soon to be broken components, and to meet your SLOs. Let's take a closer look at the process:

- Data is generated by agents on clients and then sent to a central collector for that datatype (i.e., metrics to Sensu or CollectD, events to Graphite, logs to Logstash or Splunk):

  — Occasionally a centralized monitoring system (like Sensu or Nagios) will execute checks via a pull method in addition to the aforementioned push method.

  — A benefit of distributed checking—the app generates checks and forwards them—is that there is a significantly smaller amount of configuration management required than in tightly coupled systems like Nagios for which you must configure the agent and the monitoring server together.

- The collectors store data (in systems like Graphite, InfluxDB, or ElasticSearch) or forward to event routers/processors (such as Riemann).

- Event routers uses heuristics to send data to the right places.

- Data output includes long-term storage, graphs, alerts, tickets, and external calls.

These outputs are where we get the true value of our OpViz stack.

Data In

To create outputs, we require good inputs. Wherever possible, use data already generated by your environments rather than artificial probes. When you simulate a user by sending a request into the system, it is called *blackbox monitoring*. *Blackbox monitoring* is sending "canary" users, or watching the inputs and outputs from the internet edge. Blackbox monitoring can be effective if you have low traffic periods or items that just don't run frequently enough for you to monitor. But, if you are generating sufficient data, getting real metrics, aka *whitebox monitoring*, is infinitely more appealing. *Whitebox testing* involves knowing a lot about your application, and at its most specific, includes instrumenting the internals of the application. Great tools for this include AppDynamics, NewRelic, or Honeycomb. With tools such as this you can trace the flow of a single user through the application all the way to the database.

Blackbox Testing and Queueing Theory

With the importance of latency, even with blackbox testing we can use queueing theory and information on traffic volume and and the latency of those calls to determine if the system is saturated. You can learn more about queueing theory from the VividCortex "The Essential Guide to Queueing Theory" (*https://www.vividcortex.com/resources/queueing-theory*) and the University of New Mexico's page (*http://ece-research.unm.edu/jimp/611/slides/chap6_3.html*).

One benefit of this approach is that anything creating data becomes an agent. A centralized, monolithic solution that is generating checks and probes will have challenges scaling as you grow. But with whitebox testing, you've distributed this job across your entire architecture. This kind of architecture also allows new services and components to easily register and deregister with your collection layer, which is a good thing based on our OpViz rules. That being said, there are still times when having a monitoring system that can perform remote executions as a pull can be valuable, such as checking to see whether a service is up, monitoring to see whether replication is running, or checking to see whether an important parameter is enabled on your database hosts.

Sorting Signal from Noise

More and more, we rely on larger datasets to manage distributed systems. It has come to the point at which we are creating big data systems to manage the data we collect on our applications and the infrastructures supporting them. As discussed earlier in this chapter, the use of data science and advanced math is one of the greatest shortcomings to today's observability stacks. To effectively identify the signal from all of this noise, we must rely on machines to sort the signal from the noise.

This area is still very theoretical, and most attempts at good anomaly detection have proven unusable with multimodal workloads and continuous changes to workloads due to rapid feature development and user population changes. A good anomaly detection system helps identify activity that does not fit the norm, thus directing people immediately to problems, which can reduce mean time to recover (MTTR) by getting a higher ratio of signal to noise.

Following are some systems worth evaluating:

- Reimann
- Anomaly.io
- VividCortex
- Dynatrace
- Circonus
- Prometheus

OK, so we are looking to send all of this valuable data to our OpViz platform. What kind of data are we talking about anyway?

Telemetry/Metrics

Ah metrics! So diverse. So ubiquitous. A metric is the measurement of a property that an application or a component of your infrastructure possesses. Metrics are observed periodically, creating a time-series that contains the property or properties, the time-stamp, and the value. Some properties that might apply include the host, service, or datacenter. The true value of this data comes in observing it over time through visualizations such as graphs.

Metrics are typically stored in four different ways:

Counters
> These are cumulative metrics that represent how many times a specific occurrence of something has occurred.

Gauges
> These are metrics that change in any direction, and indicate a current value, such as temperature, jobs in queue, or active locks.

Histograms
> A number of events broken up into configured buckets to show distribution.

Summaries
> This is similar to histogram but focused on proving counts over sliding windows of time.

Metrics often have mathematical functions applied to them to assist humans in deriving value from their visualizations. These functions create more value, but it is important to remember that they are derived data and that the raw data is just as critical. If you're tracking means per minute but do not have the underlying data, you won't be able to create means on larger windows, such as hours or days. The following are some of the functions:

- Count
- Sum
- Average
- Median
- Percentiles
- Standard Deviation
- Rates of Change
- Distributions

Visualizing Distributions

Visualizing a distribution is very valuable to look at the kind of data that is often generated in web architectures. This data is rarely distributed normally and often has long tails. It can be challenging to see this in normal graphs. But, with the ability to generate distribution maps over buckets of time, you enable new styles of visualization such as histograms over time and flame graphs that can really help a human operator visualize the workloads that are occurring in your systems.[1]

Metrics are the source for identifying symptoms of underlying issues, and thus are crucial to early identification and rapid resolution of any number of issues that might affect your SLOs.

Events

An event is a discrete action that has occurred in the environment. A change to a config is an event. A code deployment is an event. A database master failover is an event. Each of these can be signals that are used to correlate symptoms to causes.

Logs

A log is created for an event, so you can consider log events to be a subset of an event. Operating systems, databases, and applications all create logs during certain events. Unlike metrics, logs can provide additional data and context to something that has occurred. For instance, a database query log can tell you when a query was executed, important metrics about that query, and even the database user who executed it.

Data Out

So, data is flowing into our systems, which is nice and all but doesn't help us answer our questions or meet our SLOs, now does it? What should we be looking to create in this OpViz framework? Let's examine this more closely:

Alerts

An alert is an interrupt to a human that instructs him to drop what he's doing and investigate a rules violation that caused the alert to be sent. This is an expensive operation and should be utilized only when SLOs are in imminent danger of violation.

---

1 Latency Heat Maps (*http://www.brendangregg.com/HeatMaps/latency.html*)

Tickets/tasks
> Tickets and tasks are generated when work must be done, but there is not an imminent disaster. The output of monitoring should be tickets/tasks that go in engineer queues for work.

Notifications
> Sometimes you just want to record that an event has occurred to help create context for folks, such as when code deploy events are registered. Notifications will often go to a chat room, a wiki, or collaboration tool to make it visible without interrupting workflow.

Automation
> There are times when data, particularly utilization data, advises of the need for more or less capacity. Autoscaling groups can be called to modify resource pools in such cases. This is but one example of automation as an output of monitoring.

Visualization
> Graphs are one of the most common outputs of OpViz. These are collected into dashboards that suit the needs of a particular user community and are a key tool on which humans can perform pattern recognition.

Bootstrapping Your Monitoring

If you are like most rational people, you might be beginning to feel overwhelmed by all of these things that should be happening. That is normal! This is a good time to remind you that everything we build here is part of an iterative process. Start small, let things evolve, and add in more as you need it. Nowhere is this more true than in a startup environment.

As a brand new startup, you begin with zero. Zero metrics, zero alerting, zero visibility—just a bunch of engineers cranking out overly optimistic code. Many startups somehow end up with an instance somewhere in a public cloud that was a prototype or testbed and then it somehow turned into their master production database. Head? Meet desk!

Maybe you were just hired as the first Ops/database engineer at a young startup and you're taking stock of what the software engineers have built around monitoring or visibility, and it's effectively…zero.

Sound familiar? If you have any experience with startups, it should. It's nothing to be ashamed of! This is how startup sausage gets made. A startup that began by building out an elaborate operational visibility ecosystem in advance of their actual needs would be a stupid startup. Startups succeed by focusing hard on their core product, iterating rapidly, aggressively seeking out customers, responding to customer feedback and production realities, and making difficult decisions about where to spend their precious engineering resources. Startups succeed by instrumenting elaborate performance visibility systems as soon as they need them, not before. Startups fail all the time but usually not because the engineers failed to anticipate and measure every conceivable storage metric in advance. What we need to begin with is a *Minimum Viable Monitoring Set.*

Enumerating Moving Parts of the Database

You can think of your data as a stream from clients to databases. At the highest of levels, the database exists to take in data, to hold data, and to serve data back:

- Data in client memory
- Data across the wire between client and datastore
- Data in your databases memory structures
- Data in your OS and disk memory structures
- Data on your disks
- Data in backups and archival

Everything we seek to measure about our databases can boil down to:

- How long does it take to get data out, and why does it take that long?
- How long does it take to put data in, and why does it take that long?
- Is the data safely stored, and how is it stored?
- Is the data available in redundant locations in case primary retrieval fails?

Of course, this is quite simplistic, but it is a good top-level structure to think about while we dig into the following sections.

There are an infinite number of metrics that you can monitor between the database, system, storage, and various application layers. In the physiological needs state, you should be able to determine if your database is up or down. As you work toward fulfilling the "esteem" state, you begin by monitoring other symptoms that you have identified that correlate with real problems, such as connection counts or lock percentages. One common progression looks like this:

- Monitor if your databases are up or down (pull checks).
- Monitor overall latency/error metrics and end-to-end health checks (push checks).
- Instrument the application layer to measure latency/errors for every database call (push checks).

- Gather as many metrics as possible about the system, storage, database, and app layers, regardless of whether you think they will be useful. Most operating systems, services, and databases will have plug-ins that are fairly comprehensive.

- Create specific checks for known problems. For example, checks based on losing x percent of database nodes or a global lock percent that is too high (do this iteratively as well as proactively, see Chapter 3).

Sometimes you can take a shortcut to the "esteem" level by plugging in third-party monitoring services like VividCortex, Circonus, HoneyComb, or NewRelic. But it's kind of a hack if you're storing these database metrics in a system separate from the rest of your monitoring. Storing in disparate systems makes it more challenging to correlate symptoms across multiple monitoring platforms. We're not saying this is bad or you shouldn't do this; elegant hacks can take you a really long way! But the "self-actualization" phase generally includes consolidating all monitoring feeds into a single source of truth.

Okay. Now that you've safeguarded against your company going out of business when you lose a disk or an engineer makes a typo, you can begin asking yourself questions about the health of your service. As a startup, the key questions to ask yourself are: "Is my data safe?" "Is my service up?" and "Are my customers experiencing pain?" This is your minimum viable product monitoring set.

Is the Data Safe?

For any mission-critical data that you truly care about, you should avoid running with less than three live copies. That's one primary and two-plus secondaries for leader-follower data stores like MySQL or MongoDB or a replication factor of three for distributed data stores like Cassandra or Hadoop. Because you never, ever want to find yourself in a situation in which you have a single copy of any data you care about, ever. This means that you need to be able to lose one instance while still maintaining redundancy, which is why three is a minimum number of copies, not two. Even when you are penny-pinching and worrying about your run rate every month as a baby startup, mission-critical data is not the appropriate place to cut those costs. (We discuss availability architecture in Chapter 5, *Infrastructure Engineering*.)

But not all data is equally precious! If you can afford to lose some data or if you could reconstruct the data from immutable logs if necessary, running with n + 1, (where *n* is the required number of nodes for normal activity) copies is perfectly ok. This is a judgment call—only you can know how critical and how irreplaceable each dataset is for your company, and how tight your financial resources are. You also need backups, and you need to regularly validate that the backups are restorable and that the backup process is completing successfully. If you aren't monitoring that your backups are good, you cannot assume that your data is safe.

Sample Data Safety Monitors

Some examples of safety checks to include in your monitoring are:

- Three data nodes up
- Replication threads running
- Replication on at least one node <1 second behind
- Most recent backup success
- Most recent automated replica rebuild from backups is a success

Is the Service Up?

End-to-end checks are the most powerful tool in your arsenal because they most closely reflect your customer experience. You should have a top-level health check that exercises not just the aliveness of the web tier or application tier, but all the database connections in the critical path. If your data is partitioned across multiple hosts, the check should fetch an object on each of the partitions, and it should automatically detect the full list of partitions or shards so that you do not need to manually add new checks any time you add more capacity.

However—and this is important—you should have a simpler aliveness check for your load balancers to use that does not exercise all of your database connections. Otherwise, you can easily end up health-checking yourself to death.

Excessive Health Checking

Charity once worked on a system for which a haproxy health check endpoint did a simple SELECT LIMIT 1 from a mysql table. One day, they doubled the capacity of some stateless services, thus doubling the number of proxy servers running these health checks. Adding capacity to other systems accidentally took the entire site down by overloading the database servers with health checks. More than 95% of all database queries were those stupid health checks. Don't do that!

Speaking of lessons learned the hard way, you should always have some off-premises monitoring—if nothing else, an offsite health check for your monitoring service itself. It doesn't matter how amazing and robust your on-premises monitoring ecosystem is if your datacenter or cloud region goes down and takes your entire monitoring apparatus with it. Setting up an external check for each major product or service, as well as a health check on the monitoring service itself, is a good best practice.

Sample Database Availability Monitors

Here are some examples of ways to measure whether your system is available or close to unavailability:

- Health check at the application level that queries all frontend datastores
- Query run against each partition in each datastore member, for each datastore
- Imminent capacity issues
  - Disk capacity
  - Database connections
- Error log scraping
  - DB restarts (faster than your monitor!)
  - Corruption

Are the Consumers in Pain?

Okay, you are monitoring that your service is alive. The patient has a heartbeat. Good job!

But what if your latency subtly doubles or triples, or what if 10% of your requests are erroring in a way that cleverly avoids triggering your health check? What if your database is not writable but can be read from, or the replicas are lagging, which is causing your majority write concern to hang? What if your RAID array has lost a volume and is running in degraded mode, you have an index building, or you are experiencing hot spotting of updates to a single row?

Well, this is why systems engineering, and databases in particular, are so much fun. There are infinite ways your systems can fail, and you can probably only guess about five percent of them in advance. Yay!

This is why you should gradually develop a library of comprehensive high-level metrics about the health of the service—health checks, error rates, latency. Anything that materially affects and disrupts your customer experience. And then? Go work on something else for a while and see what breaks.

We are almost entirely serious. As discussed in Chapter 3, there is only so much to be gained by sitting around trying to guess how your service is going to break. You just don't have the data yet. You might as well go build more things, wait for things to break, and then pay a lot of attention when things actually begin failing.

Now that we've provided a bootstrapping method and an evolution method, let's breakdown what you should be measuring, with a focus on what you as the DBRE need.

Instrumenting the Application

Your application is the first place to begin. Although we can measure most things at the datastore layer, the first leading indicators of problems should be changes in user and application behavior. Between application instrumentation by your engineers and application performance management solutions (APM) such as New Relic and App-Dynamics, you can get a tremendous amount of data for everyone in the organization:

- You should already be measuring and logging all requests and responses to pages or API endpoints.
- You should also be doing this to all external services, which includes databases, search indexes, and caches.
- Any jobs or independent workflows that should be similarly monitored.
- Any independent, reusable code like a method or function that interacts with databases, caches, and other datastores should be similarly instrumented.
- Monitor how many database calls are executed by each endpoint, page, or function/method.

Tracking the data access code (such as SQL calls) called by each operation allows for rapid cross-referencing to more detailed query logs within the database. This can prove challenging with object-relational mapping systems (ORMs), for which SQL is dynamically generated.

 SQL Comments

When doing SQL tuning, a big challenge is mapping SQL running in the database to the specific place in the codebase from which it is being called. In many database engines, you can add comments for information. These comments will show up in the database query logs. This is a great place to insert the codebase location.

Distributed Tracing

Tracing performance at all stages from the application to the datastore is critical for optimizing long-tail latency issues that can be difficult to capture. Systems like New Relic or Zipkin (open source) allow for distributed traces from application calls to the external services, such as your databases. A full transaction trace from the application to datastore should ideally give timing for all external service calls, not just the database query.

Tracing with full visibility through to the database can become a powerful arsenal in educating your software engineer (SWE) teams and creating autonomy and self-reliance. Rather than needing you to tell them where to focus, they are able to get the information themselves. As Aaron Morton at the Last Pickle says in his talk, "Replacing Cassandra's Tracing with Zipkin":

> Knowing in advance which tools create such positive cultural shifts is basically impossible to foretell, but I've seen it with Git and its practice of pull requests and stable master branches, and I've seen it with Grafana, Kibana, and Zipkin.

You can read more about this on The Last Pickle's blog (*http://thelastpickle.com/blog/2015/12/07/using-zipkin-for-full-stack-tracing-including-cassandra.html*).

There are many components of an end-to-end call that can occur and be of interest to the DBRE. These include, but are not limited to, the following:

- Establishing a connection to a database or a database proxy
- Queuing for a connection in a database connection pool
- Logging a metric or event to a queuing or message service
- Creating a user ID from a centralized UUID service
- Selecting a shard based on a variable (such as user ID)
- Searching, invalidating, or caching at a cache tier
- Compressing or encrypting data at the application layer
- Querying a search layer

Traditional SQL Analysis

Laine here. In my consulting days, I can't tell you the amount of times I'd come into a shop that had no monitoring that mapped application performance monitoring to database monitoring. I'd invariably have to do TCP or log-based SQL gathering to create a view from the database. Then, I'd go back to the SWEs with my prioritized list of SQL to optimize, and they'd have no idea where to go to fix that code. Searching code bases could take a week or more of precious time.

As a DBRE, you have an amazing opportunity to work side by side with SWEs to ensure that every class, method, function, and job has direct mappings to SQL that is being called. When SWEs and DBREs use the same tools, DBREs can teach at key inflection points, and soon you'll find SWEs doing your job for you!

If a transaction has a performance "budget" and the latency requirements are known, the staff responsible for every component are incentivized to work as a team to identify the most expensive aspects and make the appropriate investments and compromises to get there.

Events and Logs

It goes without saying that all application logs should be collected and stored. This includes stack traces. Additionally, there are numerous events that will occur that are incredibly useful to register with OpViz, such as the following:

- Code deployments
- Deployment time
- Deployment errors

Application monitoring is a crucial first step, providing realistic looks at behavior from the user's perspective, and is directly related to latency SLOs. These are the symptoms providing clues into faults and degradations within the environment. Now, let's look at the supporting data that can help with root cause analysis and provisioning: host data.

Instrumenting the Server or Instance

Next is the individual host, real or virtual, on which the database instance resides. It is here that we can get all of the data regarding the operating system and physical resources devoted to running our databases. Even though this data is not specifically application/service related, it is valuable to use when you've seen symptoms such as latency or errors in the application tier.

When using this data to identify causes for application anomalies, the goal is to find resources that are over or underutilized, saturated, or throwing errors. (USE, as Brendan Gregg defined in his methodology (*http://www.brendangregg.com/useme thod.html*).) This data is also crucial for capacity planning for growth and performance optimization. Recognizing a bottleneck or constraint allows you to prioritize your optimization efforts to maximize value.

Distributed Systems Aggregation

Keep in mind that individual host data is not especially useful, other than for indicating that a host is unhealthy and should be culled from the herd. Rather, think about your utilization, saturation, and errors from an aggregate perspective for the pool of hosts performing the same function. In other words, if you have 20 Cassandra hosts, you are mostly interested in the overall utilization of the pool, the amount of waiting (saturation) that is going on, and any errors faults that are occurring. If errors are isolated to one host, it is time to remove that one from the ring and replace it with a new host.

On a Linux system, a good starting place for resources to monitoring in a linux environment includes the following:

- CPU
- Memory
- Network interfaces
- Storage I/O
- Storage capacity
- Storage controllers
- Network controllers
- CPU interconnect
- Memory interconnect
- Storage interconnect

Understanding Your Operating System

We cannot overemphasize just how much it is of value to dig deeply into the operating characteristics of your operating system. Although many database specialists leave this to system administrators, there is simply too tight of a relationship between database service levels and the operating system to not dive in. A perfect example of this is how Linux fills all of your memory with Page Cache, and thus the "Free Memory" gauge is virtually useless to monitor your memory usage. Pagescans per second becomes a much more useful metric in this case, which is not obvious without a deeper understanding of how Linux memory management works.

In addition to hardware resource monitoring, operating system software has a few items to track:

- Kernel mutex
- User mutex
- Task capacity
- File descriptors

If this is new to you, we suggest going to Brendan Gregg's USE page for Linux (*http://www.brendangregg.com/usemethod.html*) because it is incredibly detailed in regard to how to monitor this data. Its obvious that a significant amount of time and effort went into the data he presents.

Events and Logs

In addition to metrics, you should be sending all logs to an appropriate event processing system such as *RSyslog* or *Logstash*. This includes kernel, cron, authentication, mail, and general messages logs as well as process- or application-specific log to ingest, such as MySQL, or nginx.

Your configuration management and provisioning processes should also be registering critical events to your OpViz stack. Here is a decent starting point:

- A host being brought into our out of service
- Configuration changes
- Host restarts
- Service restarts
- Host crashes
- Service crashes

Cloud and Virtualized Systems

There are a few extra items to consider in these environments.

Cost! You are spending money on-demand in these environments, rather than up-front spend that you might be used to in datacenter environments. Being cost effective and efficient is crucial.

When monitoring CPU, monitor "steal time." This is time that the virtual CPU is waiting on real CPU, which is being used elsewhere. High steal times (10% or more over sustained periods) are indicators that there is a noisy neighbor in your environ-

---

ment! If steal time is the same across all of your hosts, this probably means that you are the culprit, and you might need to add more capacity and/or rebalance.

If steal time is on one or a few hosts, this means that some other tenant is stealing your time! Its best to kill that host and launch a new one. The new one will hopefully be deployed somewhere else and will perform much better.

If you can get the preceding into your OpViz stack, you will be in great shape for understanding what's going on at the host- and operating-system levels of the stack. Now, let's look at the databases themselves.

Instrumenting the Datastore

What do we monitor and track in our databases, and why? Some of this will depend on the kind of datastore. We focus here on areas that are generic enough to be universal, but specific enough to help you track to your own databases. We can break this down into four areas:

- Datastore connection layer
- Internal database visibility
- Database objects
- Database calls/queries

Each of these will get its own section, beginning with the datastore connection layer.

Datastore Connection Layer

We have discussed the importance of tracking the time it takes to connect to the backend datastore as part of the overall transaction. A tracing system should also be able to break out time talking to a proxy and time from the proxy to the backend as well. You can capture this via tcpdump and Tshark/Wireshark for ad hoc sampling if something like Zipkin is not available. You can automate this for occasional sampling or run it ad hoc.

If you are seeing latency and/or errors between the application and the database connection, you will require additional metrics to help identify causes. Taking the aforementioned USE method we recommended, let's see what other metrics can assist us.

Utilization

Databases can support only a finite number of connections. The maximum number of connections is constrained in multiple locations. Database configuration parameters will direct the database to accept only a certain number of connections, setting an artificial top boundary to minimize overwhelming the host. Tracking this maximum as well as the actual number of connections is crucial because it might be set arbitrarily low by a default configuration.

Connections also open resources at the operating system level. For instance, PostgreSQL uses one Unix process per connection. MySQL, Cassandra, and MongoDB use a thread per connection. All of them use memory and file descriptors. So, there are multiple places we want to look at to understand connection behaviors:

- Connection upper bound and connection count
- Connection states (working, sleeping, aborted, and others)
- Kernel-level Open file utilization
- Kernel-level max processes utilization
- Memory utilization
- Thread pool metrics such as MySQL table cache or MongoDB thread pool utilization
- Network throughput utilization

This should inform you as to whether you have a capacity or utilization bottleneck somewhere in the connection layer. If you are seeing 100% utilization and saturation is also high, this is a good indicator. But, low utilization combined by saturation is also an indicator of a bottleneck somewhere. High, but not full, utilization of resources is also often quite impactful to latency and could be causing latency as well.

Saturation

Saturation is often most useful when paired with utilization. If you are seeing a lot of waits for resources that are also showing 100% utilization, you are seeing a pretty clear capacity issue. However, if you are seeing waits/saturation without full utilization, there might be a bottleneck elsewhere that is causing the stack up. Saturation can be measured at these inflection points:

- TCP connection backlog
- Database-specific connection queuing, such as MySQL back_log
- Connection timeout errors
- Waiting on threads in the connection pools
- Memory swapping
- Database processes that are locked

Queue length and wait timeouts are crucial for understanding saturation. Any time you find connections or processes waiting, you have an indicator of a potential bottleneck.

Errors

With utilization and saturation, you can determine whether capacity constraints and bottlenecks are affecting the latency of your database connection layer. This is great information for deciding whether you need to increase resources, remove artificial configuration constraints, or make some architectural changes. Errors should also be monitored and used to help eliminate or identify faults and/or configuration problems. Errors can be captured as follows:

- Database logs will provide error codes when database-level failures occur. Sometimes you have configurations with various degrees of verbosity. Make sure you have logging verbose enough to identify connection errors, but do be careful about overhead, particularly if your logs are sharing storage and IO resources with your database.
- Application and proxy logs will also provide rich sources of errors.
- Host errors discussed in the previous section should also be utilized here.

Errors will include network errors, connection timeouts, authentication errors, connection terminations, and much more. These can point to issues as varied as corrupt tables, reliance on DNS, deadlocks, auth changes, and so on.

By utilizing application latency/error metrics, tracing and appropriate telemetry on utilization, saturation, and specific error states, you should have the information you need to identify degraded and broken states at the database connection layer. Next, we will look at what to measure inside of the connections.

Troubleshooting Connection Speeds, PostgreSQL

Instagram is one of the companies that chose PostgreSQL to be their relational database. It chose to use a connection pooler, PGBouncer, to increase the number of application connections that could connect to its databases. This is a proven scaling mechanism for increasing the number of connections to a datastore, and considering that PostgreSQL must spawn a new Unix process for every connection, new connections are slow and expensive.

Using the psycopg2 Python driver, the company was working with the default of `auto commit=FALSE`. This means that even for read-only queries, explicit `BEGINS` and `COM MITS` were being issued. By changing `autocommit` to `TRUE`, the company reduced its query latency, which also reduced queuing for connections in the pool.

This would initially show up as increased latency in the application as the pool was 100% utilized, causing queues to increase. By looking at the connection layer metrics and monitoring pgbouncer pools, it was clear that the *waiting* pool was increasing due to saturation, and that *active* was fully utilized most of the time. With no other metrics showing significant utilization/saturation and errors clear, it was time to look at what is going on inside of the connection that was slowing down queries. We will look into that in the next section.

Internal Database Visibility

When we look inside of the database, we can see that there is a substantial increase in the number of moving parts, number of metrics, and overall complexity. In other words, this is where things start to get real! Again, let's keep in mind USE. Our goal is to understand bottlenecks that might be affecting latency, constraining requests, or causing errors.

It is important to be able to look at this from an individual host perspective and in aggregate by role. Some databases, like MySQL, PostgreSQL, ElasticSearch, and MongoDB, have master and replica roles. Cassandra and Riak have no specific roles, but they are often distributed by region or zone. That too is important to aggregate by.

Throughput and Latency Metrics

How many and what kind of operations are occurring in the datastores? This data is a very good high-level view of database activity. As SWEs put in new features, these workloads will shift and provide good indicators of how the workload is shifting. Some examples of metrics to collect to understand these shifting workloads include the following:

- Reads
- Writes
  — Inserts
  — Updates
  — Deletes
- Other Operations
  — Commits
  — Rollbacks
  — DDL statements
  — Other administrative tasks

When we discuss latency here, we are talking in the aggregate only, meaning averages. We will discuss granular and more informative query monitoring further in this section. Thus, you are getting no outliers in this kind of data, only very basic workload information.

Commits, Redo, and Journaling

Although the specific implementations will depend on the datastore, there are almost always a set of I/O operations involved in flushing data to disk. In MySQL's InnoDB storage engine and in PostgreSQL, writes are changed in the buffer pool (memory) and operations are recorded in a redo log (or write-ahead log in PostgreSQL). Background processes will then flush this to disk while maintaining checkpoints for recovery. In Cassandra, data is stored in a memtable (memory), whereas a commit log is appended to. Memtables are flushed periodically to an SSTable. SSTables are periodically compacted, as well. Following are some metrics you might monitor:

- Dirty buffers (MySQL)
- Checkpoint age (MySQL)
- Pending and completed compaction tasks (Cassandra)
- Tracked dirty bytes (MongoDB)
- (Un)Modified pages evicted (MongoDB)
- `log_checkpoints` configuration (PostgreSQL)
- `pg_stat_bgwriter` view (PostgreSQL)

All checkpointing, flushing, and compaction are operations that have significant performance impacts on activity in the database. Sometimes, the impact is increased I/O, and sometimes it can be a full stop of all write operations while a major operation occurs. Gathering metrics here allows you to tune specific configurables to minimize the effects that will occur during such operations. So in this case, when we see latency increasing and see metrics related to flushing showing excessive background activity, we will be pointed toward tuning operations related to these processes.

Replication State

Replication is the copying of data across multiple nodes so that the data on one node is identical to another. It is a cornerstone of availability and read scaling as well as a part of disaster recovery and data safety. There are three replication states that can occur, however, that are not healthy and can lead to big problems if they are not monitored and caught. We discuss replication in detail in Chapter 10.

Replication latency is the first of the fault states. Sometimes, the application of changes to other nodes can slow down. This can be the result of network saturation, single-threaded applies that cannot keep up, or any number of other reasons. Occasionally, replication will never catch up during peak activity, causing the data to be hours old on the replicas. This is dangerous because stale data can be served, and if you are using this replica as a failover, you can lose data.

Most database systems have easily tracked replication latency metrics; you can see the difference between the timestamp on the master and the timestamp on the replica. In systems like Cassandra, with *eventually consistent models*, you are looking for backlogs of operations used to synchronize replicas after unavailability. For instance, in Cassandra, this is hinted handoffs.

Broken replication is the second of the fault states. In this case, the processes required to maintain data replication simply break due to any number of errors. Resolution requires rapid response facilitated by appropriate monitoring, followed by repair of the cause of the errors, and replication allowed to resume and catch up. In this case, you can monitor the state of replication threads.

The last error state is the most insidious: replication drift. In this case, data has lost synchronization, causing replication to be useless and potentially dangerous. Identifying replication drift for large datasets can be challenging and depends on the workloads and kind of data that you are storing.

For instance, if your data is relatively immutable and insert/read operations are the norm, you can run checksums on data ranges across replicas and then compare checksums to see if they are identical. You can do this in a rolling method behind replication, allowing for an easy safety check at the cost of extra CPU utilization on the database hosts. If you are doing a lot of mutations, however, this proves more challenging because you must either repeatedly run checksums on data that has already been reviewed or just do occasional samples.

Memory Structures

Data stores will maintain numerous memory structures in their regular operation. One of the most ubiquitous in databases is a data cache. Although it might have many names, the goal of this is to maintain frequently accessed data in memory rather than from disk. Other caches like this can exist, including caches for parsed SQL, connection caches, query result caches, and many more.

The typical metrics we use when monitoring these structures are as follows:

Utilization
    The overall amount of allocated space that is in use over time.

Churn
    The frequency that cached objects are removed to make room for other objects or because the underlying data has been invalidated.

Hit ratios

The frequency with which cached data is used rather than uncached data. This can help with performance optimization exercises.

Concurrency

Often these structures have their own serialization methods, such as mutexes, that can become bottlenecks. Understanding saturation of these components can help with optimization as well.

Some systems, like Cassandra, use Java Virtual Machines (JVMs) for managing memory, exposing whole new areas to monitor. Garbage collection and usage of the various object heap spaces are also critical in such environments.

Locking and Concurrency

Relational databases in particular utilize locks to maintain concurrent access between sessions. Locking allows mutations and reads to occur while guaranteeing that nothing might be changed by other processes. Even though this is incredibly useful, it can lead to latency issues as processes stack up waiting for their turn. In some cases, you can have processes timing-out due to deadlocks, for which there is simply no resolution for the locks that have been put in place but to roll back. The details of locking implementations are reviewed in Chapter 11.

Monitoring locks includes monitoring the amount of time spent waiting on locks in the datastore. This can be considered a saturation metric, and longer queues can indicate application and concurrency issues or underlying issues that affect latency, with sessions holding locks taking longer to complete. Monitoring rollbacks and deadlocks is also crucial because it is another indicator that applications are not releasing locks cleanly, causing waiting sessions to timeout and roll back. Rollbacks can be part of a normal, well-behaved transaction, but they often are a leading indicator that some underlying action is affecting transactions.

As discussed in the memory structures section earlier, there are also numerous points in the database that function as synchronization primitives designed to safely manage concurrency. These are generally either mutexes or semaphores. A mutex (Mutually Exclusive Lock) is a locking mechanism used to synchronize access to a resource such as a cache entry. Only one task can acquire the mutex. This means that there is ownership associated with mutexes, and only the owner can release the lock (mutex). This protects from corruption.

A semaphore restricts the number of simultaneous users of a shared resource up to a maximum number. Threads can request access to the resource (decrementing the semaphore) and can signal that they have finished using the resource (incrementing the semaphore). Examples of using mutexes/semaphores to monitor MySQL's InnoDB storage engine are listed in Table 4-1.

Table 4-1. InnoDB semaphore activity metrics

Name	Description
Mutex Os Waits (Delta)	The number of InnoDB semaphore/mutex waits yielded to the OS.
Mutex Rounds (Delta)	The number of InnoDB semaphore/mutex spin rounds for the internal sync array.
Mutex Spin Waits (Delta)	The number of InnoDB semaphore/mutex spin waits for the internal sync array.
Os Reservation Count (Delta)	The number of times an InnoDB semaphore/mutex wait was added to the internal sync array.
Os Signal Count (Delta)	The number of times an InnoDB thread was signaled using the internal sync array.
Rw Excl Os Waits (Delta)	The number of exclusive (write) semaphore waits yielded to the OS by InnoDB.
Rw Excl Rounds (Delta)	The number of exclusive (write) semaphore spin rounds within the InnoDB sync array.
Rw Excl Spins (Delta)	The number of exclusive (write) semaphore spin waits within the InnoDB sync array.
Rw Shared Os Waits (Delta)	The number of shared (read) semaphore waits yielded to the OS by InnoDB.
RW Shared Rounds (Delta)	The number of shared (read) semaphore spin rounds within the InnoDB sync array.
RW Shared Spins (Delta)	The number of shared (read) semaphore spin waits within the InnoDB sync array.
Spins Per Wait Mutex (Delta)	The ratio of InnoDB semaphore/mutex spin rounds to mutex spin waits for the internal sync array.
Spins Per Wait RW Excl (Delta)	The ratio of InnoDB exclusive (write) semaphore/mutex spin rounds to spin waits within the internal sync array.
Spins Per Wait RW Shared (Delta)	The ratio of InnoDB shared (read) semaphore/mutex spin rounds to spin waits within the internal sync array.

Increasing values in these can indicate that your datastores are reaching concurrency limits on specific areas in the code base. You can resolve this via tuning configurables and/or by scaling out to maintain sustainable concurrency on a datastore to satisfy traffic requirements.

Locking and concurrency can truly kill even the most performant of queries once you start experiencing a tipping point in scale. By tracking and monitoring these metrics during load tests and in production environments, you can understand the limits of your database software and identify how your own applications must be optimized to scale up to large numbers of concurrent users.

Database Objects

It is crucial to understand what your database looks like and how it is stored. At the simplest level, this is an understanding of how much storage each database object and its associated keys/indexes takes. Just like filesystem storage, understanding the rate of growth and the time to reaching the upper boundary is as crucial, if not more, than the current storage usage.

In addition to understanding the storage and growth, monitoring the distribution of critical data is helpful. For instance, understanding the high and low bounds, means and cardinality of data is helpful to understanding index and scan performance. This is particularly important for integer datatypes and low cardinality character-based datatypes. Having this data at your SWE fingertips allows you and them to recognize optimizations on datatypes and indexing.

If you have sharded your dataset using key ranges or lists, understanding the distribution across shards can help ensure you are maximizing output on each node. These sharding methodologies allow for hot spots because they are not even distributions using a hash or modulus approach. Recognizing this will advise you and your team on needs to rebalance or reapproach your sharding models.

Database Queries

Depending on the database system you are working with, the actual data access and manipulation activity can prove to be highly instrumented or not at all. Trying to drink at the firehose of data that results in logging queries in a busy system can cause critical latency and availability issues to your system and users. Still, there is no more valuable data than this. Some solutions, such as Vivid Cortex and Circonus, have focused on TCP and wire protocols for getting the data they need, which dramatically reduces performance impact of query logging. Other methods include sampling on a less loaded replica, only turning logging on for fixed periods of time or only logging statements that execute slowly.

Regardless of all this, you want to store as much as possible about the performance and utilization of your database activity. This will include the consumption of CPU and IO, number of rows read or written, detailed execution times and wait times, and execution counts. Understanding optimizer paths, indexes used, and statistics around joining, sorting, and aggregating is also critical for optimization.

Database Asserts and Events

Database and client logs are a rich source of information, particularly for asserts and errors. These logs can give you crucial data that can't be monitored any other way, such as the following:

- Connection attempts and failures
- Corruption warnings and errors
- Database restarts
- Configuration changes
- Deadlocks
- Core dumps and stack traces

You can aggregate some of this data and push it to your metrics systems. You should treat others as events to be tracked and used for correlations.

Wrapping Up

Well, after all of that, I think we all need a break! You've come out of this chapter with a solid understanding of the importance of operational visibility, how to start an OpViz program, and how to build and evolve an OpViz architecture. You can never have enough information about the systems you are building and running. You can also quickly find the systems built to observe the services that have become a large part of your operational responsibilities! They deserve just as much attention as every other component of the infrastructure.

CHAPTER 5

Infrastructure Engineering

Let's begin the process of actualizing our database clusters for consumption by applications and analysts. Previously, we've discussed a lot of the preparatory work: service-level expectations, risk analysis, and, of course, operational visibility. In the next two chapters, we discuss the techniques and patterns for designing and building the environments.

In this chapter, we discuss the various hosts a datastore can run on, including *serverless* or *Database as a Service* options. We discuss the various storage options available to those datastores.

Hosts

As discussed previously, your datastores do not exist in a vacuum. They must always run as processes on some host. Traditionally, database hosts were physical servers. Over the past decade, our options have grown, including virtual hosts, containers, and even abstracted services. Let's look at each in turn, discuss the pros and cons of using them for databases, and examine some specific implementation details.

Physical Servers

In this context, a physical server is a host that has an operating system and is 100% dedicated to running services directly from that operating system. In immature environments, a physical server might run many services on it while traffic is low and resources are abundant. One of the first steps a database reliability engineer (DBRE) will take is to separate datastores to their own servers. The workloads required by a datastore are generally quite intensive on CPU, RAM, and Storage/IO. Some applications will be more CPU-bound or IO-bound, but you don't want them competing with other applications for resources. Tuning these workloads is also quite specific and thus requires isolation to properly accomplish.

When you run a database on a dedicated physical host, your database will be interacting with and consuming a large number of components that we will discuss briefly in just a moment. For the purposes of this discussion, we will assume that you are running a Linux or Unix system. Even though much of this can be applied to Windows, the differences are significant enough that we will not be using them as examples.

We've tried to break out a significant chunk of the best practices here to show the depth of operating system (OS) and hardware knowledge that a DBRE can utilize to solve problems that can dramatically increase availability and performance of databases. As we go upward in abstractions to virtual hosts and containers, we will add in relevant information where appropriate.

Operating a System and Kernel

As the DBRE, you should collaborate directly with software reliability engineers (SREs) to define appropriate kernel configurations for your database hosts. These should become gold standards that automatically deploy along with database binaries and other configurations. Most database management systems (DBMS's) will come with vendor-specific requirements and recommendations that should be reviewed and applied where possible. Interestingly, there can be very different approaches to this depending on the type of database you are using. So, we will go through a few high-level categories and discuss them.

User resource limits

There are a number of resources that databases utilize at much higher numbers than typical servers. These include file descriptors, semaphores, and user processes.

I/O scheduler

Input/Output (I/O) scheduling is the method that operating systems use to decide the order in which block level I/O operations will be submitted to storage volumes. By default, these schedulers often assume they are working with spinning disks that have high seek latency. Thus, the default is usually an *elevator algorithm* that attempts to order requests by location and to minimize seek times. In Linux, you might see the following options available:

```
wtf@host:~$ cat /sys/block/sda/queue/scheduler
[noop] anticipatory deadline cfq
```

The noop scheduler is the proper choice when the target block device is an array of SSDs with a controller that performs I/O optimization. Every I/O request is treated equally because seek times on solid-state drives (SSDs) are relatively stable. The deadline scheduler will optimize by seeking to minimize I/O latency by imposing dead-lines to prevent starvation and by prioritizing reads over writes. The Deadline Scheduler has shown to be more performant in highly concurrent multithreaded environments, such as database loads.

Memory allocation and fragmentation

No one can deny that databases are some of the most memory-hungry applications a server can run. Understanding how memory is allocated and managed is critical to utilizing it as effectively as possible. Database binaries are compiled using a variety of memory allocation libraries. Here are some examples:

- MySQL's InnoDB, as of version 5.5, uses a custom library that wraps glibc's mal loc. GitHub claims to have saved 30% latency by switching to tcmalloc, whereas Facebook uses jemalloc.

- PostgreSQL also uses its own custom allocation library, with malloc behind it. Unlike most other datastores, PostgreSQL allocates memory in very large chunks, called memory contexts.

- As of version 2.1, Apache Cassandra off-heap allocation supports jemalloc over native.

- MongoDB's version 3.2 implementation uses malloc by default but can be config-ured with tcmalloc or jemalloc.

- As of version 2.4, Redis uses jemalloc.

jemalloc and tcmalloc have both proven to provide significant improvements in concurrency for most database workloads, performing significantly better than glibc's native malloc while also reducing fragmentation.

Memory is allocated in pages that are 4 KB in size by default. Thus, 1 GB of memory is the equivalent of 262,144 pages. CPUs use a *page table* that contains a list of these pages, with each page referenced through a *page table entry*. A *translation lookaside buffer* (TLB) is a memory cache that stores recent translations of virtual memory to physical addresses for faster retrieval. A TLB *miss* is where the virtual-to-physical page translation is not in a TLB. A TLB miss is slower than a hit, and can require a page walk, requiring several loads. With large amounts of memory, and thus pages, TLB misses can create thrashing.

Transparent Huge Pages (THP) is a Linux memory management system that reduces the overhead of TLB lookups on machines with large amounts of memory by using larger memory pages, thus reducing the number of entries required. THPs are blocks of memory that come in 2 MB and 1 GB sizes. Tables used for 2 MB pages are suitable for gigabytes of memory, whereas 1 GB pages are best for terabytes. However, defrag-mentation of these large page sizes can cause significant CPU thrashing, which has been seen on Hadoop, Cassandra, Oracle, and MySQL workloads, among others. To mitigate this, you might need to deal with disabling defragmentation and losing up to 10% of your memory because of it.

Linux is not particularly optimized for database loads requiring low latency and high concurrency. The kernel is not predictable when it goes into reclaim mode, and one of the best recommendations we can give is to simply ensure that you never fully use your physical memory by reserving it to avoid stalls and significant latency impacts. You can reserve this memory by not allocating it in configuration.

Swapping

In Linux/UNIX systems, *swapping* is the process of storing and retrieving data that no longer fits in memory and needs to be saved to disk to alleviate pressure for memory resources. This is a very slow operation by orders of magnitude compared to memory access, and thus should be considered a last resort.

It is generally accepted that databases should avoid swapping because it can immediately increase latency beyond acceptable levels. That being said, if swap is disabled, the operating system "Out of Memory Killer" (*OOM Killer*) will shut down the database process.

There are two schools of thought here. The first, and more traditional, approach is that keeping a database up and slow is better than the database not being available at all. The second approach, and the one that aligns more closely with the DBRE philosophy, is that latency impacts are as bad as performance impacts; thus, swapping in from disk should not be tolerated at all.

Database configurations will typically have a realistic memory usage high watermark as well as a theoretical one. Fixed memory structures like buffer pools and caches will consume fixed amounts, making them predictable. At the connection layer, however, things can get messier. There is a theoretical limit based on the maximum number of connections and the maximum size of all per-connection memory structures, such as sort buffers and thread stacks. Using connection pools and some sane assumptions, you should be able to predict a reasonably safe memory threshold by which you can avoid swapping.

This process does allow for anomalies such as misconfigurations, runaway processes, and other pear-shaped events to push you past your memory bounds, which would shut down your server in an OOM event. This is a good thing, though! If you have effective visibility, capacity, and failover strategies in place, you have effectively shut out a potential Service-Level Objective (SLO) violation on latency.

Disabling Swap

You should do this only if you have rock-solid failover processes. Otherwise, you will absolutely find yourself affecting availability to your applications.

Should you choose to allow swapping in your environment, you can reduce the operating system's chance of swapping out your database memory for file cache, which is generally not helpful. You can also adjust the OOM scores for your database processes to reduce the chance that your kernel memory profiler will kill your database process for memory needs elsewhere.

Non-Uniform memory access

Early implementations of multiple processors used an architecture called *Symmetric Multiprocessing* (SMP) to provide equal access to memory for each CPU via a shared bus between the CPUs and the memory banks. Modern multiprocessor systems utilize *Non-Uniform Memory Access* or *NUMA*, which provides a local bank of memory to each processor. Access to memory banked to other processors is still done over a shared bus. Thus, some memory access has much lower latency (local) versus others (remote).

In a Linux system, a processor and its cores are considered a *node*. The operating system attaches memory banks to their local nodes and calculates cost between nodes based on distance. A process and its threads will be given a *preferred node* to utilize for memory. Schedulers can change this temporarily, but affinity will always go to the preferred node. On top of this, after memory is allocated, it will not be moved to another node.

What this means in an environment in which large memory structures are present, such as database buffer pools, is that memory will be allocated heavily to the preferred node. This imbalance will cause the preferred node to be filled, with no available memory on it. This means that even if you are utilizing less memory than physically available on the server, you will still see swapping.

Solving NUMA and MySQL at Twitter

Jeremy Cole has produced two impressive posts about this issue and how Twitter resolved it.[1] Initially, the following approach was utilized: forcing interleaved allocation by using `numactl --interleave=all`.

---

[1] "A brief update on NUMA and MySQL" (*http://bit.ly/2zxNuPe*) and "The MySQL 'swap insanity' problem and the effects of the NUMA architecture" (*http://bit.ly/2zxXnfP*), both available on his blog.

By interleaving, allocation could effectively spread itself across all nodes. This was not 100% effective, however, as an OS buffer cache can be quite full if the MySQL process was restarted after running for awhile in production. By adding on two more solution points, the process proved repeatable and reliable:

- Flushing Linux's buffer caches just before `mysqld` startup by using `sysctl -q -w vm.drop_caches=3`. This helps to ensure allocation fairness, even if the daemon is restarted while significant amounts of data are in the operating system buffer cache.
- Forcing the OS to allocate InnoDB's buffer pool immediately upon startup, using `MAP_POPULATE` where supported (Linux 2.6.23+), and falling back to `memset` otherwise. This forces the NUMA node allocation decisions to be made immediately, while the buffer cache is still clean from the aforementioned flush.

This is a perfect example of the kind of value that a DBRE can provide to a very large population of SWEs and SREs. In this case, excessive swapping led to a deep dive into OS memory management. Using a deep knowledge of MySQL's memory management in conjunction with this led to immediate fixes that eventually were rolled into main MySQL forks.

At this point, for most DBMS requests, you set interleaving for NUMA in the kernel. Stories abound for PostgreSQL, Redis, Cassandra, MongoDB, MySQL, and Elastic-Search about the same issues.

Network

The assumption of this book is that all datastores are distributed. Network traffic is critical for the performance and availability of your databases, period. You can break up network traffic into the following categories:

- Internode communications
- Application traffic
- Administrative traffic
- Backup and recovery traffic

Internode communications include data replication, consensus and gossip protocols, and cluster management. This is the data that let's the cluster know its own state and keeps data replicated in the amounts defined. Application traffic is the traffic that comes from application servers or proxies. This is what maintains application state and allows for the creation, mutation and deletion of data by applications.

Administrative traffic is the communication between management systems, operators, and the clusters. Administrative traffic is the communication between management systems, operators, and clusters. This includes starting and stopping services, deploying binaries, and making database and configuration changes. When things go badly elsewhere, this is the lifeline to systems that allows for manual and automated recovery. Backup and recovery traffic is just what it says. This is the traffic created when archiving and copying data, moving data between systems or recovering from backups.

Isolation of traffic is one of the first steps to proper networking for your databases. You can do this via physical *network interface cards* (NICs), or by partitioning one NIC. Modern server NICs generally come in 1 Gbps and 10 Gbps sizes, and you can bond them in a pair to allow for redundancy and load balancing. Although this redundancy will increase mean time between failures (MTBF), it is an example of creating robustness rather than resiliency.

Databases need a lean transport layer to manage their workloads. Frequent and fast connections, short round trips, and latency-sensitive queries all require a specific tuning effort. This can be broken down into three areas:

- Tuning for large numbers of connections by expanding the amount of TCP/IP ports.
- Reducing the time it takes to recycle sockets to avoid large amounts of connections sitting in TIME_WAIT, and thus rendering it unusable.
- Maintaining a large TCP backlog so that saturation will not cause connections to be refused.

TCP/IP will become your best friend in troubleshooting latency and availability problems. We strongly suggest that you deep-dive into this. A good book to do so is *Internetworking with TCP/IP, Vol 1* by Douglas E. Comer (Pearson). It is updated as of 2014 and is an excellent reference.

Storage

Storage for databases is a huge topic. You need to consider the individual disks, the grouped configuration of disks, controllers providing access to disks, volume management software, and the filesystems on top of this. It is quite possible to geek out on any single section of this for days, so we will try to stay focused on the big picture here.

In Figure 5-1, you can see the ways in which data is propagated to storage. When you read from a file, you go from user buffer, to page cache, to disk controller, to disk platter for retrieval, and then step back through that for delivery to the user.

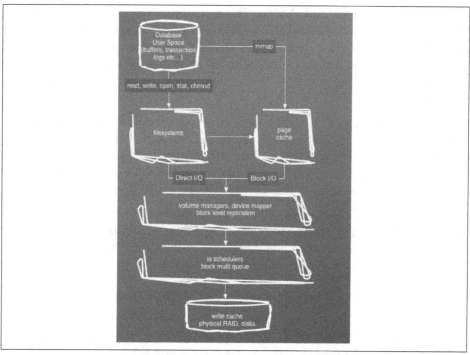

Figure 5-1. The linux storage stack

This elaborate cascade of buffers, schedulers, queues, and caches is used to mitigate the fact that disks are very slow compared to memory, with the difference being 100 nanoseconds versus 10 milliseconds (*http://bit.ly/2zyKIt1*).

For database storage, you will have five major demands, or objectives:

- capacity
- throughput (or IO per second, aka *IOPS*)
- latency
- availability
- durability

Storage capacity

Capacity is the amount of space available for the data and logs in your database. Storage can be via large disks, multiple disks striped together (RAID 0), or multiple disks functioning as individual mount points (known as JBOD, or just a bunch of disks). Each of these solutions has a different failure pattern. Single large disks are single points of failure, unless mirrored (RAID 1). RAID 0 will have its MTBF reduced by a factor of N, where N is the number of disks striped together. JBOD will have more frequent failures, but unlike RAID 0, the other N–1 disks will be available. Some databases can take advantage of this and stay functional, if degraded, while the replacement disk is acquired and installed.

Understanding a database's total storage needs is only one piece of this picture though. If you have a 10 TB storage need, you can create a 10 TB stripe set, or mount ten 1 TB disks in JBOD and distribute data files across them. However, you now have a 10 TB database to back up at once, and if you have a failure, you will need to recover 10 TB, which takes a long time. During that time, you will have reduced capacity and availability for your overall system. Meanwhile, you must consider if your database software, the operating system, and the hardware can manage the concurrent workloads to read and write to this monolithic datastore. Breaking this system up into smaller databases will improve resiliency, capacity, and performance for applications, for backup/restores, and for copying the dataset.

Storage throughput

IOPS is the standard measure of input and output operations per second on a storage device. This includes reads and writes. When considering the needs, you must consider IOPS for the peak of a database's workload rather than the average. When planning a new system, you will need to estimate the number of IOPS needed per transaction, and the peak transactions in order to plan appropriately. This will obviously vary tremendously depending on the application. An application that does constant inserts and single row reads can be expected to do four or five IOPs per transaction. Complex multiquery transactions can do 20 to 30 easily.

Database workloads tend to be mixed read/write, and random, rather than sequential. There are some exceptions, such as append-only write schemas (such as Cassandra's SSTables), which will write sequentially. For hard disk drives (HDDs), random IOPs numbers are primarily dependent upon the storage device's random seek time. For SSDs, random IOPs numbers are instead constrained by internal controller and memory interface speeds. This explains the significant improvement in IOPS seen by SSDs. Sequential IOPS indicate the maximum sustained bandwidth that the disk can produce. Often sequential IOPS are reported as megabytes per second (MBps), and are indicative of how a bulk load or sequential writes might perform.

When looking at SSDs, remember to consider the bus, as well. Consider installing a PCIe bus flash solution, such as FusionIO 6 GBps throughput with microsecond latency. As of this writing, 10 TB will cost you around $45,000, however.

Traditionally, IOPS was the constraining factor over storage capacity. This is particularly true for writes, which you could not optimize away via caching like reads. Adding disks via striping (RAID 0) or JBOD would add more IOPS capacity just like storage. RAID 0 will give you uniform latency and eliminate hot spots that might show up in JBOD, but at the expense of a reduced MTBF based on the number of disks in the stripe set.

Storage latency

Latency is the end-to-end client time of an I/O operation; in other words, the time elapsed between sending an I/O to storage and receiving an acknowledgement that the I/O read or write is complete. As with most resources, there are queues for pending requests, which can back up during saturation. Some level of queuing is not a bad thing, and, in fact, many controllers are designed to optimize queue depth. If your workload is not delivering enough I/O requests to fully use the performance available, your storage might not deliver the expected throughput.

Transactional database applications are sensitive to increased I/O latency and are good candidates for SSDs. You can maintain high IOPS while keeping latency down by maintaining a low queue length and a high number of IOPS available to the volume. Consistently driving more IOPS to a volume than it has available can cause increased I/O latency.

Throughput-intensive applications like large MapReduce queries are less sensitive to increased I/O latency and are well-suited for HDD volumes. You can maintain high throughput to HDD-backed volumes by maintaining a high queue length when performing large, sequential I/O.

The Linux page cache is another bottleneck to latency. By using direct IO (O_DIRECT), you can avoid multimillisecond latency impacts by bypassing the page cache.

Storage availability

Performance and capacity are critical factors, but unreliable storage must be accounted for. Google did an extensive study on HDD failure rates in 2007 titled "Failure Trends in a Large Disk Drive Population (*http://bit.ly/2zyKZfx*)" (see Figure 5-2). From this, you can expect about 3 out of 100 drives to fail in their first three months of service. Of disks that make it through the first six months, you will find approximately 1 in 50 fail between six months and one year in service. This doesn't seem like a lot, but if you have six database servers with eight drives each, you can expect to have a disk failure during that period.

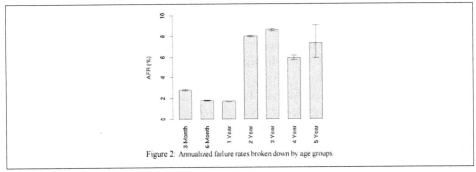
Figure 2: Annualized failure rates broken down by age groups

Figure 5-2. HDD failure rates, according to Google

This is why engineers began mirroring drives, à la RAID 1, and enhancing stripe sets with a parity drive. We don't talk much about the parity variants (e.g., RAID 5) because their write penalty is so large. Modern storage subsystems will typically find disks in JBOD or grouped in stripes (RAID 0), mirrors (RAID 1), or mirrors that are striped (RAID10). With that in mind, it is easy to extrapolate that RAID 1 and RAID 10 are most tolerant of single-disk failures, whereas RAID 0 is most prone to complete service loss (and greater chances the more disks in the stripe). JBOD shows the ability to tolerate failures while still serving the rest of the storage.

Availability is not just the MTBF of your volumes. It is also the time it would take to rebuild after a failure, or the mean time to recover (MTTR). The choice of RAID 10 versus RAID 0 is dependent on the ability to easily deploy replacement database hosts during a failure. It can be tempting to stay with RAID 0 for performance reasons. RAID 1 or 10 requires double the IOPS for writes, and if you are using high-end drives, the duplication of hardware can become expensive. RAID 0 is performant and predictable, but somewhat fragile. After all, a five-drive stripe set of HDDs can be expected to have about a 10% failure rate in the first year. With four hosts, you can reasonably expect a failure every year or two.

With a mirror, you can replace the disk without the need to rebuild the database. If you are running a 2 TB database with fairly fast-spinning disks, database backup copy time is measured in hours, and you will likely need more hours for database replication to sync the delta from the last backup. To be comfortable with this, you will need to consider if you have enough capacity to support peak traffic with one, or even two, failed nodes while this recovery is going on. In a sharded environment, where one dataset is only a percentage of users, this might be perfectly acceptable, meriting more fragile data volumes for the benefits of cost and/or write latency.

Durability

Finally, there is durability. When your database goes to commit data to physical disk with guarantees of durability, it issues an operating system call known as `fsync()`

rather than relying on page cache flushing. An example of this is when a redo log or write-ahead log is being generated and must be truly written to disk to ensure recoverability of the database. To maintain write performance, many disks and controllers utilize an in-memory cache. `fsync` instructs the storage subsystem that these caches must be flushed to disk. If your write cache is backed by a battery, and can survive a power loss, it is much more performant to not flush this cache. It is important to validate that your particular setup does truly flush data to stable storage, whether that is a non-volatile RAM (NVRAM), write cache or the disk platters themselves. You can do this via a utility such as diskchecker.pl (*https://gist.github.com/bradfitz/3172656*) by Brad Fitzpatrick.

Filesystem operations can also cause corruption and inconsistency during failure events, such as crashes. Journaling filesystems like XFS and EXT4 significantly reduce the possibility of such events, however.

Storage Area Networks

In opposition to direct storage, you can use a storage area network (SAN) with an external interface, typically Fibre Channel. SANs are significantly more expensive than direct attached, and by centralizing storage, you reduced management expense and allow a significant amount of flexibility.

With top-of-the-line SANs, you get significantly more cache. Additionally, there are a lot of features that can be useful for large datasets. Being able to take snapshots for backups and data copies is incredibly useful. Realistically, data snapshots and movement are some of the nicest features in modern infrastructures, where SSDs provide better IO than traditional SANs.

Benefits of Physical Servers

Physical servers are the simplest approach to hosting databases. There are no abstractions that hide implementation and runtime details or add additional complexity. In most cases, you have as much control as is possible with your OS, and as much visibility. This can make operations fairly straightforward.

Cons of Physical Servers

Still, there can be some drawbacks to using physical servers. First among them is that you can find yourself wasting capacity that has been dedicated to specific servers. Additionally, deployment of these systems can take quite a lot of time, and it can be difficult to ensure that every server is identical from the hardware and software perspectives. With that in mind, let's discuss virtualization.

Virtualization

In virtualization, software separates physical infrastructures to create various dedicated resources. This software makes it possible to run multiple operating systems that run multiple applications on the same server. With virtual machines (VMs), for example, you could alternately run four instances of Linux on one server, each with dedicated computing, memory, networking, and storage.

Virtualization allows an infrastructure's resources, including compute, storage, and networking, to be combined to create pools that can be allocated to virtual servers. This is often referred to as cloud computing. This is what you work with if you are running on a public cloud infrastructure such as Amazon Web Services (AWS). This can also be done within your own data centers.

Essentially, whether in a public, private, or hybrid solution, you are able to define what your server resources and the related operating systems look like via code. This allows for consistent deployments for database systems, which means the DBREs users are empowered to build their own database clusters, which have been configured according to the standards set by the DBRE. These standards include the following:

- OS
- Database software version
- OS and database configurations
- Security and permissions
- Software packages and libraries
- Management scripts

This is all a wonderful thing, but adding an abstraction layer on top of physical resources does create its own set of complexities to manage. Let's look at some of them.

Hypervisor

A *hypervisor* or virtual machine monitor (VMM) can be software, firmware, or hardware. The hypervisor creates and runs VMs. A computer on which a hypervisor runs one or more VMs is called a *host machine*, and each VM is called a *guest machine*. The hypervisor presents the guest operating systems with a virtual operating platform and manages the execution of the guest operating systems.

Concurrency

Databases running within hypervisors show lower boundaries for concurrency than the same software on bare metal. When designing for these virtualized environments, the focus should be on a horizontally scaled approach, minimizing concurrency within nodes.

Storage

Storage durability and performance are not what you would expect in the virtualized world. Between the page cache of your VM and the physical controller lies a virtual controller, the hypervisor, and the host's page cache. This means increased latency for I/O. For writes, hypervisors do not honor `fsync` calls in order to manage performance. This means that you cannot guarantee that your writes are flushed to disk when there is a crash.

Additionally, even though you can easily spin-up a VM in 10 minutes or less, that does not necessarily create the data that an existing database needs to be functional. For instance, if you are deploying a new replica, you will need to bootstrap the data for that replica from somewhere.

When looking at storage in virtualized environments, there are two major categories: local storage and persistent block storage. Local storage is ephemeral. Its data cannot survive the life of the VM. Persistent block storage can be attached to any VM and utilized. If the virtual machine is shut down, another VM can attach to that storage. This externalized, persistent storage is ideal for databases. This block storage often will allow snapshots for easy data movement, as well.

This block storage is much more network dependent than traditional physical disks, and congestion can quickly become a performance killer.

Use Cases

With all of these caveats, the DBRE must consider virtual and cloud resources carefully when planning to use them for database infrastructure. When designing for these infrastructures, you must consider all of the aforementioned factors, which we summarize here:

- Relaxed durability means data loss must be considered an inevitability.
- Instance instability means automation, failover, and recovery must be very reliable.
- Horizontal scale requires automation to manage significant numbers of servers.
- Applications must be able to tolerate latency instability.

Even with all of this in mind, there can be tremendous value to virtualized and cloud infrastructures for databases. The ability to create self-service platforms that your users can build on and work with is a force multiplier for DBRE resources. This allows dissemination of knowledge and best practices even with only a few DBREs on staff.

Rapid deployment also allows for extensive testing of applications and prototyping. This allows for development teams to be much more productive without bottlenecking on the DBRE for deployments and configuration. This also means developers are less likely to go off on their own when deploying new application persistence tiers.

Containers

Containers sit on top of a physical server and its host OS. Each container shares the host OS kernel, binaries, and libraries. These shared components are read-only, and each container can be written to through a unique mount. Containers are much lighter than VMs. In fact, they are only megabytes in size. Whereas a VM might take 10 minutes or so to spin up, a container can take seconds to start.

For datastores, however, the advantages of a quick spin up in Docker are often outweighed by the need to attach, bootstrap, and synchronize data. Additionally, kernel-level customizations, IO heavy workloads, and network congestion often make a shared OS/host model challenging. Docker is a great tool for rapidly spinning up deployments for tests and development environments, however, and DBREs will still find useful places for it in their toolkits.

Database as a Service

Increasingly, companies are looking to third-party solutions for their virtualization and cloud services. Taking the self-service model we discussed in Chapter 6 further, you end up with third-party-managed database platforms. All of the public cloud providers offer these, the most famous being Amazon's Relational Database Service (RDS), which offers MySQL, PostgreSQL, Aurora, SQL Server, and Oracle. In these environments, you are given the opportunity to choose fully deployed database environments to place in your infrastructure.

Database as a Service (DBaaS) has gained significant adoption rates because of the idea that the automation of many of the more mundane aspects of operations frees up time from valuable engineering resources. Typical features can include:

- Deployment
- Master failover
- Patches and upgrades

- Backup and recovery

- Exposure of metrics

- High performance due to *"special sauce,"* such as Amazon's Aurora

All of this does free up time, but also can lead software engineers (SWEs) to think that database specialists are not needed. This could not be further from the truth. Abstracted services add their own challenges, but more important, they allow you to focus where your specialized knowledge can create the most value.

Challenges of DBaaS

Lack of visibility is one of the biggest challenges. With no access to the OS, network devices, and hardware, you will be unable to diagnose many significant issues.

DBaaS and Network Time Protocol (NTP)

We were using one well-known DBaaS, and our client decided to be one of the first to use a new database version the vendor was providing. We begged the client not to, but incentives were given and we found ourselves beta testing. In this case, an intrepid operations member neglected to synchronize Network Time Protocol (NTP) between all of the DB hosts. After hours of troubleshooting replication lag that could not be explained, we called support to find out what exactly had been going on. That night was a whiskey night!

Although many monitoring systems are now gathering database SQL data at the TCP level to manage data gathering at scale, they must fall back to logs or internal snapshots such as MySQL's *performance schema* for data. Additionally, time-tested tracing and monitoring tools like `top`, `dtrace`, and `vmstat` are unavailable.

Durability issues are similar to other virtualized environments, and implementation of important components such as replication and backups are often *black boxes* that rely on your vendor to do the right thing.

The DBRE and the DBaaS

In the world of marketing, DBaaS platforms are often sold as ways to eliminate the need for expensive and difficult-to-hire/retain database specialists. The DBaaS platform does allow for more rapid introduction of an operationally sound database infrastructure, which can delay the need for hiring or engaging a specialist. This is far from the elimination of the need for the specialist that is being sold however.

If anything, with the DBaaS abstracting away toil and easy-to-solve issues, you create risk that a difficult-to-solve issue will come up before you have the appropriate data-

---

base specialists dialed into your environment. Additionally, there are key decisions to be made early that do require someone with depth in the database engine you have chosen. These decisions include the following:

- Which database engine to use
- How to model your data
- An appropriate data access framework
- Database security decisions
- Data management and growth/capacity plans

So, even though software engineers may be more empowered by the DBaaS, you as the DBRE should work harder than ever to help them choose correctly and to ensure that they understand where your expertise can make the difference in success or failure of the DBaaS deployment.

DBaaS can be very attractive to an organization, particularly in its early days when every engineering minute is incredibly critical. As a DBRE in such an environment, it is strongly recommended that you consider a migration path and a disaster recovery path to your own infrastructure. Everything that your DBaaS solution can do you and your operations team can automate at the right time, giving you full control and visibility into your datastores for better or for worse.

Wrapping Up

In this chapter, we looked at the various combinations of hosts that you might find yourself working with—physical, virtual, containers, and services. We discussed the impact of processing, memory, network and storage resources, and the impacts that under-allocation and misconfiguration can cause.

In Chapter 6, we discuss how to manage these database infrastructures through appropriate tooling and process to scale and to manage risk and failure. We will cover configuration management, orchestration, automation and service discovery, and management.

CHAPTER 6

Infrastructure Management

In Chapter 5, we looked at the various infrastructure components and paradigms on which you might run your datastores. In this chapter, we discuss how to manage those environments at scale. We begin with the smallest unit, the individual host's configuration and definition. From this point, we zoom out to the deployment of hosts and orchestration between components. After this, we zoom out even further to the dynamic discovery of the current state of infrastructure, and the publishing of that data—aka service discovery. Finally, we will go to the development stack, discussing how to create development environments that are similar to these large production stacks.

Gone are the days of one or two boxes that can be manually managed with ease and relative stability. Today, we must be prepared to support large, complex infrastructures with only a few sets of hands. Automation is critical in ensuring that we can deploy datastores repeatably and reliably. Application stability and availability, and the speed at which new features can be deployed, relies on this. Our goals must be to eliminate processes that are repetitive and/or manual and to create easily reproducible infrastructures via standardized processes and automation.

What are good opportunities for this?

- Software installations, including operating system (OS), database, and associated packages and utilities
- Configuring software and the OS for desired behaviors and workloads
- Bootstrapping data into new databases
- Installing associated tools such as monitoring agents, backup utilities, and operator toolkits
- Testing of infrastructure for appropriate setup and behaviors

- Static and dynamic compliance testing

If we were to boil all of this down, our goals are to ensure that we can consistently build and/or reproduce any component of our database infrastructures, and that we can know the current and previous state of any of these components as we carry out troubleshooting and testing.

Admittedly, this is a fairly high-level overview. Should you want to deep-dive, we'd suggest *Infrastructure as Code*, by Kief Morris (O'Reilly). The goal for this chapter is to explain the various components of infrastructure management via code that you will be asked to contribute to, and point out the ways in which they can make your life as a database reliability engineer (DBRE) easier.

Version Control

To achieve these goals, we must use version control for all components required in the process. This includes the following:

- Source code and scripts
- Libraries and packages that function as dependencies
- Configuration files and information
- Versions of OS images and database binaries

A *version control system* (VCS) is the core of any software engineering workflow. The database and systems engineers working with software engineers (SWEs) to build, deploy, and manage applications and infrastructures work together within the VCS. Traditionally, this was the case. The systems and database engineers would often not use any VCS. If they did happen to use one, it would be separate from the SWE team's VCS, leading to an inability to map infrastructure versions to code versions.

Some examples of popular VCS platforms include:

- GitHub
- Bitbucket
- Git
- Microsoft Team Foundation Server
- Subversion

The VCS must be the source of truth for everything in the infrastructure. This includes scripts, configuration files, and the definition files you will use to define a database cluster. When you want to introduce something new, you check it into the VCS. When you want to modify something, you check it out, perform your changes, and commit the changes back into the VCS. After commits are in place, review, testing, and ultimately deployment can occur. It is worth noting that passwords should be masked in someway before being stored in the VCS.

Configuration Definition

To define how your database cluster should be configured and built, you will be utilizing a series of components. Your configuration management application will use a *domain-specific language* (DSL), though you might also find yourself working with scripts in Windows PowerShell, Python, Shell Scripts, Perl, or other languages. Following are some popular configuration management applications:

- Chef
- Puppet
- Ansible
- SaltStack
- CFEngine

By defining configuration, rather than scripting it, you create easily readable components which you reuse across your infrastructure. This creates consistency, and often reduces the amount of work needed to add a new component to configuration management.

These applications have primitives, which are called recipes in Chef or manifests in Puppet. These are rolled up into cookbooks or playbooks. These rollups incorporate the recipes with attributes that can be used to override defaults for different needs such as test versus production, file distribution schemes, and extensions such as libraries and templating. The end result of a playbook is code to generate a specific component of your infrastructure such as installing MySQL or Network Time Protocol (NTP).

These files can become quite complex in and of themselves and should share certain attributes. They should be parameterized so that you can run the same definition across different environments, such as dev, test, and production based on your inputs. The actions taken from these definitions and their application also need to be *idempotent*.

Idempotency

An idempotent action is one that can be run repeatedly with the same outcomes. An idempotent operation takes a desired state and does whatever is necessary to bring the component to that state regardless of its current state. For instance, if you are updating a configuration file to set the size of your buffer cache, you can assume the entry exists, which is naive and error prone. Instead, you can insert the line into the file. If you insert this line automatically, but it already exists, you will duplicate it. Thus, the action is not idempotent.

Instead, you can have the script look to see if the entry exists. Then, if the line does exist, you can modify it. If the line is nonexistent, you can insert it. This is an idempotent approach.

We can break up into sections an example of the configuration definition required by a distributed system such as Cassandra as follows:

- Core Attributes
  - Installation method, location, hashes
  - Cluster name and version
  - Group and user permissions
  - Heap sizing
  - JVM tuning and configuration
  - Directory layout
  - Service configuration
  - JMX setup
  - Virtual nodes
- JBOD setup and layout
- Garbage collection behavior
- Seed discovery
- Configuration of the YAML config file
- OS resource configs
- External services
  - PRIAM
  - JAMM (Java metrics)
  - Logging
  - OpsCenter

- Data center and rack layout

In addition to idempotency and parameterization, each of these components should have appropriate pre and post tests and integration into monitoring and logging for error management and continuous improvement.

Pre and post tests will include validation that state starts and ends up where expected. Additional tests can focus on using features that might be enabled or disabled by the change to see if functional behavior is expected. We assume that operational, performance, capacity, and scale tests are done prior to determine if these changes are even necessary. This means that testing will focus on validation that the implementation worked and desired behaviors are occurring. You'll find an example of a real-world case study with idempotency on the Salesforce Developers blog (*http://sforce.co/2zxYrjG*).

Building from Configuration

After you have your server specifications, acceptance tests, and modules for automation and building defined, you have everything in source code you need to build your databases. There are two approaches regarding how this should be done, and they are called *baking* and *frying*. Baking, frying, recipes, chefs...getting hungry yet? Check out John Willis's presentation on DevOps and Immutable Delivery (*https://www.nginx.com/blog/devops-and-immutable-delivery/*).

Frying involves dynamic configuration at host deployment time. Hosts are provisioned, operating systems are deployed, and then configuration occurs. All of the configuration management applications mentioned in the previous section have the ability to build and deploy infrastructure via frying.

For instance, if you are frying up a MySQL Galera Cluster, you might see the following:

- Server hardware provisioned (three nodes)
- Operating systems installed
- Chef client and knife (CLI) installed, cookbooks uploaded
- Cookbooks for OS permissions and configuration applied
- Cookbooks for default package installations applied
- Databag created/uploaded for /clusternode level attributes to be used (IP, init node, package names)
- Node roles applied (Galera Node)
  - MySQL/Galera binaries installed
  - MySQL utility packages and scripts installed

— Basic configuration set up

— Tests run

— Services started and shut down

— Cluster created/primary node set up

— Remaining nodes setup

— Tests run

• Register cluster with infrastructure services

Baking involves taking a base image and configuring that base image at build time. This creates a "golden image," which becomes the standard template for all hosts built for the same role. This is then snapshotted and stored for future use. Amazon AMIs or virtual machine (VM) images are examples of the artifacts output from this baking process. In this scenario, nothing is dynamic.

Packer is a tool from Hashicorp that creates images. The interesting thing about Packer is that it can create images for different environments (such as Amazon EC2 or VMWare images) from the same configuration. Most configuration management utilities can create baked images as well.

Maintaining Configuration

In an ideal world, use of configuration management will help you mitigate and potentially eliminate configuration drift. Configuration drift is what happens after a server is deployed after frying or baking. Although all instances of this component might start identical, people will inevitably log in, tweak something, install something, or run a few experiments and leave some trace behind.

An *immutable infrastructure* is one that is not allowed to mutate, or change, after it has been deployed. If there are changes that must happen, they are done to the version controlled configuration definition, and the service is redeployed. Immutable infrastructures are attractive, because they provide the following:

Simplicity
By not allowing mutations, the permutations of state in your infrastructure are dramatically limited.

Predictability
State is always known. This means that investigations and discovery are much faster, and everything is easily reproducible during troubleshooting.

Recoverability
> State can easily be reintroduced by redeploying the golden image. This reduces mean time to recover (MTTR) significantly. These images are known, tested, and ready to deploy at any time.

That being said, immutable infrastructures can have fairly dramatic overhead. For instance, if you have a 20-node MySQL Cluster and you want to modify a parameter, you must then redeploy every single node of this cluster in order to apply the change after it is checked in.

In the interest of moderation and middle ground, there can be some mutations that are frequent, automated and predictable, and can be allowed in the environment. Manual changes are still prohibited, keeping a significant amount of the value of predictability and recoverability while minimizing operational overhead (*http://chad fowler.com/2013/06/23/immutable-deployments.html*).

Enforcement of Configuration Definitions

How are these policies enforced?

Configuration synchronization

Many of the configuration management tools already discussed will provide synchronization. This means that any mutations occurring are overwritten on a schedule as the configuration is forcibly overwritten back to standard. This requires the synchronized state to be extraordinarily complete, however, or some areas will be missed, and thus allowed to drift.

Component redeploys

With appropriate tooling, you should be able to identify differences, and redeploy cleanly to eliminate them. Some environments might go so far as to constantly redeploy, or redeploy after any manual login/interaction has occurred on the component. This is generally more attractive in a baked solution, where the overhead of post-deployment configuration has been eliminated.

Using configuration definition and management can help ensure that your individual servers or instances are built correctly and stay that way. There is a higher level of abstraction in the deployment process, which is the definition of cross-service infrastructures and orchestration of those deployments.

Infrastructure Definition and Orchestration

Now that we've looked at the configuration and deployment of individual hosts, whether they be servers, VMs, or cloud instances, let's zoom out to look at groups of hosts. After all, we will rarely be managing a single database instance in isolation.

With the assumption that we are always working with a distributed datastore, we need to be able to build, deploy, and operate multiple systems at once.

Orchestration and management tools for provisioning infrastructures integrate with deployment (either frying or baking) applications to create full infrastructures, including services that might not use a host, such as virtual resources or platform as a service configurations. These tools will ideally create a solution for codifying the creation of an entire datacenter or service, giving developers and operations staff the ability to build, integrate, and launch infrastructures from end to end.

By abstracting infrastructure configurations into archivable, version-controlled code, these tools can integrate with configuration management applications to automate the provisioning of hosts and applications while handling all of the set up of underlying infrastructure resources and services required for automation tools to effectively do their jobs.

When discussing infrastructure definitions, we often use the term stack. You might have heard of a LAMP stack (Linux, Apache, MySQL, PHP), or a MEAN stack (MongoDB, Express.js, Angular.js, Node.js). These are generic solution stacks. A specific stack might be focused on a specific application or group of applications. A stack takes an even more specific meaning when you discuss the definition of infrastructures for the purpose of automation and orchestration via tooling. That is the definition we will be referring to here.

The structure of these stacks has a significant impact on how you meet your responsibilities as the DBRE on your team. Let's discuss these permutations, and the impacts to the DBRE role.

Monolithic Infrastructure Definitions

In this stack, all of the applications and services that your organization owns are defined together in one large definition. In other words, all database clusters will be defined in the same files. In such an environment, any number of applications and services will typically be using one or more databases. You might find five different applications with their associated databases in the same definition.

There are really no pros to a monolithic infrastructure definition, but there are plenty of cons. From an overall orchestration/infrastructure as code point of view, the problems can be elaborated as follows:

- If you want to make a change to the definition, you will need to test against the entire definition. This means that tests are slow and fragile. This will cause people to avoid making changes, creating a calcified and fragile infrastructure.

- Changes are also more prone to break everything rather than being isolated to one component of the infrastructure.

- Building a test or development environment means that you have to build every-thing together rather than a smaller section that is isolated that you can focus on.
- Changes will often be restricted to small groups of individuals who are able to know the entire stack. This creates bottlenecks of changes, slowing velocity.

Teams can find themselves in a monolithically defined stack if they have introduced a new tool, like Terraform, and simply reverse engineered their entire infrastructure into it. When considering an infrastructure definition, you have horizontal consider-ations (various tiers within one stack) and vertical considerations (breaking up your stack functionally so that one service is in one stack, rather than putting all services in one).

Separating Vertically

By breaking out the definition to individual services per definition, as illustrated in Figure 6-1, you can reduce size and complexity. So, what once was one definition file can become two, one for each service. This reduces the failure domain during changes to one service only. It will also reduce testing by half, and the size of your development and test environments commensurately.

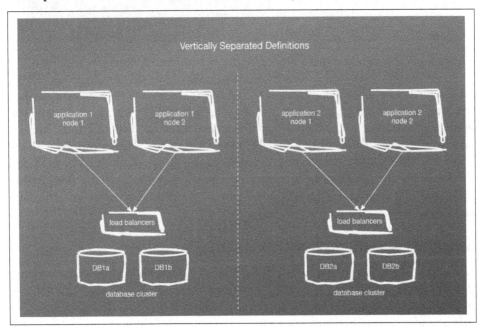

Figure 6-1. Separating vertically

If you have multiple applications using the same database tier, which is rather com-mon, this will prove more challenging. At this point, you will need to create three definitions. One will be a shared database definition, and the other two will be the individual service definitions, excluding the database tier, as demonstrated in Figure 6-2.

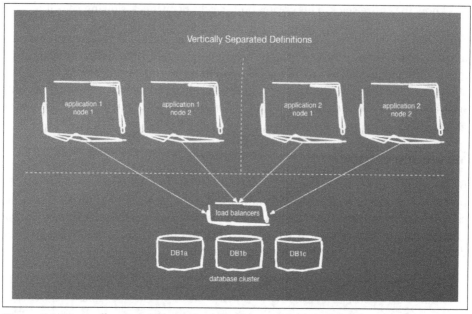

Figure 6-2. Vertically separated service definitions, with shared database

Now your failure domain for changes to the definition file are reduced even further, because each definition is smaller and more focused. However, you still have two applications coupled to the database, which means that there will need to be integration testing to ensure that changes made to the database tier work effectively with the other application stacks. So, testing will still require all applications to be built and deployed. Having applications separated does mean that you have the flexibility to build and test applications serially or in parallel depending on your infrastructure constraints.

Separated Tiers (Horizontal Definitions)

If you take the application definitions that have been separated out, you can break definition files out by tiers, also called *horizontally separating*. So, a standard web app might have a web server stack, an application server stack, and a database stack. The primary advantage of breaking out your infrastructure definition in this matter is that you have now reduced your failure domain even further. In other words, if you need to change configuration to your database servers, you don't need to worry about potentially breaking the build for web servers.

After you have separated tiers vertically and potentially horizontally, you find yourself dealing with new and interesting complexities. Specifically, you now have communication paths across stacks that require sharing of data. Your database load balancer virtual IPs must be shared with your application servers, but the stacks have their own definitions. This dynamic infrastructure requires a *service catalog* to ensure that any component of your infrastructure can effectively share its state to any other component for communication and integration.

Acceptance Testing and Compliance

Utilizing automation and infrastructure as code obviously gives us a lot of benefits. One more that we haven't mentioned yet is acceptance testing and compliance. With images of infrastructure in place, you can utilize tools such as ServerSpec, which uses descriptive language to define tests for your infrastructure images. This brings test-driven development (TDD) to your infrastructure, which is a great opportunity to continue to align infrastructure and software engineering.

With a framework such as ServerSpec for automated testing, you can delve into compliance and security, which are ideal customers of this. Working with these teams you can create a test suite focused on database security and compliance. Inspec is a plug-in for ServerSpec that does this work quite well. You can find more information about it at the Chef blog (*https://blog.chef.io/2015/11/04/the-road-to-inspec/*).

Service Catalog

With dynamic environments being built, scaled, and destroyed automatically, there must be a source of truth for current state that all infrastructure components can use. Service discovery is an abstraction that maps specific designations and port numbers of your services and load balancers to semantic names. For instance, mysql-replicas is a semantic that can include any number of MySQL hosts replicating data from the primary write host. The utility of this is being able to refer to things by semantic names instead of IP address, or even hostnames. Information in the catalog can be accessed via HTTP or DNS.

The following are some of the most common service discovery tools available as of this writing:

- Zookeeper
- Consul.io
- Etcd
- Build your own!

There are numerous use cases for such a server catalog that the DBRE might encounter. Here are a few. (We discuss more in later chapters as we explore specific architectures.)

Database failovers
By registering *Write IPs* to the catalog, you can create templates for load balancers. When IP is switched, load balancer configurations rebuild and reload.

Sharding
Share information about writeable shards to application hosts.

Cassandra Seed Nodes
Let bootstrapping nodes know where to go for seeds.

A service catalog can be very simple, storing service data to integrates services, or it can include numerous additional facilities, including health checks to ensure that data in the catalog provides working resources. You can also store key–value pairs in many of these catalogs (*http://bit.ly/2zxRX4D*).

Bringing It All Together

That was a lot of information, and a lot of it high-level. Let's discuss a day in the life of a DBRE using these concepts for MySQL. Hopefully, this will add some valuable context. For simplicity, we will assume that this environment runs in Amazon's EC2 environment. You've been tasked with bringing up a new MySQL cluster for your primary user database, which is sharded and requires more capacity. Here are the tools you've been given:

- MySQL Community, 5.6
- MySQL MHA for replication management and failover
- Consul for cluster state database

The Terraform files and the Chef Cookbooks for MySQL shards for the user database are checked into GitHub, of course. There should be no manual changes that need to occur in order to build this. You grumble about the fact that you should probably automate capacity analysis and deployment of new shards, but this is only your third month and you just haven't had the time yet.

Checking your deployment logs, you see the last time a MySQL shard was deployed, and you compare that to the current versions of the terraform and chef code to validate that nothing has changed since then. Everything checks out, so you should be good to go. First, you run terraform with the plan option, to show the execution path and verify nothing untoward will happen. Assuming that is good, you go ahead and run the terraform commands to build the shard.

Terraform executes a chef provisioner that queries Consul for the latest `shard_id`, and increments it by one. Using that `shard_id`, it runs its way through a series of steps that include the following:

1. Launch three EC2 instances in two availability zones (AZs) using the appropriate Amazon Machine Images (AMIs) for MySQL Shard Hosts
2. Configuring MySQL on these hosts and bringing the service up
3. Register each node into consul, under the `shard_id` namespace

   - First one will register as master, the following will register as failovers
   - Start replication using this data

4. Launch two EC2 instances in two AZs using the appropriate AMIs for MySQL MHA Manager Hosts
5. Register Master High Availability (MHA) manager to consul, under the `shard_id` namespace
6. Configure MHA using node data from consul
7. Start MHA replication manager
8. Run through a series of failover tests

At this point, you have an MHA managed MySQL cluster that is registered in Consul. Some things will happen automatically from here, including the following:

- Backups start snapshotting from the master automatically, as scripts use Consul.
- Monitoring agents are in the AMIs, and automatically begin sending metrics and logs to the operational visibility stack.

Finally, when you are satisfied, you mark the shard as active in Consul. At this point, proxy servers begin adding it to their templates and reloading. Application servers identify it as available, and start sending data to it as appropriate.

Development Environments

Testing locally in a development environment or sandbox is crucial to this workflow. You should feel confident in the impacts of your changes before committing it to the VCS. One of our goals with everything we've discussed in this chapter is repeatability. This means that the sandbox must be as close as possible in software and configuration as your actual infrastructure. This means the same OS, the same configuration management, orchestration, and even service catalogs.

When discussing deployment, we mentioned Packer. To reiterate, Packer allows you to create multiple images from the same configuration. This includes images for virtual machines *on your workstation*. Using a tool like Vagrant on your workstation allows you to download the latest images, build the VMs, and even run through a standard test suite to verify that everything works as expected.

After you've done your changes, tested them, brought down any new changes from your VCS and tested again, you can commit this right back into the team VCS in preparation for integration and deployment.

Wrapping Up

Using infrastructure as code, automation, and version control are crucial skillsets for any reliability engineer, and the DBRE is no exception. With the tools and techniques discussed in this chapter, you can begin eliminating toil, reducing mistakes, and creating self-service deployments for your engineering teams.

In Chapter 7, we begin digging deeper into a crucial component of infrastructure: backup and recovery. One key difference in the database tiers is the importance of persistence and availability of data. Although most other environments can be built as artifacts and deployed fast and easily, databases require large working sets of data to be attached and maintained safely. There is a broad toolkit available to do this, which is what we will go over next.

CHAPTER 7
Backup and Recovery

In Chapters 5 and 6, we focused on infrastructure design and management. This means that at this point we have a good feeling for how to build, deploy, and manage distributed infrastructures running databases. This includes techniques for rapidly adding new nodes for capacity or to replace a failed node. Now, it's time to discuss the serious meat and potatoes: data backup and recovery.

Let's face it. Everyone considers backup and recovery dull and tedious. Most think of it as the epitome of toil. It is often relegated to junior engineers, outside contractors, and third-party tooling that the team is loathe to interact with. We've worked with some pretty horrible backup software before. Trust me, we empathize.

Still, this is one of the most crucial processes in your operations toolkit. Moving your precious data between nodes, across datacenters, and into long-term archives is the constant movement of your business' most precious commodity: its data. Rather than relegating this to a second-class citizen of Ops, we strongly suggest you treat it as a VIP. Everyone should understand not only the recovery targets, but be intimately familiar with operating and monitoring the processes. Many DevOps philosophies propose that everyone should have an opportunity to write and push code to production. We propose that every engineer should participate at least once in the recovery processes of critical data.

We create and store copies of data, otherwise known as backups and archives, as a means to the real need. That need is recovery. Sometimes, this recovery is something nice and leisurely, such as building an environment for auditors or configuring an alternate environment. More often though, the recovery is needed to rapidly replace failed nodes or to add capacity to existing clusters.

Today, in distributed environments, we face new challenges in the backup and recovery realm. Now, as before, most local datasets are distributed to reasonable sizes, of up to a few terabytes at most. The difference is that those local datasets are only one fraction of a larger distributed dataset. Recovering a node is a relatively manageable task, but keeping state across the cluster becomes more challenging.

Core Concepts

Let's begin by discussing core concepts around backup and recovery. If you are an experienced database or systems engineer, some of this might be rudimentary. If so, please feel free to fast forward a bit.

Physical versus Logical

When backing up a database physically, you are backing up the actual files in which the data resides. This means that the database-specific file formats are maintained, and there is usually a set of metadata within the database that defines what files exist, and what database structures reside within them. If you back up files and expect another database instance to be able to utilize them, you will need to back up and store the associated metadata that the database relies on in order to make the backup portable.

A logical backup exports the data out of the database into a format that is, theoretically, portable to any system. There will usually be some metadata still, but it is more likely to be focused on the point in time at which the backup was taken. An example of this is an export of all of the insert statements needed to populate an empty database to bring it up to date. Another example could be each row in a JSON format. Due to this, logical backups tend to be very time consuming because it is a row-by-row extraction rather than a physical copy and write operation. Similarly, recovery involves all of the normal overhead of the database, such as locking and generation of redo or undo logs.

An excellent example of this dichotomy is the difference between row-based and statement-based replication. In many relational databases, statement-based replication means that upon commit, a log of data manipulation language (DML; aka insert, update, replace, delete) statements is appended to. Those statements are streamed to replicas, where they are replayed. Another approach to replication is row-based, or change data capture (CDC).

Online versus Offline

An offline, or cold, backup is one in which the database instance that utilizes the files is shutdown. This allows files to be quickly copied with no worries about maintaining a point in time state while other processes are reading and writing data. This is an ideal, but very rare state in which to work.

In an online, or hot, backup, you are still copying all of the files, but you have the added complexity of needing to get a consistent, point-in-time snapshot of the data that must exist for the amount of time it takes a backup to occur. Additionally, if live traffic is accessing the database during the backup, you also must be careful not to overwhelm the Input/Output (IO) throughput of the storage layer. Even throttled, you can find that the mechanisms used to maintain consistency add unreasonable amounts of latency to application activity.

Full, Incremental, and Differential

A full backup, regardless of the approach, means that the entire local dataset is backed up fully. On small datasets, this is a fairly trivial event. For 10 terabytes, it can take an impossible amount of time.

A differential backup allows you to take a backup of only the changed data since the last full backup. In practice, there is usually more data backed up than just that which has changed because your data will be in structures such as a page. A page will be of a particular size, such as 16 K or 64 K, and will have many rows of data in it. An incremental backup will back up any page that has modified data in it. Thus, larger page sizes will backup significantly more than just the changed data.

An incremental backup is similar to a differential backup, except that it will use the last backup, incremental or full, as the point in time at which it will look for changed data. Thus, if you are restoring an incremental backup, you might need to recover the last full backup, and one or more incremental backups, as well, to get to the current point in time.

With these concepts in mind, let's discuss various things to consider when deciding on an effective backup and recovery strategy.

Considerations for Recovery

When you first evaluate an effective strategy, you should look back to your Service-Level Objectives (SLOs), as discussed in Chapter 2. Specifically, you need to consider availability and durability indicators. Any strategy that you choose will require you to be able to recover data within the predefined uptime constraints. And, you need to back up fast enough to ensure that you meet the necessary parameters for durability. If you back up every day, and your transaction logs between backups remain on node-level storage, you can very well lose those transactions before the next backup.

Additionally, you need to consider how the dataset functions within the holistic ecosystem. For instance, your orders might be stored in a relational system, where everything is committed in transactions, and is thus easily recovered in relation to the rest of the data within that database. However, after an order is set, a workflow may be triggered via an event stored in a queuing system or a key–value store. Those systems might be eventually consistent, or even ephemeral, relying on the relational system for reference or recoverability. How do you account for those workflows when recovering?

If you are in an environment with rapid development, you might also find that data stored in a backup was written and utilized by a different version of the application than the version running after the restore is done. How will the application interact with that older data? Hopefully the data is versioned to allow for that, but you must be knowledgeable of this and prepared for such eventualities. Otherwise, the application could logically corrupt that data and create even larger issues down the road.

Each of these, and many other variables that you cannot plan for, must be taken into account when planning for data recovery. As we discussed in Chapter 3, we simply can't prepare for every eventuality. But, this is a critical service. Data recoverability is one of the most significant responsibilities of the database reliability engineer (DBRE). So, your plan for data recoverability must be able to be as broad as possible, taking into account as many potential issues as possible.

Recovery Scenarios

With that in mind, let's discuss the types of incidents and operations that might require recovery so that we can plan on supporting each need. We can first sort these into planned versus unplanned scenarios. Treating recovery as an emergency tool only will limit your team's exposure to the tool to emergencies and emergency simulations. Instead, if we can incorporate recovery into daily activities, we can expect a higher degree of familiarity and success during an emergency. Similarly, we will have more data to determine whether the recovery strategy supports our SLOs. With multiple daily runs, it is easier to get a sample set that can include upper bounds and can be represented with some level of certainty for planning purposes.

Planned Recovery Scenarios

What are the day-to-day recovery needs that can be incorporated? Here is a list that we've seen at various sites:

- Building new production nodes and clusters
- Building different environments
- Extract, Transform, and Load (ETL) and pipeline processes for downstream data-stores
- Operational tests

When performing these operations, be sure to plug the process into your operational visibility stack:

Time

How long does each component, as well as the overall process, take to run? Uncompress? Copy? Log applies? Tests?

Size

How big is your backup compressed and uncompressed?

Throughput

How much pressure are you putting on the hardware?

This data will help you stay ahead of capacity issues, allowing you to ensure that your recovery process stays viable.

New production nodes and clusters

Whether your databases are part of an immutable infrastructure or not, there are opportunities for regular rebuilds that will, of necessity, utilize recovery procedures. Databases are rarely set into autoscaling automation because of the amount of time it can take for a new node to be bootstrapped and brought into a cluster. Still, there is no reason that a team can't set up a schedule to regularly introduce new nodes into a cluster to test these processes. Chaos Monkey (*http://bit.ly/2zy1qsE*), a tool developed by Netflix that randomly shuts down systems, can do this in such a way that the entire process of monitoring, notification, triage, and recovery can be tested. If you're not there yet, though, you can still do this as a planned part of a checklist of processes your operations team should be performing at regular enough intervals to keep them all familiar with the procedure. These activities allow you to test not only a full and incremental recovery, but incorporation into the replication stream and the process to take a node into service.

Building different environments

It is inevitable that you will be building environments for development, for integration testing, for operational testing and for demos among others. Some of these environments will require complete recovery, and should utilize node recovery and full cluster recovery. Some will have other requirements, such as subset recovery for feature testing and data scrubbing for user privacy purposes. This allows for you to test point-in-time recovery as well as the recovery of specific objects. Each of these are very different from a standard full dataset recovery and are useful for recovering from operator and application corruption. By creating APIs that allow for object-level and point-in-time recovery, you can facilitate the automation and familiarization with these processes.

ETL and pipeline processes for downstream datastores

Similarly to your environment builds, the process of pushing data from production databases into pipelines for downstream analytics and streaming datastores is a perfect place to utilize point-in-time and object-level recovery processes and APIs.

Operational tests

During various testing scenarios, you will need copies of data. Some testing, such as capacity and load testing, requires a full dataset, which is an excellent opportunity for utilizing full-recovery processes. Feature testing might require smaller datasets, which is an excellent opportunity to use point-in-time and object-level restores.

Recovery testing itself can become a continuous operation. In addition to utilizing recovery processes in everyday scenarios, you can set restores to constantly be run, allowing for automated testing and validation to rapidly bring up any issues that might have occurred to break the backup process. When we bring up this process, many people ask how to test the success of a restore.

When taking the backup, you can produce a lot of data that can be used for testing, such as the following:

- The most recent ID in an auto increment set.
- Row counts on objects.
- Checksums on subsets of data that are insert only and thus can be treated as immutable.
- Checksums on schema definition files.

As with any testing, this should be a tiered approach. There are some tests that will succeed or fail quickly; these should be the first layer of testing. Examples of this are checksum comparisons on metadata/object definitions, the successful starting of a database instance, and the successful connection to a replication thread. Operations that might take longer, such as checksumming data and running table counts, should be run later into the validation process.

Unplanned Scenarios

With all of the day-to-day planned scenarios that can be used, the recovery process should be quite finely tuned, well documented, well practiced, and reasonably free of bugs and issues. Thus, the unplanned scenarios are rarely as scary as they could be otherwise. The team should see no difference in these unplanned exercises. Let's list and dive into each to discuss the possibilities that might cause us to need to exercise our recovery processes:

- User error

- Application errors
- Infrastructure services
- Operating system and hardware errors
- Hardware failures
- Datacenter failures

User error

Ideally, user error should be somewhat of a rare occurrence. If you are creating guard rails for engineers, you can add a lot of prevention. Still, there will always be an occasion when an operator accidentally does damage. Some examples of this include the ubiquitous absence of a WHERE clause when executing an UPDATE or DELETE in the database client. Or, perhaps a data cleansing script is executed in the production, rather than the testing environment. There are also many cases when something executes correctly, just at the wrong time, or against the wrong hosts. All of these are user errors. These errors are often immediately identified and recovered. However, there can be occasions when the impacts of these changes might not be known for days or weeks, thus hindering detection.

Application errors

Application errors are the scariest of the scenarios discussed because they can be so insidious. Applications are constantly modifying how they interact with datastores. Many of these applications are also managing referential integrity and external pointers to assets such as files or third-party IDs. It is frighteningly simple to introduce a change that destructively mutates data, removes data, or adds incorrect data in ways that might not be noticed for quite a long time.

Infrastructure services

Chapter 6 covers the magic of infrastructure management services. Unfortunately, these systems can be as destructive as they can be helpful, with wide-ranging consequences from editing a file, pointing to a different environment, or pushing an incorrect configuration.

OS and hardware errors

Operating systems and the hardware they interface with are still systems built by humans, and thus can have bugs and unintended consequences from undocumented or poorly known configurations. In the context of data recovery, this is quite true regarding the path of data from the database through OS caches, filesystems, controllers, and ultimately disks. Data corruption or data loss is much more common than we think. Unfortunately, our trust and reliance on these mechanisms creates cultures in which data integrity is expected rather than something to be skeptical of.

 ### Silent Corruption

This kind of OS and hardware error impact happened to Netflix in 2008. Error detection and correction on disks utilizes error correction code (ECC). ECC corrects single-bit errors automatically, and detects double-bit errors. Thus, an ECC can detect an error up to twice the hamming distance of what it can correct. So, if it can correct 46 bytes in your 512-byte sector hard drive, it can detect up to 92 bytes of error. What isn't correctable is reported to the controller as uncorrectable, and the disk controller increments the "uncorrectable error" counter in S.M.A.R.T. Errors larger than 92 bytes are passed straight to the controller as good data. That propagates to backups. Terrifying right?

This is what makes cloud and so-called "serverless" computing something that should be approached with great skepticism. When you do not have access to implementation details, you cannot be sure that data integrity is being treated as top priority. Too often it is ignored, or even tuned down for performance. Without knowledge, there is no power.

Checksumming filesystems like ZFS will checksum each block, ensuring detection of bad data. If you are using RAID that involves mirroring or parity, it will even fix the data.

Hardware failures

Hardware components fail, and in distributed systems they fail regularly. You get regular failures of disks, memory, CPUs, controllers, or network devices. These failures of hardware can cause node failures, or latency on nodes that make the system unusable. Shared systems like network devices can affect entire clusters, making them unavailable, or causing them to break into smaller clusters that aren't aware of the network having been partitioned. This can lead to rapid and significant data divergence that will need to be merged and repaired.

Datacenter failures

Sometimes, hardware failures at the network level can cascade into datacenter failures. Occasionally, congestion of storage backplanes cause cascading failures as in the case of Amazon Web Services in 2012 (*http://bit.ly/2zxSpzR*). Sometimes hurricanes, earthquakes, and tractor trailers can create conditions that cause the failure of entire datacenters. Recovery from this will test even the most robust of recovery strategies.

Scenario scope

Having enumerated the planned and unplanned scenarios that might create the need for a recovery event, let's further add the dimension of scope to these events. This will be useful to determine the most appropriate response. Here are ranges we'll consider:

- Localized or single-node
- Cluster-wide
- Datacenter or multiple clusters

In a *local or single-node scope*, the recovery is limited to a single host. Perhaps you are adding a new node to a cluster for capacity or for the replacement of a failed node. Perhaps you are doing a rolling upgrade, and restores are being done node by node. Any of these are *local scope.*

In a *cluster-wide scope*, the need to execute recovery is global to all members of that cluster. Perhaps a destructive mutation or data removal occurred and cascaded to all nodes via replication. Or, perhaps you need to build a new cluster for capacity testing.

Datacenter or multiple cluster scope indicates that all data in a physical location or region needs recovery. This could be due to failure of shared storage, or a disaster that has caused the catastrophic failure of a datacenter. This might also be deployment of a new redundant site for planning purposes.

In addition to the locality scope, there is dataset scope. This can be enumerated into three potential types:

- Single object
- Multiple objects
- Database metadata

In *single-object scope*, one specific object requires recovery of some or all data. The incident discussed previously, in which a DELETE ends up removing more data than planned, is a single-object scope. In *multiple objects*, the scope is against more than one, and possibly all, objects in a particular database. This can occur in application corruption or during a failed upgrade or shard migration. Finally, there is *database metadata scope*, in which the data stored in the database is fine, but the metadata that makes the database usable, such as user data, security permissions, or mapping to OS files, is lost.

Scenario Impact

In addition to defining the scenario requiring recovery and the scope enumerated, it is also crucial to define the potential impacts because they will be significant in determining how the recovery option is approached. You can approach data loss that doesn't affect the SLO methodically and slowly to minimize escalating the impact. More destructive changes that are causing SLO violation must be approached with an eye toward triage and rapid service restoration before any long-term clean up. We can separate the approaches into three categories:

- SLO impacting, application down, or majority of users affected
- SLO threatening, some users affected
- Features affected, non-SLO threatening

With recovery scenario, scope, and impact, we have a potential combination of 72 different scenarios to consider. That's a lot of scenarios! Too many really to give each the level of focus they need. Luckily, many scenarios can utilize the same recovery approach. Still, even with this overlap, there is no way that we can fully plan for every eventuality. Thus, building a multitiered approach to recovery is required to help make sure we have as extensive of a toolkit as possible. In the next section, we use the information we just went through in this section to define the recovery strategy.

Anatomy of a Recovery Strategy

There is a reason why we say "recovery strategy" rather than "backup strategy." Data recovery is the very reason we do backups. Backups are simply a means to the end, and thus are dependent on the true requirement: recovery within parameters. The simple question "Is your database backed up?" is a question that should be followed with the response, "Yes, in multiple ways, depending on the recovery scenario." A simple yes is naive and promotes a false sense of security that is irresponsible and dangerous.

An effective database recovery strategy not only engages multiple scenarios with the most effective approaches, but also includes the detection of data loss/corruption, recovery testing, and recovery validation.

Building Block 1: Detection

Early detection of potential data loss or corruption is crucial. In our discussion of user and application errors in "Unplanned Scenarios" on page 118, we noted that these problems can often go for days, weeks, or even longer before being identified. This means that backups might even be aged-out by the time the need for them is noticed. Thus, detection must be a high priority for all of engineering. In addition to building early detection around data loss or corruption, ensuring that there is as long of a window as possible in place to recover in case early detection fails is also critical. Let's look at the different failure scenarios discussed, and identify some real-world approaches to detection and lengthened recovery windows.

User error

One of the biggest impacts in reducing time to identifying data loss is through not allowing manual or ad hoc changes to be executed in production environments. By creating wrappers for scripts, or even API-level abstractions, engineers can be guided through effective steps for ensuring all changes are as safe as possible, tested, logged, and pushed up to the appropriate teams.

An effective wrapper or API will be able to do the following:

- Execute in multiple environments via parameterization
- A dry-run stage, in which execution results can be estimated and validated
- A test suite for the code execution
- Validation post-execution to verify that changes met expectations
- Soft-deletion or easy rollback via the same API
- Logging by ID of all data modified, for identification and recovery

By removing the ad hoc and manual components of these processes, you can increase the likelihood that all changes will be trackable by troubleshooting engineers. All changes will be logged so that there is traceability and the change cannot simply disappear into the day-to-day noise. Finally, by soft-staging mutations or deletions and building in easy rollbacks of any data, you give greater windows of time for problems with the change to be identified and corrected. This is not a guarantee. After all, manual processes can be extremely well logged, and people can forget to set up logging in automated processes, or they can bypass them.

Application errors

A key to early detection of application errors is data validation. When engineers introduce new objects and attributes, database reliability engineers should work with them to identify data validation that can be done downstream, outside of the application itself.

Like all testing, initial work should focus on quick tests that provide fast feedback loops on critical data components, such as external pointers to files, relationship mapping to enforce referential integrity, and personal identification information (PII). As data and applications grow, this validation becomes more expensive and more valuable. Building a culture that holds engineers accountable for data quality and integrity rather than the storage engines pays dividends in terms of not only flexibility to use different databases, but also by helping people feel more confident about experimenting and moving fast on application features. Validation functions as a guard rail, helping everyone to feel braver and more confident.

Infrastructure services

Any catastrophic infrastructure impacts that require recovery should be caught rapidly by monitoring the operational visibility stack. That being said, there are some changes that can be quieter and potentially cause data loss, data corruption, or availability impacts. Using golden images and comparing them regularly to your infrastructure components can help identify straying from the test images quickly. Similarly, versioned infrastructure can help identify straying infrastructure and alert the appropriate engineers or automation.

OS and hardware errors

As with infrastructure services, the majority of these problems should be rapidly caught by monitoring of logs and metrics. Edge cases that are not standard will require some thought and experience to identify and add to monitoring for early detection. Checksums on disk blocks is an example of this. Not all filesystems will do this, and teams working with critical data need to take the time to consider the appropriate filesystems that can identify silent corruption via checksumming.

Hardware and datacenter failures

As with infrastructure services, these failures should be easily identifiable via the monitoring that we've already gone over in Chapter 4. Isn't it great that we already did that?

Building Block 2: Tiered Storage

An effective recovery strategy relies on data being placed on multiple storage tiers. Different recovery needs can be served by different storage areas, which not only ensure the right performance, but also the right cost and the right durability for any number of scenarios.

Online, high performance storage

This is the storage pool most of your production datastores will run on. It is characterized by a high amount of throughput, low latency, and thus, a high price point. When recovery time is of the utmost importance, putting recent copies of the datastore, and associated incremental backups on this tier is paramount. Generally speaking, only a few copies of the most recent data will reside here, allowing for rapid recovery for the most common and impactful of scenarios. Typical use cases will be full database copies to bring new nodes into production service after failures, or in response to rapid escalations of traffic that result in a need for additional capacity.

Online, low-performance storage

This storage pool is often utilized for data that is not sensitive to latency. Larger-sized disks that have low throughput and latency profiles—and a lower price point—make up this pool. These storage pools are often much larger due to this, and thus more copies of data from further back in time can be stored in this tier. Relatively infrequent, low-impact, or long-running recovery scenarios will utilize these older backups. Typical use cases will be finding and repairing application or user errors that slipped by early detection.

Offline storage

Tape storage or even something like Amazon Glacier are examples of this kind of storage. This storage is off-site, and often requires movement via vehicle to bring it to an area where it can be made available for recovery. This can support business continuity and auditory requirements but does not have a place in day-to-day recovery scenarios. Still, due to the size and cost, vast amounts of storage are available here, allowing for the potential of storing all data for the life of the business, or at least for a full legal compliance term.

Object storage

Object storage is a storage architecture that manages data as objects, rather than files or blocks. Object storage gives features not available through traditional storage architectures, such as an API available to applications, object versioning, high degrees of availability via replication and distribution. Object storage allows for scalable and self-healing availability of large amounts of objects with full versions and history. This can be ideal for easy recovery of specific objects that are unstructured, and that are not reliant on relationships to other data for coherence. This gives an attractive opportunity to allow for recovery of application or user errors. Amazon S3 is a classic example of an inexpensive, scalable, and reliable object-level storage tier.

Each of these tiers plays a part in a comprehensive strategy for recoverability across multiple potential scenarios. Without being able to predict every possible scenario, it is this level of breadth that is required. Next, we will discuss the tools that utilize these storage tiers to provide recoverability.

Building Block 3: A Varied Toolbox

So, now it is time to evaluate the required recovery processes by going through the scenarios and evaluating options. We know from various sections in this chapter that we have a series of tools available to us. Let's look at them a little more closely.

Replication Is Not a Backup!

You will note that nowhere do we discuss replication as a way to effectively back up data for recovery. Replication is blind, and can cascade user errors, application errors, and corruption. You must look at replication as a necessary tool for data movement and synchronization, but not for creating useful recovery artifacts. If anyone tells you that they are using replication for backups, give them some side eye and move on. Similarly, RAID is not a backup. Rather, it is a redundancy.

Full physical backups

We know that we will need to do full restores at each level of scope: node level, cluster level, and datacenter level. Rapid, portable full restores are incredibly powerful and mandatory in dynamic environments. They allow rapid node builds for capacity or for deployment of replacements during failures. A full backup can be done via full data copies over the network, or via volumes that can easily be attached and detached from specific hosts/instances. To do this, you need full backups.

Full backups of a relational database require either the opportunity to lock the database to get a consistent snapshot from which you can copy, or the ability to shut the database down for the duration of the copy. In an asynchronously replicated environment, the replicas cannot be completely trusted to be synchronized with the primary writer, so you should perform these full backups from the primary if at all possible. After the snapshot is created within the database or via a filesystem or infrastructure snapshot, you can copy that snapshot to staging storage.

Full backups of an appending write datastore, such as Cassandra, involve a snapshot that utilizes an OS hard link at the OS level. Because the data in these distributed datastores is not on all nodes, the backup is considered an *eventually consistent* backup. Recovery will require the node being brought back into a cluster at which point regular consistency operations will eventually bring it up to date.

A full backup on online, high-performance storage is for immediate replacement into an online cluster. These backups are typically uncompressed because uncompression takes a lot of time. Full backups on online, low-performance storage are utilized for building different environments, such as for testing, or for analytics and data forensics. Compression is an effective tool to allow for longer timelines of full backups on limited storage pools.

Incremental physical backups

As discussed earlier, incremental backups allow for bridging the gap between the last full backup and a place in time after it. Physical incremental backups are generally done via data blocks that have a changed piece of data in it. Because full backups can be expensive, both in terms of performance impact during the backup and storage, incremental backups allow you to quickly bring a full backup that might be older up to date for use in the cluster.

Full and incremental logical backups

A full logical backup provides for portability and simpler extraction of subsets of data. They will not be used for rapid recovery of nodes, but instead are perfect tools for use in forensics, moving data between datastores, and recovering specific subsets of data from large datasets.

Object stores

Object stores, like logical backups, can provide for easy recovery of specific objects. In fact, object storage is optimized for this specific use case, and it can easily be used by APIs to programmatically recover objects as needed.

Building Block 4: Testing

For such an essential infrastructure process as recovery, it is astonishing how often testing tends to fall by the wayside. Testing is an essential process to ensure that your backups are usable for recovery. Testing is often set up as an occasional process, to be run on an intermittent basis such as monthly or quarterly. Although this is better than nothing, it allows for long periods of time between tests during which backups can stop working.

There are two effective approaches to adding testing into ongoing processes. The first one is incorporating recovery into everyday processes. This way, recovery is constantly tested, allowing for rapid identification of bugs and failures. Additionally, constant recovery creates data about how long your recovery takes, which is essential in calibrating your recovery processes to meet Service-Level Agreements (SLAs). Examples of constant integration of recovery into daily processes includes the following:

- Building integration environments
- Building testing environments
- Regularly replacing nodes in production clusters

If your environment does not allow for enough opportunities to rebuild datastores, you can also create a continuous testing process, whereby recovery of the most recent backup is a constant process, followed by verification of the success of that restore. Regardless of the presence of automation, even offsite backup tiers do require occasional testing.

With these building blocks, you can create an in-depth defense for different recovery scenarios. By mapping out the scenarios and tools used to recover them, you can then begin evaluating your needs in terms of development and resources.

A Recovery Strategy Defined

As we discussed earlier in this chapter, we have multiple failure scenarios to prepare for. To do this, we need a rich toolset, and a plan for utilization of each of those tools.

Online, Fast Storage with Full and Incremental Backups

This portion of the strategy supports the meat and potatoes of daily recovery. When you need to build a new node for rapid introduction into production or for testing, you use this strategy.

Use Cases

The following scenarios are the primary use cases for this portion of strategy:

- Replacing failed nodes
- Introducing new nodes
- Building test environments for feature integration
- Building test environments for operations testing

Running a daily full backup is often the highest frequency possible due to latency during backups. Keeping up to a week's worth allows for rapid access to any recent changes and is usually more than enough. This means seven full copies of the database, uncompressed, plus the amount of data required to track all changes for incremental backups. Some environments do not have the capacity or money for this, so permutations can occur in *retention period* and *frequency* as levers for tuning.

Detection

Monitoring informs you when there is a node or component failure requiring recovery to new nodes. Capacity planning reviews and projections let you know when you need to add more nodes for capacity purposes.

Tiered storage

Online, high-performance storage is required because production failures require rapid recovery. Similarly, testing must be as fast as possible to support rapid development velocity.

Toolbox

Full and incremental physical backups provide the fastest recovery option, and are the most appropriate here. These backups are left uncompressed due to recovery time needs.

Testing

Because integration testing happens frequently, these recovery scenarios occur frequently. In virtual environments, daily reintroduction of one node into the cluster allows for similar frequent exercising of recovery processes. Finally, a continuous recovery process is introduced due to the significant importance of this process.

Online, Slow Storage with Full and Incremental Backups

Here, we have slower storage with cheaper, more plentiful space.

Use cases

The following scenarios are the primary use cases for this portion of strategy:

- Application errors
- User errors
- Corruption repair
- Building test environments for operations testing

When new features, failed changes, or inappropriate migrations occur and cause damage to data, you need to be able to access and extract large amounts of data for recovery. That is where this tier comes in. This is perhaps the messiest stage of recovery because there are too many permutations of potential damage to account for. Code often must be scripted during the recovery effort, which itself can lead to more bugs and errors without effective testing.

Copying full backups from high-performance to low-performance storage through a compression mechanism is an easy way to get full backups into this portion of our strategy. Due to compression and cheaper storage, keeping up to a month or even longer is possible depending on budget and needs. In highly dynamic environments, the opportunity for missing corruption and integrity issues is much higher, which means you need to account for a longer amount of time.

Detection

Data validation is the key for identifying the need for recovery from this pool. When validation fails, engineers can use these backups to identify what happened, and when, and begin extracting clean data for reapplication into production.

Tiered storage

Online, low-performance storage is required because a long window of time is required for this part of the strategy. Cheap, large storage is the key.

Toolbox

Full and incremental physical backups are the most appropriate here. These backups are compressed due to recovery time needs as well. Here, you can also utilize logical backups, such as replication logs, in addition to physical ones to allow for more flexibility in recovery.

Testing

Because this recovery does not happen as often, continuous automated recovery processes are critical to ensure that all backups are usable and in good shape. Occasional "game day" practice runs of specific recovery scenarios such as a table, or a range of data, are also good to keep teams familiar with the processes and tools.

Offline Storage

By far the least expensive, this is also the slowest of storage tiers from which to extract data.

Use cases

The following scenarios are the primary use cases for this portion of strategy:

- Audits and compliance
- Business continuity

So, this part of the solution is really focused on rare, but highly critical needs. Audits and compliance often require data going back seven years or more. But, they are not time sensitive, and can take quite a while to prepare and present. Business continuity requires copies of data away from the same physical locations of the current production systems to ensure that if there are disasters, you can rebuild. Although this is time sensitive, it can be restored in staged approaches that allow for flexibility.

Copying full backups from low-performance to offline storage through a compression mechanism is an easy way to get full backups into this portion of our strategy. Keeping up to seven years or even longer is not only possible, but required.

Detection

Detection is not a substantial part of this component of the strategy.

Tiered storage

Cheap storage in vast sizes is required because a long window of time is required for this part of the strategy. Tape or solutions like Amazon Glacier are often the choices here.

Toolbox

Full backups are the most appropriate here. These backups are compressed due to recovery time needs also.

Testing

Testing strategies here are similar to the online, slow storage tier.

Object Storage

An example of object storage is Amazon's S3. It is characterized by programmatic access, rather than physical.

Use cases

The following scenarios are the primary use cases for this portion of the strategy:

- Application errors
- User errors
- Corruption repair

Object storage inspection, placement, and retrieval APIs are given to software engineers for integration into applications and administrative tools to effectively recover from user error and application errors. With versioning, it becomes trivial enough to recover from deletes, unexpected mutations, and other potential time-sinks for administrators without these tools.

Detection

Data validation and user requests are key for identifying the need for recovery from this pool. When validation fails, engineers can identify the date ranges of the occurrence and programmatically recover from the incident.

Testing

Because object-level recovery becomes a part of the application, standard integration testing should be more than enough to ensure that this works.

With these four approaches to data recovery, we are able to provide a fairly comprehensive strategy for recovering from most scenarios, even those for which we don't expect or plan. There is fine tuning to be done based on recovery service-level expectations, budget, and resources. But, overall, we've set the stage for an effective plan that incorporates detection, metrics, and tracking, and continuous testing.

Wrapping Up

You should be finishing this chapter with a solid understanding of the potential risks to your environment that could require data recovery. These risks are legion and unpredictable. One of the most important points is that you can't plan for everything, and you need to build a comprehensive strategy to ensure you can tackle anything that comes up. Some of this includes working with software engineers to incorporate recovery into the application itself. In other places, you need to build some pretty solid recovery software yourself. And in all cases, you must build off of the previous chapters on service-level management, risk management, infrastructure management. and infrastructure engineering to get there.

In Chapter 8, we discuss release management. It is our hope that going into the rest of this book, data recovery stays in the forefront of your mind. Every step forward in an application and infrastructure brings risks to data and stateful services. The prime directive of the DBREs world is to ensure that data is recoverable.

CHAPTER 8

Release Management

As we automate and ease the burdens of infrastructure management, the database reliability engineer (DBRE) is able to devote more time to the highly valuable parts of their job. One of these high-value activities is working with software engineers to build, test and deploy application features. Traditionally, the database administrator (DBA) would be a gatekeeper to production. They would expect to see each database migration, database object definition, and code accessing the database to ensure that it was done correctly. When satisfied, the DBA would plan an appropriate hand-crafted change and husband it through into production.

You might already be thinking that this is not necessarily a sustainable process for environments experiencing significant amounts of deployments and changes in their database structures. In fact, if you've been part of one of these processes you are already keenly aware of how quickly a DBA can go from gatekeeper to bottleneck, leading to burnout on the DBA end and frustrations in software engineering.

Our goal in this chapter is to look at how DBREs can effectively utilize their time, skills, and experience to support a software engineering process that utilizes continuous integration (CI) and even continuous deployment (CD) without becoming a bottleneck.

Education and Collaboration

One of the first steps the DBRE must take is educating the developer population about the datastores with which they are working. If the SWEs can make better choices about their data structures, their SQL, and the overall interaction strategies, there will be fewer needs for direct intervention by the DBRE. By taking on the role of conduit of database knowledge to the SWE teams, you can have quite a significant impact on the continuous learning processes of your peers. This also fosters better relationships, trust, and communication, all things critical to the success of the technical organization.

To be clear, we are not advocating that the DBRE attempt a hands-off relationship with the software engineering team. Instead, we are suggesting an interaction wherein the DBRE uses regular interactions and strategic efforts to create a knowledgeable team that has access to resources and can function autonomously for a high degree of its day-to-day decisions with respect to the databases.

Remember to keep everything that you do specific, measurable, and actionable. Define key metrics for your team's success in this, and as you implement strategies and changes, see how they help the team. Some key metrics to consider in this process are:

- Number of database stories that require DBRE interaction.
- Success/Failure of DB story deployments.
- Feature velocity. How quickly can a SWE get a story into production?
- Downtime caused by DB changes.

Agile methodology and DevOps cultures require cross-functional interactions between people of different backgrounds, skill levels, and, of course, professional contexts to collaborate closely. Education and collaboration are a huge part of this process, and are great opportunities for you as the DBRE to shift out of the legacy "DBA" mode and become an integrated part of your technical organization.

Become a Funnel

You will undoubtedly find yourself following blogs, twitter feeds, and social accounts of people and organizations that you consider to be exceptional in the world of data and databases. In doing this, you will find articles, Q&A sessions, podcasts, and projects that have relevance and value to what you and your teams are doing. Curate these and share them. Create a regular newsletter, forum, or even a channel in chat where you can post relevant information and bring it up for discussion. Show the engineering team that you and the other DBREs are invested in their success and continued development.

Foster Conversations

The next step is to create active dialogue and interactions with software engineers. This is where you and the team begin to dig into relevant content that you have shared to generate ideas, learn to apply the information and even improve upon it by identifying gaps and teaming up for further study and experimentation. There are multiple ways to do this, and it will depend significantly on the culture of learning and collaboration in your environment. Here are just a few examples:

- Weekly tech talks
- Brown bag lunches
- Online AMAs ("ask me anythings")
- Chat channel focused on knowledge sharing

Similarly, you can hold open office hours, where people are encouraged to ask you questions, interact on specific topics, and explore things together.

Domain-Specific Knowledge

Although the previous components provide general foundation and knowledge relevant to the appropriate datastores and architectures in use at your organization, there is still a need for knowledge transfer specifically related to your organization's domains.

Architecture

We are not fans of documentation that is static and untied to the processes that actually build and deploy our architectures. With configuration management and orchestration systems, you get a lot of documentation for free that is always up to date. Putting tools on top of these to allow for easy discovery, borrowing, and annotation of notes and comments creates a living, breathing document for teams.

On top of this comes the ability to understand context and history. There is a reason that certain datastores, configurations, and topologies are made. Helping engineers find out what architecture is in place, why it is in place, how to find documentation about how to interact with it, and, finally, what trade-offs and compromises have been made to get to where we are now.

As the DBRE, it is your job to make this knowledge, context, and history available to engineers who are making decisions daily while working on features without your oversight. Building a knowledge base of design documents creates the structure necessary to build context and history around the architecture. These documents can apply to full projects that require new architectural components, or they might relate to smaller incremental changes or subprojects. For instance, you would definitely need a design document to show the process of moving from statement- to row-based replication, but it would not necessarily have the same requirements as the first Kafka installation to support building a distributed log file for event-driven architectures.

Creating and disseminating templates for these documents is a team exercise. It is critical, however, that certain pieces of information are included:

Executive summary
> For those looking for the basics.

Goals and anti-goals

What was expected out of this project? What was out of scope?

Background

Context a future reader might need.

Design

From high-level to quite detailed, you should find diagrams, sample configurations, or algorithms.

Constraints

What did you need to keep in mind and work around, such as compliance for PCI, IaaS-specific needs or staffing?

Alternatives

Did you evaluate other options? What methodology did you use and why were they discarded?

Launch Details

How was it rolled out? What problems arose and how were they managed? Scripts, processes and notes go here also.

As you can see, these documents can potentially grow quite large. For some projects, that is ok. Distributed systems and multitier services are complex and there is a lot of information and context that must be absorbed. Remember that a big goal here is giving that context to engineers without requiring more time from you than necessary.

Data model

Just as important as the architecture, data flow and physical pipelines is the information about the kind of data that is being stored. Letting software engineers know what kind of data is already stored and where they can find it can eliminate a significant amount of redundancy and investigative time from the development process. Additionally, this allows you to share how the same data should be represented in various paradigms—relational, key–value, or document oriented. This is also the opportunity to give best practices for which data stores are not appropriate for certain kinds of data.

Best Practices and Standards

Giving engineers standards for the activities they engage in regularly is another effective method for optimizing the amount of value you are able to generate. You can do this incrementally as you help engineers and make decisions. Some examples of this include the following:

- Datatype standards

- Indexing
- Metadata attributes
- Datastores to use
- Metrics to expose
- Design patterns
- Migration and DB change patterns

Publishing these as you work with engineers allows for a self-service knowledge base (*https://martinfowler.com/articles/evodb.html*), accessible at any time rather than forcing teams to bottleneck on you.

Tools

Giving software engineers effective tools for their development process is the ultimate enabler. You might be helping them with benchmarking tools and scripts, data consistency evaluators, templates, or even configurators for new data stores. Ultimately, what you are doing is enabling greater velocity in the development process while simultaneously freeing up your time for higher-value efforts.

Following are some excellent examples of tools:

- Etsy's Schemanator
- Percona Toolkit, particularly online schema changes
- SQL Tuning and Optimzation suites
- SeveralNines Cluster Configurator
- Checked in Change plan templates and examples
- Checked in migration scripts and pattern examples
- Benchmark suites for easy testing, visualization, and analysis

Treat software engineering teams as your customers, and practice lean product development. Get them a minimally viable tooling on how to do their jobs and consistently interview, monitor, and measure their successes, failures, pain points, and wishes. This will guide you toward what tools will give them the most benefits.

Collaboration

If you're regularly educating, creating tools, and empowering engineers, good relationships will naturally be created. This is critical, because they lead to ongoing collaboration. Any software engineer should be empowered to reach out to the DBRE team to ask for information or for the chance to pair while they work. This gives great value bidirectionally, as the software engineers (SWEs) learn more about how the

DBRE team works and what they look for, and the DBRE team learns more about the software development process.

DBREs can facilitate this further by proactively reaching out to engineers. There are stories that obviously have a large dependency and reliance on DB development and refactoring. This is where DBREs should be focusing their efforts, to help guarantee success and efficiency. Ask to pair or be part of a team on these stories. Similarly, keeping an eye on migrations being committed into mainline will help the DBRE team cherry pick where it needs to perform reviews.

It goes without saying, but making sure that DBREs are not segregated into their own cave, deep underground and away from where code is being built will help ensure that this collaboration can actually occur. Rotating DBREs and SWEs into each other's projects and work can also do this.

Throughout this section, we have been discussing ways in which you can help software engineers in the development process to be as self-sufficient as possible. As development teams grow, you need to utilize effective education, standards, and tooling to ensure that your teams are making good decisions without needing your direct intervention. Simultaneously, you are able to educate engineers regarding when they do need you to review upcoming changes and solutions so that you can assist at the appropriate times.

Next, we discuss how to effectively support the various components of the delivery pipeline as DBREs. Although Continuous Delivery (CD) is not a new concept by any means, organizations have struggled to incorporate databases into the process. In each of the following sections, we discuss how to effectively introduce the database layers into the full delivery cycle.

Integration

Frequent integration of database changes allows for smaller, more manageable changesets and creates quicker feedback loops by identifying breaking changes as soon as possible. Many organizations strive for Continuous Integration (CI), enabling automatic integration of all checked-in changes. A large portion of the value of CI is the automated tests that prove that the database is meeting all expectations for the application. These tests are applied any time that code is committed.

Throughout the software development life cycle, any change to the database code or components should trigger a fresh build, followed by integration and its tests. You and the software engineering team are responsible for establishing the working definition of the database. Integration continues to verify that the database remains in a working state while the software engineers refactor the data model, introduce new datasets, and find new and interesting ways to query the database.

Doing CI for the database tier proves to be very challenging. In addition to the functional aspects of any applications utilizing database objects, there are operational requirements around availability, consistency, latency, and security. Changes to objects can affect stored code (functions, triggers, or views among others), and even queries from other parts of the applications. Additionally, advanced features, such as events, in databases can create more fragility. Beyond testing for functionality, there are numerous potential edge cases involving data integrity. Even though sometimes constraints can enforce integrity, these rules must be tested. Even more concerning are environments in which no constraints exist.

Prerequisites

To establish CI at the database level, there are five requirements that you must satisfy. Let's take a look at each one.

Version control system

Just as with infrastructure code and configurations, all database migrations must be checked in to the same version control system (VCS) as the rest of the application. It is critical that you are able to build from the latest configurations in order to understand how a recent database configuration change could potentially disrupt and break your application builds in new and interesting ways.

At this risk of being redundant, *everything* must be checked in to code. This includes the following:

- DB object migrations
- Triggers
- Procedures and functions
- Views
- Configurations
- Sample datasets for functionality
- Data cleanup scripts

This provides a lot of useful things outside of CI:

- You can easily find all related items in one place.
- It supports all of the automated builds necessary for automated deployments (see Chapter 6).
- You can find all history and versions of the database, which helps for recoveries, forensics, and troubleshooting.

- You know that the application and database versions will be synchronized, at least in an ideal world.

As you continue to run integrations, validating checked in code and infrastructure changes against known working state, software engineers can apply the latest database versions to their development environments.

Database build automation

Assuming that you're utilizing the configuration management and automation techniques discussed in the Chapter 6, you should be able to automatically build databases for integration. This includes applying the latest data definition language (DDL) scripts and loading representative datasets for testing. This can prove more challenging than you might expect because production data often must be cleaned up or scrubbed to ensure that no compliance issues occur with exposing customer data.

Test data

Empty databases almost always perform extremely well. Small datasets often do the same. You will need three different sets of data. First is all metadata needed for lookup tables. This is where you find IDs for customer types, location IDs, workflow, and internal tables. These datasets are generally small and crucial for the application to work correctly.

Next, you need a working set of functional data, such as customers or orders. This is generally just enough to let those quick tests that run in the early stages of integration succeed before investing time in the more intensive tests.

Finally, you need large datasets to help understand what things look like under production load. These usually need to be built from production sets and scrubbed to ensure that you don't expose customer data, accidentally send emails to thousands of users, or other interesting and exciting opportunities for customer and legal interaction.

Metadata and test datasets should be versioned, checked in, and applied as part of the builds. Larger datasets often come from production, and the scripts needed to restore and cleanse the data should be versioned and checked in to ensure that there is synchronization between application and persistence layer.

Database migrations and packaging

This is all presupposed on the concept that database changes are applied as migrations (incremental coded changes). Each set of changes, such as an alter table, or adding metadata or adding a new column family will be checked in and given a sequence number. Because all changes are applied sequentially, you have a version number for the database at any time based on the most recently applied migration.

Traditionally, DBAs would either get a list of changes from developers or do a *schema diff* between development and production to get the information needed for them to apply the necessary changes for a release. The benefit of this is that large, potentially highly impactful changes can be managed very carefully by the DB specialists. This can minimize potential downtime and impacts during expensive migrations.

The negative side of this traditional approach, however, is that it can be challenging to see which changes map to which features. If something must be rolled back, it can be challenging to identify the incremental database change related to the particular feature. Similarly, if a database change fails, all features waiting on those changes will be delayed, affecting time for stories to get to production.

The incremental approach allows for all of the things we want from agile approaches: rapid time to market, incremental and small changes, clear visibility, and fast feedback loops. But this means that SWEs must be more knowledgeable about creating safe migrations, and about when they should get the DBRE team in to help them. Additionally, there is risk that migrations might conflict. If two SWEs are modifying the same objects, their migrations would run serially which could cause two alters instead of one. If the object has a lot of data in it, this could greatly increase migration time. You must consider trade-offs in these cases, which means that SWEs must be aware that they are potentially stepping on one another's toes.

CI server and test framework

It is assumed that your software integration is already utilizing these things. A good CI system will provide all of the necessary functionality for integration. Testing frameworks will provide both the system level tests as well as the code component tests.

At the system level, frameworks such as Pester for Windows or Robot for Linux are available. Additionally, you can utilize Jepsen (*http://jepsen.io/*), a distributed systems testing framework specifically built to validate data consistency and safety in distributed storage.

With these prerequisites, you can begin the work of using your company's CI platform for database migrations. As the name implies, continuous integration means that anytime a database change is committed, integration is performed automatically. For this to happen and for the engineering team to be confident that the changes will not adversely affect the application's functionality and service-level expectations, testing becomes the key tool.

Testing

So, you have all engineers checking their database changes into the VCS. The CI server is able to trigger automated database builds synchronized with the application releases and you have a testing framework. What's next? We need to verify that integration works and what kind of effects it will have in the next phase: deployment.

Unfortunately, we're here to tell you that this stuff is hard! Database changes are notorious for affecting huge amounts of code and functionality. That being said, there are ways to build applications that can make this easier.

Test-Friendly Development Practices

When designing development processes, you can make things easier for testing with any number of choices. We've included two here as examples.

Abstraction and encapsulation

There are numerous ways in which you can abstract database access away from SWEs. Why would you do this? Centralizing database access code creates a standard, easily understood way of implementing new objects and accessing objects. It also means that you don't have to find code all over the code base in order to make a database change. This simplifies testing and integration tremendously. There are a few different ways to do this abstraction:

- Data access objects (DAOs)
- APIs or web services
- Stored procedures
- Frameworks meant for this

With these in place, your integration can focus on testing the primitives around accessing and updating data first, to see if changes have affected the ability to use them. As with any testing, you want high-impact, quick-execution tests first, and centralized data access code makes this much easier to accomplish.

Being efficient

Often you might find engineers using a "select *," or retrieving an entire row of an object to work with. This is done to "future proof" or ensure that whatever might need data gets it. Perhaps they want to be sure that if an attribute is added to the object, they automatically retrieve it. This is dangerous, and like any "future proofing," is wasteful and puts applications at risk during changes. A "select *" will retrieve all columns, and if code is not ready to handle that, it will break. All of the data retrieved also must be shipped over the network, which requires more bandwidth if you are retrieving multiple rows and begin overfilling your TCP packets. Being selective about what you are retrieving is crucial. You can modify object access code when the right time comes, and you'll be prepared for it when it does.

Post-Commit Testing

The goal of post-commit testing is to validate that changes apply successfully and that the application is not broken. Additionally, impact analysis and rules-based validation for security and compliance can occur at this level. After code has been committed, the build server should immediately build an integration datastore, apply changes, and begin a series of tests that are quick enough to run that the feedback loop to engineers is as tight as possible. This means a quick database build using a checked-in minimal dataset containing all necessary metadata, user accounts, and test data necessary to exercise the appropriate functions on all data access objects. This allows for a fast turnaround to engineers to see if they've broken the build.

Early in an organization's life, much of this might be done manually. As rules come into play, tools and automation can be applied to make these processes faster and more bulletproof.

Pre-build

Prior to applying changes, the following validation against established rules for impact analysis and for compliance can be performed at this time:

- Validation that SQL is formed correctly
- Validation of the number of rows potentially affected by changes
- Validation of index creation for new columns
- Validation that defaults are not applied to new columns on tables with existing data
- Validation of impact to stored code and referential constraints
- Report that sensitive database objects and attributes are being updated
- Report when rules required for compliance are being violated

Build

When the build runs, validation of SQL occurs again. In this case, based on actual application of the changes rather than rules based analysis.

Post-build

After the changes have been applied to the build, you can run functional test suites. You can also create reports that show analysis of impact and any rules violations that occurred in the change.

Full Dataset Testing

It is assumed that after the application runs against a full production dataset, there is the potential for the service to no longer meet service-level expectations. This means that the test suite should be run against production datasets at appropriate loads. This requires more preparation and resources to do, so this test suite can be scheduled asynchronously from the standard commit integration tests. Depending on the frequency of integration and code pushes, you might find a weekly or even daily schedule makes the most sense for these tests.

The steps taken for this extensive testing vary but will generally follow a blueprint such as the following:

- Provision datastore and application instances
- Deploy code
- Recover full dataset
- Anonymize data
- Hook up metrics collection
- Apply changes to the datastore
- Launch functional, quick tests
- Perform load tests, ramping up concurrency
- Deprovision instances
- Post-test analysis

Some things that you will want to look at in these tests include the following:

- Latency changes for tests compared to previous runs on smaller datasets
- Database access path changes in optimizers that could affect latency or resource utilization
- Database metrics that indicate potential performance or functionality impacts (locking, errors, waits on resources)
- Changes in resource utilization from previous runs

You can automate some analysis, such as registration of queries into a centralized datastore and comparison of historical plan changes. Some, such as metrics analysis would require an operator to review and perform effective review to determine if any changes are passable or not.

If any red flags come up, automated or not, the DBREs are able to narrow down the changes requiring analysis by reviewing changes applied since the last test run.

Although this does not allow for immediate flagging of a specific committed change, it does allow for a much quicker identification.

In addition to fast and slow analysis of applications, there are additional tests that must periodically be performed on a rapidly evolving datastore. These tests ensure that the evolving database will continue to be a good citizen in the overarching ecosystem. These are downstream tests and operational tests.

Downstream Tests

Downstream tests are used to ensure that any data pipelines and consumers of the datastore are not adversely affected by any changes applied as part of the migrations. Like full dataset testing, downstream tests are best done asynchronously from the commit process. Here are some examples of downstream tests:

- Validating event workflows triggered by data in the database
- Validation of extraction, transform, and loading of data into analytics datastores
- Validation of batch and scheduled jobs that directly interact with the database
- Validation that job times have not increased significantly, potentially affecting delivery at specific times for required delivery or downstream processes

Similarly to full-dataset testing, these tests are often much more extensive and require larger datasets for consumption. By running them asynchronously but regularly, it is easier to identify potential changes that have affected the downstream processes that have been flagged in testing. If tests are failed, pushes to production can be stopped, and DBREs can have tickets automatically put in queue for them when rules are violated.

Operational Tests

As datasets increase and schemas evolve, there are opportunities for operational processes to run longer and potentially fail. These process tests include the following:

- Backup and recovery processes
- Failover and cluster processes
- Infrastructure configuration and orchestration
- Security tests
- Capacity tests

These tests should regularly perform automated builds from production datasets, with all pending and committed changes applied before tests are run. Failed tests can advise the build server that there is a problem that must be evaluated and resolved before changes can be pushed to production. Although it is rarer for database changes to affect these processes, the impact can be severe at the service level, and thus require a high level of diligence.

With a combination of continuous, lightweight builds and tests, and strategically scheduled more-intensive tests, you can foster a greater degree of confidence in reliability engineering, software engineering, operations, and management that database changes can be safely introduced into production without direct intervention by the DBRE team.

These integration processes are a perfect example of DBREs providing high amounts of value through process, knowledge sharing, and automation to empower software engineers without bottlenecking them. In the next section, we will discuss the largest elephant in the room: deployment. Recognizing that a database change is safe is the first step, but safely getting those changes into a production environment is just as important.

Deployment

In the previous section on integration, we touched on the concept of database migrations and some of the pros and cons. Because we discussed how significant these can be, it makes sense to decompose data migrations in such a way that SWEs can easily and incrementally modify environments safely. Or, at least in as safe a way as possible.

In an ideal world, our goals should be to empower SWEs to recognize when their database changes require analysis and management by DBREs in order to be effectively introduced into production. Additionally, we would be able to give those engineers the tools to safely and reliably introduce most changes into production themselves. Finally, we would give SWEs the ability to push their changes to production at any time, rather than during restrictive maintenance windows. Creating a reasonable approximation of this world is what we will review in this section.

Migrations and Versioning

As discussed in "Prerequisites" on page 139, each changeset that is applied to the database should be given a numeric version. This is generally done with incrementing integers that are stored in the database after a changeset is applied. This way your deployment system can easily look at the database and discover the current version. This allows easy application of changes when preparing to push code. If a code deployment is certified for database version 456, and the current database version is 455, the deployment team knows that it must apply the changeset for 456 prior to pushing code.

So, an SWE has committed changeset 456 into the code base and integration has been successfully run with no breaking changes. What comes next?

Impact Analysis

We discussed impact analysis in the previous section under post-commit testing. Some impacts, such as the invalidation of stored code in the database, or violation of security controls, are gates that cannot be passed. The SWE must go back and modify her changes until these impacts have been mitigated.

In this section, we discuss the impact of *performing* the database migration on production database servers. Database changes can affect a production service in multiple ways.

Locking of objects

Many changes can cause a table or even a group of tables to be inaccessible for writes, reads, or both. In these cases, the amount of time the objects are inaccessible should be estimated and determined to be acceptable or not. Acceptable locking really will be part of the service-level objectives (SLOs) and business needs, and thus is subjective. Previous changes on these objects can be recorded with specific metrics around the time it took to run the change. This will allow some objective data to be used to determine impact time, even though the time it takes to do changes to objects will lengthen as dataset size and activity increases.

If unacceptable, the DBRE should work with the deployment team to determine a plan to either reduce the time to a point of acceptability, or to redirect traffic until such time as the change has successfully finished.

Saturation of resources

A change can also utilize significant amounts of Input/Output (I/O), which can increase latency for all other transactions utilizing the datastore. This can cause service levels to be violated, and eventually cause processes to back up to a point at which the application becomes unusable and other resources are also saturated. This can easily cause a cascading failure.

Data integrity issues

As part of these changes, there are often transitional periods during which constraints might be relaxed or deferred. Similarly, locking and invalidation can cause data to not be stored in the way SWEs would expect.

Replication stalls

Database changes can also cause increased activity and lagged replication. This can affect the usefulness of replicas and even put failover at risk.

It is these impacts that we as DBREs must help SWEs proactively identify and avoid.

Migration Patterns

After impact analysis, the SWE should be able to make a decision on the appropriate way to deploy the migration. For many migrations, there is no reason to go through a lot of incremental changes and extensive review work to execute. New objects, data inserts, and other operations can be easily pushed through to production.

After data is in the system, however, changes or removal of existing data, and modification or removal of objects with data in them, create opportunities for your migration to affect service levels as discussed earlier. It is at this time that the SWE should bring the DBRE in. Luckily, there is a relatively finite set of changes for which you can plan. As you work with SWEs to plan and execute on these migrations, you can build a repository of patterns for database changes to be applied. At some point, if they happen frequently and painlessly enough, you can automate them.

For example, you can set up deployment gates in integration and testing that utilize rules-based analysis and testing results to determine whether migrations are safe to be deployed. Some flagged operations could include the following:

- Updates and deletes without a WHERE clause to filter rows
- Number of rows impacted is greater than N
- Alters on tables with a certain dataset size
- Alters on tables stored in metadata as too busy to have live alters on them
- New columns with defaults
- Certain datatypes in create/alter statements such as BLOB (Binary Large Object) files
- Foreign keys without indexes
- Operations on particularly sensitive tables

The more flags and safeguards you put in place to enable safety in production for everyone, the more confidence you create in all teams. This results in development velocity. Now, let's assume that our intrepid SWE who has checked in changeset 456 has had his change flagged due to an alter that is deemed to be impactful. At this point, he can use a migration pattern for that operation if it has been applied and documented. Otherwise, he should create one in collaboration with the DBRE team.

Pattern: locking operations

Adding a column is a very typical operation in most database environments. Depending on the DBMS that you are using, these operations can be quick and simple, without locking the table. Other DBMSs will require a re-creation of the table. When adding the column, you might want to put a default value in the column as well. This

---

will definitely create a significant impact because the value must be entered into each existing row of the table before the change is completed and the lock is released.

One way to avoid some locking operations is to utilize code. For example:

- Add empty column
- Perform regression tests
- Utilize conditional code in the select statement at access time to determine if a row needs updating rather than performing it as a batch statement
- Set up a watcher to advise when the attribute is fully populated and conditional code can be removed

For some operations, locking of the object is unavoidable. In these cases, you must give a pattern, automatic or manual, to engineers. This might be a tool for performing online changes via triggers and table renames. Or, it might be a rolling migration utilizing proxies and failovers to apply the changes node by node on out-of-service nodes.

It can be tempting to have two processes: one that is lightweight and one that has more steps. This way, you only roll out the complex pattern for major impacting changes. However, this can cause you to rely too heavily on one process, leaving the other underpracticed and perhaps buggy. It is best to be consistent with the process that works most effectively for all locking operations.

Pattern: high resource utilization operations

There are multiple patterns that you can utilize here, depending on the operations that are being executed.

For data modification, throttling by performing the updates in batches is a simple pattern to give engineers when performing bulk operations. For larger environments, it often makes more sense to utilize code to do lazy updating upon login of a user, or querying of a row for example.

For data removal, you can encourage SWEs to utilize *soft deletes* in their code. A soft delete flags a row as deleteable, which means it can be filtered out of queries in the application and removed at will. You can then throttle the deletes, removing them asynchronously. As with bulk updates, for large datasets this might prove to be impossible. If deletes are regularly performed on ranges, such as dates or ID groupings, you can utilize partitioning features to drop partitions. By dropping a table or partition, you do not create undo I/O which can reduce resource consumption.

Should you find that DDL operations such as table alters create enough I/O that latency is affected, you should consider this a red flag that capacity might be reaching its limits. Ideally, you would work with operations to add more capacity to the data stores. However, if this is not possible or is delayed, these DDL operations can be treated like blocking operations, with the appropriate pattern being applied.

Pattern: rolling migrations

As discussed in the previous sections, it often makes sense to give engineers the ability to apply changes incrementally across each node in a cluster. This is often called a *rolling upgrade*, because you are rolling the change through each node. You accomplish this somewhat differently depending on whether the cluster can be written to via any node, or if only one node can function as a target write node.

In a write anywhere cluster, such as Galera, you can take one node out of service by removing the node from a service directory or proxy configuration. After draining the traffic from the node, the change can be applied. The node is then reintroduced into the appropriate configuration or directory to put it back in service.

In a write leader cluster, where writes go to one node, you would take the followers in the replication chain out of service individually as in the write anywhere cluster. However, after this has been done for all nodes but the master, there must be a failover to a node with the changeset already applied.

Obviously both of these choices require a lot of orchestration. Understanding what operations are expensive and might require rolling upgrades is a critical part of choosing a datastore. It is also why many people are exploring database solutions that allow for low-impact-only schema evolution.

Migration testing

Even though it might seem evident, it is imperative to recognize that if a changeset's implementation details are modified, the revised migration must be committed and fully integrated before deployment in post-integration environments, including production.

Rollback testing

In addition to testing migrations and their impact, the DBRE and her supported teams must consider the failure of migrations/deploys and the rolling back of partial or full changesets. Database change scripts should be checked-in at the same time as migrations. There can be autogenerated defaults for some migrations, such as table creations, but there must be an accounting for data that comes in. Therefore, we don't recommend reverting by simply dropping an object. Renaming tables allows them to still be accessible in case data was written and must be recovered.

Migration patterns also enable ease in the process of defining rollbacks. The lack of an effective rollback script can be a gating factor in the integration and deployment process. To validate that the scripts work, you can use the following deployment and testing pattern:

- Apply changeset
- Quick integration tests
- Apply rollback changeset
- Quick integration tests
- Apply changeset
- Quick integration tests
- Longer and periodic testing

Much like testing recoveries, testing fallbacks is critical and you must incorporate it into every build and deploy process.

Manual or Automated

Another advantage of using migration patterns is that a migration pattern can allow for automatic approval and deployment rather than waiting for review and execution by the DBRE team. It also means that certain patterns can automatically flag DBREs for implementation outside of the automated process.

There is no reason to rush the path to automation, particularly when dealing with critical data. Community best practices posit that anything run frequently should be automated if at all possible, but this is mitigated by the impact of failed automation. If you have built an environment that has tested and reliable fallbacks, rapid and practiced recovery processes, and mature engineers, you can begin to take migration patterns and automate the application of those changes. But, just moving toward standardized models, push-button deploys and fallbacks, and guard rails/flags provides significant progress toward our goals.

Wrapping Up

In this chapter, we covered the ways in which a DBRE team provides oversized value to software engineering teams through the development, integration, testing and deployment phases of software development. We can't emphasize enough how much of this relies on collaboration and very close relationships between DBRE, operations, and SWE teams. As the DBRE in this equation, you must consider yourself teacher, diplomat, negotiator, and student. The more you invest in education and relationships, the greater dividends will be paid as you apply the knowledge shared in this section.

A natural progression from release management is that of security. Your data is one of the most significant attack vectors in the infrastructure. Every change and feature potentially creates vulnerabilities that must be planned for and mitigated. In Chapter 9, we discuss how to bring value to security planning and processes.

Security

The function of security has always been a significant part of the database administrator's job. Just as with recovery, the security of the organization's most critical asset is paramount. Security incidents and attempts are occurring with greater and greater frequency. You need only read the news to learn about high-profile cases of hundreds of thousands (even millions) of user profiles, credit cards, and emails being stolen and resold regularly.

In the siloed world, the database administrator (DBA) would focus on his database security controls only, hardening in isolation and recognizing that security was the job of someone else. As the stewards of the organization's data, however, the database reliability engineer (DBRE) must take a more holistic approach to the job.

We've already spoken about continuous deployment (CD) pipelines, cloud environments, and infrastructure as code in earlier chapters of this book. Each of these areas represents new attack vectors for potential thieves and vandals to get at your data. In this chapter, we craft a paradigm for database security for the DBRE to match today's organizations and infrastructures. We will then approach the craft, discussing the potential attack vectors, a methodology and strategy for mitigation, and a holistic model that the DBRE can champion.

The Purpose of Security

It goes without saying that security is a crucial role equal to that of data recovery, as discussed in Chapter 7. Depending on the data, stolen data is as bad as corrupted data. But, just as recovery is a function with broad use cases outside of just emergency recovery, so does security have multiple functions.

Protecting Data from Theft

This is the classic use case. In most cases, each opportunity to store data has someone who wants access to that data outside of its normal use. Individuals both internal and external might want to gain access to databases to resell customer data, to get at competitive secrets, or simply to cause damage using the data that they have acquired. Attack vectors for this include the following:

- Data in the online databases
- Data moving between datastores
- Data in backups and archives
- Data going from datastores to applications and clients
- Data in memory on application servers
- Data going from applications across the internet to users

As we just mentioned, not all thieves are external. Internal users who already might have knowledge of systems and authenticated access are even more dangerous than the many imagined bogeymen out on the internet. Regardless of location, the DBRE works with InfoSec, Ops and software engineers (SWEs) to make certain that data can be read, duplicated, or moved out of its appropriate place.

Protecting from Purposeful Damage

Sometimes, the intent of a malicious actor is purely to hurt the organization. Corrupting or manipulating data, shutting down databases, or utilizing all of the IT resources until they are no longer accessible are all ways someone can damage an organization's databases and data. These can take the form of Denial of Service (DOS) attacks, exploitation of bugs that will shut down databases, and access that allows manipulation of data or storage. The good thing about these attacks is they often are recoverable via backups. But, damaging backups often is easier than damaging an online store.

Protecting from Accidental Damage

Although we often think of security as a function to protect us from bad actors, security is just as important in ensuring that someone does not accidentally wander into the wrong environment, wrong schema, object, or row and cause damage unintentionally. A fence can keep out outsiders and help people to know they are straying in areas they didn't mean to. Just as internal actors are more dangerous than external when you're protecting data from theft, accidental vandals and saboteurs often come with tools and credentials that can quickly cause catastrophes.

Protecting Data from Exposure

Even without a witting or unwitting actor, there are still risks. In complex, distributed and decoupled systems, it is rather easy for a bug or misplaced set of credentials to expose sensitive clear-text data in logs, in the wrong customer's browser or email, or even allow unauthorized people to log in as a user to another person's account. This kind of exposure can rightfully and rapidly erode trust in your organization's ability to safeguard and husband data.

Compliance and Auditing Standards

Organizations are under intense scrutiny from numerous standards and laws that help to protect customers and individuals. It is security's job to educate the organization regarding these standards and to ensure that the organization complies. It is a thankless job, and one that often frustrates people looking to focus on new features and scaling. Still, it is essential if the organization doesn't want to find itself shut down or fined large sums of money.

Database Security as a Function

Throughout this book, we've pushed strongly on the notion of cross-functional relationships and approaches to database reliability. The DBRE has become much more of a liaison, subject matter expert, and educator to the rest of the organization. With developer teams growing exponentially, this is the only way to scale. Information security experts are often one of the most understaffed positions in the organization, making it even more challenging for the DBRE and information security (IS) teams to effectively guard company data in the face of constant development and change.

This is exactly what we discussed in Chapter 8, in which we focus on enabling safe, effective and rapid development via self-service, education, and cherry picking methods. The developers are the front line of security, as well, and the approaches we discuss will be done with a similar thrust. Security must first and foremost be integrated into the development processes for applications and for infrastructures, rather than being a side note or a checkbox on a compliance sheet at release time.

How do you do this? You do it using the same tools (*http://bit.ly/2zw896p*) we've been discussing throughout the book. Let's review those now.

Education and Collaboration

We discuss this in greater detail in Chapter 8, so we will summarize the three approaches here:

- Fostering conversations

- Creating domain-specific knowledge bases

- Collaborating via pairing and reviews

You do this to teach SWEs how to more effectively and safely develop on their own defenses against attacks on the organization's datastores. This increases the performance and effectiveness of the application, it reduces the amount of downtime and degradation of service from implementations and poor design, and it increases the velocity of development teams. Similarly, this constant grassroots effort must be done to educate on database security. This includes the following:

- Secure database access configuration and controls.

- Effective use of security features such as encryption, fine-grained access control, and data management.

- What data is exposed by the database that can be brought into instrumentation, logs, and telemetry to help expose malicious or damaging activity.

- Database specific vulnerabilities that must be managed at other layers, including updates as new *CVEs* are released.

CVEs

The acronym CVE stands for Common Vulnerabilities and Exposures. (See the CVE database (*https://cve.mitre.org*).) You can also generate custom feeds to follow based on topics of interest such as SQL Injection vulnerabilities. This is an excellent resource to keep you updated on newly discovered vulnerabilities, or updates to existing ones.

By continued education and collaboration, database security becomes a regularly discussed topic, one that is explored, critiqued, and researched within the organization.

Self-Service

The next step to fostering a rigorous and mature security process that can scale with development team size and feature velocity is to create self-service approaches to database security. You'll never be able to review every feature, every new service, and every new datastore on your own. Instead, you will find yourself constantly blocking requests as your backlog grows and grows. Partnering with InfoSec to create reusable, approved security patterns that engineers can check out and use at will enables a scalable security process.

As we discussed in Chapter 5, *Infrastructure Engineering*, infrastructure as code allows you to create approved deployments of all datastores that might be created and released into the wild. This means that a large portion of your time is spent on building these gold standards, researching vulnerabilities, and revising or updating the playbooks in your platform to mitigate those vulnerabilities, including the following:

- Approved software build numbers
- Removal of default accounts and passwords that come with datastores
- Locking down of unnecessary ports
- Setting up effectively constrained access lists to reduce the points of entry to your datastores
- Removing features and configurations that allow exploits via filesystem or network
- Install and set up keys for secure sockets layer (SSL) communications
- Scripts to check and enforce password policies
- Configuring auditing and log forwarding to ensure that all access can be reviewed and protected from tampering

By checking in all of this and making it available to people deploying new datastores, you can allow preapproval of these infrastructures due to the use of the gold standard. The DBRE and InfoSec teams do not need to spend time reviewing and reporting on vulnerabilities with these known installs.

In addition to infrastructure self-service, code libraries such as logging, authentication, password hashing, and encryption can all be checked-in and made available. This includes client software.

Building Your Own Database Clients

Similar to self-service for infrastructure, providing self-service clients and libraries is an effective mitigation technique. Clients provided by vendors often already have workarounds that you might not be aware of, thus exposing you unknowingly to vulnerabilities in the future. These clients will often use older protocols also, to ensure backward compatibility. By writing your own, you reduce the risk of unknown factors, and you take control of a core part of the database tier: the access layer.

Integration and Testing

Integration and testing processes represent excellent opportunities to catch vulnerabilities early and often, rather than at the end of the development process when fixes are exponentially more expensive. Alternately, they represent high-risk opportunities for exploitation given that the infiltrator who owns the testing and integration server can bypass all tests and inject malicious code quite easily.

During integration, standard tests that have been approved by security can be applied to automatically validate that vulnerabilities are not being introduced. This can include, but is not limited to the following:

- SQL injection vulnerabilities in database access functions
- Testing the authentication layer for common flaws including plaintext communications, plain-text credential storage or connecting as elevated administrative users
- Testing new stored code for exploits such as buffer overflows

In addition to the immediate post-commit tests that are always run, more intensive tests can be run asynchronously on a regular time schedule. This includes penetration tests at the application level, but also rigorous testing within the network for vulnerabilities that can be exploited via unauthenticated and authenticated means that will grant access to the database or operating system (OS).

Operational Visibility

Integrating all outputs of security function into standard logging and telemetry as well as their outputs is crucial. This data comes from everywhere in the stack, including application layer, database layer, and OS layers. You also saw much more of this in Chapter 4.

Application layer instrumentation

Tracking every failed and successful SQL statement sent to database is critical for identifying SQL injection attacks. SQL syntax errors can be a leading indicator. It alerts you that someone or something is trying to pass unplanned SQL through the application into the database. Syntax errors in a working, tested application should be very rare. Similarly, SQL injection patterns, if studied, will show strings that often indicate an attack is underway. This includes UNION and LOAD_FILE statements. We discuss this further in "Vulnerabilities and Exploits" on page 160.

Audit data also should be collected around personally identifiable information (PII) or critical data. Using metadata to flag API endpoints as PII/critically impacting or not allows you to collect granular data on accessing, changing, or removing data such as passwords, emails, credit cards, or document blobs. Although auditing will also occur at the database layer, this application-level auditing can easily give appropriate staff members access to see if application code is being accidentally or purposefully abused.

Database layer instrumentation

At the database layer, any and all activity should be logged and pushed into the operational visibility stack for analysis. Following are some activities to look for:

Configuration Changes
These can occur in a file or in memory. Configuration file changes can open a system up completely to exploitation.

Database User Changes
Privilege or password changes and new users should all be inspected for corresponding migrations that have been checked in to code and integrated. Otherwise, these changes could be deliberately creating security holes.

All select, insert, update, and delete data
Auditing at the database level provides a good supplement and foil to application-level auditing. Excessive querying or modifications, queries coming from unexpected users, and unexpectedly large result sets can all indicate problems.

New database objects, particularly stored code
New or modified functions, procedures, triggers, views, and user-defined functions (UDFs) should all be correlated to database migrations because they can be indications of exploits.

Logins, successful and failed
There should be expected traffic patterns for any database. Application users will come from specific hostgroups, and, generally speaking, no one should be directly logging in to a database. In some environments, you might go so far as to mark a datastore suspect if there is a login that does not occur from an application server, proxy, or other approved client.

Patches and binary changes
Hot patches can occur from a user who has received OS access. This might be through network buffer overflows or other exploits. These changes can create backdoors and potentially malicious code.

OS instrumentation

Just as with the database, operating systems must be carefully monitored and logged, as well. This includes the following:

Configuration Changes
Just as with database changes.

New software, scripts, or files
New or modified software, scripts, and files are almost always bad signs outside of temporary directories, log directories, or other expected landing zones for new files. Comparing these regularly to golden images can indicate malicious activity.

Logins, successful and failed
Just as with database logins.

Patches and binary changes
Just as with database changes.

Comprehensive data gathering combined with effective tools for comparison and anomaly detection are critical for identifying malicious activity that has gotten past security. There is no security strategy that can be comprehensive and up-to-date enough to keep everyone out, so effective visibility is required, and the DBRE team works hand in hand with Ops, InfoSec, and SWE to ensure this instrumentation.

Vulnerabilities and Exploits

We've spoken at a high level about the DBRE's primary job duties for helping build a scalable security function. Throughout this section, we discussed various potential threats at a very high level. In this section, we discuss the potential vulnerabilities that must be considered and planned for as the DBRE goes about training and educating the organization, building self-service configurations, and setting up monitors, templates, and playbooks for response.

When modeling threats, it is important to classify and prioritize. Balancing and prioritizing with all of your other priorities is critical. There are already structured approaches to do this. For example, Microsoft has populated STRIDE for classification and DREAD for prioritization.

STRIDE

STRIDE is a classification scheme for characterizing known threats according to the kinds of exploit that are used (or motivation of the attacker). The STRIDE acronym (*http://bit.ly/2zxfqCJ*) is formed from the first letter of each of the following categories:

Spoofing identity
Identity spoofing allows for a user to assume another identity in order to bypass access controls. Because most multiuser applications end up with a single user into the database, there is significant risk.

Tampering with data

Users can change data via application POST activities in addition to actions taken with spoofed or assumed identities. Data validation and APIs even for administrative activities are critical for protecting against that.

Repudiation

Without proper levels of auditing, customers and internal users can dispute activities that they have taken. This can lead to financial losses in disputes, failing of audits and inability to find malicious activities.

Information disclosure

Customer and private details can be revealed to the public, to competitors and to malicious buyers. This also can include accidental disclosure.

Denial of service

Applications and specific infrastructure components are also subject to denial of service. This can come from expensive operations or simply masses of activities distributed across the world.

Elevation of privilege

Users can potentially move into roles with higher degrees of privilege. At the highest level, application users can achieve root access on servers.

DREAD

DREAD classification allows for risk analysis and prioritization based on the risk presented by each evaluated threat. The DREAD algorithm (*http://bit.ly/2zjZfrL*) shown here is used to compute a risk value, which is an average of all five categories.

Damage potential

If a threat exploit occurs, how much damage will be caused?

- 0 = Nothing
- 5 = Individual user data is compromised or affected
- 10 = Complete system or data destruction

Reproducibility

How easy is it to reproduce the threat exploit?

- 0 = Very difficult or impossible, even for administrators of the application
- 5 = One or two steps required, may need to be an authorized user
- 10 = Just a web browser and the address bar is sufficient, without authentication

Exploitability

What is needed to exploit this threat?

- 0 = Advanced programming and networking knowledge, with custom or advanced attack tools
- 5 = Malware exists on the internet, or an exploit is easily performed, using available attack tools
- 10 = Just a web browser

Affected users

How many users will be affected?

- 0 = None
- 5 = Some users, but not all
- 10 = All users

Discoverability

How easy is it to discover this threat?

- 0 = Very hard to impossible; requires source code or administrative access
- 5 = Can figure it out by guessing or by monitoring network traces
- 9 = Details of faults like this are already in the public domain and can be easily discovered using a search engine
- 10 = The information is visible in the web browser address bar or in a form

While we walk through each of the potential attack vectors, utilizing categorization like this can allow you to determine where to focus your energy and resources.

Basic Precautions

In this section, we discuss multiple possible precautions, with examples from various datastores. This includes general mitigating techniques that will be expanded on in the section on strategy. There are some mitigation techniques that are more general and can be applied to multiple categories. These include the following:

Configuration

Remove all unnecessary features and configurations from the database. Many database systems are feature rich, and most applications will not utilize even a small portion of those features. Shutting these down can reduce attack vectors.

Patching
> Continued scanning of vulnerability databases will give you regular security patches to be applied. Keeping these up to date will reduce the risk of exploitation.

Removing unnecessary users
> Default users and passwords are well known and create significant risk.

Network and host access
> Use firewalls and security groups to minimize which hostgroups have access to the databases, and over which ports. Similarly, using restrictions via roles and privileges to minimize the ability for anyone to access systems is of top priority.

The Dangers of Defaults

During this writing, there has been a staggeringly significant—and preventable—security exploit against MongoDB and ElasticSearch databases listening on Public IPs. In 2015, Shodan wrote an article (*https://blog.shodan.io/its-the-data-stupid/*) revealing that more than 30,000 MongoDB instances were publicly accessible because the default listing IP was 0.0.0.0 and no authentication was enabled. That's more than 595.2 TB of data exposed simply because no one paid attention to defaults in early versions of the server.

Here are the categories we will be discussing:

- Denial of Service
- SQL injection
- Network and authentication protocols

Denial of Service

Denial of Dervice (DoS) attacks are a family of attacks designed to make a service or application unavailable by throwing so many requests at them its resources are saturated and cannot fulfill requests from actual users. This often takes the form of exhausting network bandwidth via a distributed network of clients flooding a network with requests. The other category these attacks can take involves exhausting the resources of a specific server or cluster, such as a database. By consuming all CPU, memory, or disk, the critical server can become unresponsive, effectively taking all services down that depend on it.

These attacks are typically not destructive in that they do not damage or steal data. They are designed to take down a service, whether for general nuisance, for anti-competitive actions, or as a cover to distract InfoDec and Ops teams while other attacks are taking place.

Large network flooding attacks are the norm, and thus most defensive techniques focus on these. This has caused attackers to go up the stack to service components that are more vulnerable, have fewer resources available to them, and that function as lynchpins. Unfortunately, databases are a perfect target here, and thus the DB-DoS (Database Denial of Service) was born. With minimal effort, database logic can be executed at exponential levels, saturating resources in ways that do not look very different from normal elevated traffic.

Following are some potential impacts of a DB-DoS attack that we will want to mitigate:

- Consumption of user connections until application servers are starved out
- Disrupting the optimizer with a huge variance of queries that require parsing, hashing, and inspection during query optimization
- Autoscaling of resources until a budget measure shuts down the service
- Removal of valid data from caches, causing extensive disk I/O
- Increased memory usage potentially causing swapping
- Table growth and logs that consume all disk space
- Excessive replication lag due to large amounts of writes
- Starving of OS resources including file descriptors, processes, or shared memory

These can be instigated easily by using a number of different tactics. The easiest is simply to use the application functionality itself. Here are a few examples:

- Building large shopping carts
- Searches with no input or broad input
- API calls that return slowly can tell an abuser that a query might not be optimized or indexed, and thus be a target for repetitive calls
- Adding UNIONs to inputs in forms that can cause huge numbers of joins and scans (this is a SQL injection technique also)
- Sorting large result sets
- Creating edge cases such as a huge number of posts in a forum application, or a huge number of friends in a social application

Similar to abusing application functionality, a knowledgeable attacker who can identify the database in use can often find ways to shut it down. For instance, locking out users by logging in incorrectly, running administrative commands via SQL injection that can clear caches, or sending malformed XML can cause overflows in parsers.

Mitigation

In addition to standard mitigation techniques that we have already discussed, the most effective approaches to mitigate a DB-DoS are quite similar to the techniques used for surviving heavy traffic and growth issues. There is a tripod that supports the ability to survive these sudden surges in resource utilization, whether from legitimate or illegitimate traffic sources. You will notice that automated capacity scaling is not included. There is always an upper bound to capacity, whether due to hardware, software, or budget, and any DB-DoS can probably get you there.

Resource management and load shedding

Over time, the technical teams will begin to understand the general workload characteristics of their applications. It can be reasonably assumed then that they should be able to build a set of tools to effectively handle surges in load. As the DBRE, your responsibility is to help educate and support SWEs in understanding these workloads and prioritizing work to reduce the risks effectively. These tools can include the following:

Client-side throttling
Rather than letting a robot hit an endpoint repeatedly, putting in a throttle regarding the time between submitting a request and resubmitting it can effectively stop or slow down surges. You can do this via basic counters, exponential degradation, ratios of calls to retries, or combined with data coming back from the application regarding service-level quotas being exceeded.

Quality of service
You can classify traffic going to the application based on criticality also. Marking expensive queries, such as search, that can be exploited as less critical allows the application to enforce quality-of-service quotas that make DB-DoSes more difficult to achieve.

Degrade the results
For expensive queries and remote procedure calls (RPCs), you might want to develop two execution paths. For normal loads, a full execution path will be fine, but perhaps you want to reduce the number of rows scanned or shards queried during heavy loads such as what could be generated during a DB-Dos.

Query killers and heavy-handed approaches
If you do not have the ability to do more comprehensive code-based approaches, you might need to use brute force. Killing long-running queries or putting performance profiles at the database layer to reduce the number of resources a query

can consume are effective enough, at the cost of a lack of control and potentially bad user experience that is difficult to mitigate at the code level.

Continual improvement of database access and workloads

If you ever needed a justification to devote DBRE and SWE resources to cleaning up the most expensive queries in the database tiers, the potential for DB-DoS is it. Because these queries often might not be part of normal workload patterns, they might be ignored in a methodology where you are tuning based on the aggregate consumption of resources at the database tier. If these outliers are only called infrequently it is easy to ignore them. But, a clever sleuth can find them and exploit them. This means that a good performance process should ideally be looking for the most expensive queries regardless of execution frequency in order to push these into a tuning queue.

Logging and monitoring

Regardless of the aforementioned efforts, a persistent actor can still affect your database. Effective monitoring of execution calls by endpoint should be able to identify significant spikes and reveal them to triage teams for throttling or even shutting down. Similarly, if there are queries or activities that have no upper bounds, monitoring of the number of items in "in clauses," memory structures, permanent or temporary tables, or similar structures can help to identify potential problems.

It is important to remember that attacks can include destructive forms in addition to theft or vandalism. DB-Dos attacks can be easily forgotten when planning a security function. Now, let's go on to the next threat to consider.

SQL Injection

SQL injection is a class of exploits in which database code, usually SQL, is injected into an application input. This is done in order to bypass security and execute code in the database that has nothing to do with the application's expected input. SQL injection can be used to exploit bugs that cause buffer overflows. Buffer overflows can shut down a database, perform a DbDoS, or they can give a user elevated privileges at the database, and even the OS level. An example of this can be found here (*http://bit.ly/ 2zAiKxa*).

Another attack vector that utilizes SQL injection is stored code in the database itself. Stored code such as stored procedures can often execute arbitrary statements at elevated privileges. This can be exploited by an internal user or someone who has managed to get access via credential guessing or sniffing.

SQL injection can also be used to access data by utilizing UNION statements to get datasets from other tables with identical numbers of columns as the tables being queried in the original form. For instance, if a search form queries a table with five columns, a union injected into the form could allow you to add result sets to any other table with five columns. Data can be effectively stolen without needing to exploit a bug.

Mitigation

SQL injection mitigation at the application layer begins with education of your software engineering team. When coding, software engineers must avoid dynamic queries and must prevent input with malicious SQL from modifying queries.

Prepared statements

The first step is ensuring that engineers use some variant of prepared statements. A prepared statement is also known as a *parameterized statement*. In a prepared statement, the structure of the query is defined in advance. Form input is then bound to a variable that is used to run the query. The opposite of this is to dynamically define and build SQL at runtime. A prepared statement is safer because the bad actor will not be able to modify query logic. If SQL injection occurs, the SQL will simply be considered a string for comparison, sorting, or filtering, rather than as a separate SQL statement for execution.

Example 9-1. Example prepared statement in Java

```
String hostname = request.getParameter("hostName");

String query = "SELECT ip, os FROM servers WHERE host_name = ? ";

PreparedStatement pstmt = connection.prepareStatement( query );
pstmt.setString( 1, hostName);
ResultSet results = pstmt.executeQuery( );
```

Input validation

There are times when prepared statements cannot protect you. Dynamic table names, or inputs to the ordering of a sort cannot be prepared in advance. This requires validation of input against which to be protected. In such a case, the application checks a defined list of valid table names, or Desc and Asc, to see if the query can be safely executed. Validation can also be performed to ensure that zip codes are five integers, strings have no spaces, and lengths are specific or within bounds.

Harm reduction

There are other mitigations that you can perform outside of the application that reduce the impact of SQL injection for cases in which precautions are unable to protect the application inputs. You cannot guarantee that SQL injection will not occur, so it is best to establish defense in depth. This includes patching of database binaries in order to reduce the number of exploitable bugs. Eliminating unnecessary stored code and unnecessary privileges from database users used by the application is critical also. Additionally, giving each application its own database user can reduce the damage a hijacked account can cause.

Monitoring

As with almost any other malfunction or dysfunction, instrumentation and monitoring of that data is crucial to mitigation. It is also critical to make sure to log and analyze dumps and stack traces and query log pattern matching for unions, semicolons, and other strings that are indicative of SQL injection.

SQL injection is very easy to prevent, and yet it is one of the most common ways to exploit databases. A consistent and ongoing platform of education and collaboration, as well as shared libraries that have been approved by infosec and DBRE, is a must for large, growing software engineering teams to ensure safety as well as velocity.

Network and Authentication Protocols

There are a number of ways to attack a database server through the various communications protocols available to a malicious actor. If there is a bug in the network protocol, the exploiting user can potentially gain direct server access. This was done in the "hello" bug (CAN-2002-1123), which was in session setup code on TCP port 1433. There are also exploits that can occur after authentication over the network, gaining OS or database access, or elevated privileges. Similarly, database protocols can be rife with vulnerabilities. Some servers actually allow unencrypted communications, which can allow credentials to be stolen and used. Other times, bugs can allow a user to send signals of authentication without actual credentials.

The mitigation techniques discussed in the beginning of this section are all critical to reducing attack vectors in your database infrastructure. Using those techniques and building a deep understanding of authentication protocols and database features in your engineering organization can ensure that your configurations are as secure as possible.

Now that we've given an overview of the potential attack vectors and their mitigation strategies, let's discuss the protection of data in case intrusion, elevation of privileges, or even full access to databases and servers is gained. The natural place to transition to in this conversation is encryption.

Encryption of Data

There are inevitably going to be times when someone malicious, someone who is unwittingly trespassing, or even someone friendly will be able to access data that they shouldn't. You've already locked down all your known network and OS paths, you've minimized access and privileges for every user, you've patched every known bug, and you've blocked all known application holes that could be exploited. Yet, you still need to prepare for the inevitable.

Encryption is the process of transforming data using an agreed upon set of keys or secrets. Theoretically, only people who have these keys should be able to transform the encrypted data back into a usable format. Encryption is often a last form of defense for data, even after it has been stolen and is in the hands of malicious actors.

In this section, we discuss encryption at three different layers:

- Data in transit
- Data at rest within the database client
- Data at rest on the filesystem

Each of these is a potential attack vector that can be secured via encryption. And, such encryption methods bring about overhead and cost in various forms, requiring consideration and trade-offs in most organizations.

In each of these layers, we must take into account another dimension of data, which is the type of data. Data can be considered sensitive or not, and that sensitivity of data can be broken out into categories described in the subsections that follow. If you are storing and managing any of this kind of data, the DBRE team should be working very closely with the InfoSec and SWE teams to ensure that all parties understand the obligations and standards and are building the self-service platforms, libraries, and monitoring required to meet those regulations. Data comes in many different forms, and we will review some of the more common forms of regulated data that you can manage.

Financial Data

This includes account numbers and associated data around accounts that can be used for authentication or identification. It also includes transaction histories and data that reveals the financial status of an individual or organization such as credit scores, financial reports, balances, and more. Financial data in the United States alone is regulated by numerous laws, bodies, and standards including PCI DSS requirements for credit card data, GLBA, SOX/J-SOX, NCUA, data privacy and data residency laws, and the Patriot Act. We can find similar bodies in other countries as well.

Personal Health Data

Information about patients and their health is covered within this category. It includes personally identifiable information such as social security numbers, names, and contact information, as well as data regarding patients' health, their treatments and procedures, and their insurance information. Health data in the US is regulated predominantly by the Health Insurance Portability and Accountability Act of 1996 (HIPAA).

Private Individual Data

This is often referred to as Personally Identifiable Information or (PII). It includes social security numbers, addresses, phone numbers, and emails. This information can be used for identity theft, harassment, and unwanted contact. The Privacy Act of 1974 was the basis for the US standards currently in place for this data.

Military or Government Data

Any data related to government operations or personnel is considered very sensitive. Information regarding military operations and personnel is more so. There are very strict procedures in place for any organization supporting and storing this.

Confidential/Sensitive Business Data

This includes any data that must be kept secret to protect a business' competitiveness. It includes Intellectual Property (IP), trade secrets, financials, and performance/activity reporting. Customer and sales information falls into this, also.

Understanding the nature of the data being stored in individual datastores is critical to being able to make appropriate choices around encryption and protections. This is also why it is so important that organizational collaboration and education occurs. Otherwise, in fast-moving organizations, it would be easy for an unwitting engineer to begin putting sensitive data into datastores that have not been locked down for such.

There are also some basic standards that should simply always be applied. Even though we even feel embarrassed mentioning these, the aforementioned MongoDB case and defaults should tell us just how important these reminders are. These include the following:

- Web administrative interfaces speaking directly to databases should always use SSL, or use a secure proxy service. We use SSL to refer to both. Transport Layer Security (TLS) is the successor of SSL 3.0 and most people refer to both as SSL. TLS 1.0 suffers from vulnerabilities and should be considered inadequate (*http:// bit.ly/2zxqT5t*).

- You should use SSH2 or remote desk protocol (RDP) for connecting to servers.

- Administrative connections to databases should use a separate administrative network and should use TLS 1.1 or 1.2 if the database allows it.

- Each SSL protocol should use an appropriately strong encryption cypher. The strength of a an encrypted session comes from the cipher negotiated between the server and client.

Let's first look at the encryption of data in transit.

Data in Transit

Data must be moved across networks. This is an inevitable and sad fact for the DBRE looking to secure her data. Just as money must be moved in armored trucks, or valuable goods must be transported for delivery, so must data be transported. This is a highly vulnerable time, and depending on where in the transit process, this vulnerability becomes greater. This is also called "Data in flight."

Before digging in further, its worthwhile to ensure that any DBRE worth his or her salt (really hoping you get that joke...) understands the various components and best practices in a cipher suite.

Anatomy of a cipher suite

Each database server will communicate with clients over a negotiated *cipher suite*. It is important to understand the implications of a particular databases implementation of a cipher suite to ensure that data is protected at the levels necessary. Your InfoSec team should be able to set standards, but if this is left to you, understanding the implications of a specific databases implementation is critical. Here's an example of a cipher suite:

```
ECDHE-ECDSA-AES128-GCM-SHA256
```

The first part of the suite, ECDHE is the key exchange algorithm. This particular example uses *elliptic curve version* of the key–exchange using ephemeral keys. Other values here could be RSA, DH, and DHE. Ephemeral key exchanges are based on Diffie-Hellman (*https://www-ee.stanford.edu/~hellman/publications/24.pdf*) and use per-session, temporary keys during the initial TLS handshake. They provide perfect forward secrecy (PFS), which means a compromise of the server's long-term signing key does not compromise the confidentiality of past session. When the server uses an ephemeral key, the server signs the temporary key with its long-term key (the long-term key is the customary key available in its certificate).[1] DHE is considered stronger than EDHE and should be favored.

The next part, ECDDSA, is the signature algorithm that is used to sign the key–exchange parameters. RSA is preferred here over DSA or DSS, which can be very weak depending on the signing entropy source.

---

1 Check out the Transport Layer Protection Cheat Sheet (*http://bit.ly/owasp-cheat-sheet*).

Next, AES128 refers to the cipher in the suite. In this case, it is Advanced Encryption Standard (AES) with a 128-bit key. This is followed by the mode of operation for the cipher, in this case Galois/Counter mode (GCM), which provides authenticated encryption. GCM supports only AES, Camellia, or Aria, and thus those ciphers are ideal. For AES, the National Institute of Standards and Technology (NIST) selected three members, each with a block size of 128 bits, but three different key lengths: 128, 192, and 256 bits as the standard.

Finally, SHA-256 refers to the keyed message authentication code (MAC) function e. SHA-256 is a hashed MAC (HMAC) function used by certification authorities to sign certificates and certificates revocation lists (CRLs). You use this algorithm to create the master secret. Recipients of messages use this to verify that the contents are correct. After a side has sent its finished message and received and validated the finished message from its peer, it can begin to send and receive application data over the connection. SHA2 is a preferred implementation of this algorithm. It includes four kinds of hash functions: SHA224, SHA256, SHA384, and SHA512.

When evaluating a database's implementation of SSL, understanding the cipher list is important because this list shows the order in which ciphers are scanned until a matching cipher that is available for both the client and server is found.

When evaluating the needs of communications encryption, you must consider not only the types of data discussed previously but also the transit paths and boundaries, specifically:

- Communications within the network
- Communications outside of the network

Each of these transport areas requires consideration and an agreed upon set of assumptions. Each of those assumptions creates a set of requirements, and each of those requirements creates a need for implementation.

Communication within the network

Communications within a secured subnet are generally assumed to be secured at the network layer, and thus most regulations do not require the communications channels (aka the network connection itself) to be further protected. This means that application servers requesting or sending data and replication between servers and other internetwork communications do not need to set up encrypted communications in a secured network. This is good, as this is the majority of the activity a database will be engaged in, and encryption is quite CPU intensive. That being said, if the database is storing sensitive data, it still is required to be encrypted somehow. This is ideally done at the application layer when the data is being placed into the database itself. We will discuss this further when we discuss data at rest.

If sensitive data within a database cannot be secured, whether due to legacy reasons or other constraints, the organization should consider requiring encrypted communications for anything connecting to the database.

Communications outside of the network

For cases in which you are connecting between two networks owned and managed by your organization or between your network and the internet, you must use a virtual private network (VPN) using IPSec or SSL when transporting any data, sensitive or not.

Similarly, internet clients should be communicating to load balancers via SSL/TLS for most communications. This does add CPU overhead to clients and load balancers, but it should be relatively rare that you want data being transferred as clear text between your clients and you.

With an understanding of the needs for SSL, let's look at the architectural choices that go into making this happen.

Establishing secure data connections

Modern database systems typically have SSL support of various degrees. There are exceptions, such as Redis, and it is important when determining if a datastore fits your needs that you verify this. Sensitive data that is not encrypted should not be cached!

It is worth pointing out that SSL overhead is generally quite minimal as compared to myths that persist. The majority of computational overhead is done on initiation of the connection, and that rarely exceeds 2% CPU overhead and an increase of 5 millisencond latency (*http://bit.ly/2zykkiT*). Some ciphers, such as AES, have instructions built into most modern CPUs, substantially increasing speed compared to software-based ciphers.

There is a layered set of approaches that you can apply to securing connections.

Basic connection encryption.   At the most basic of levels, you first configure a database server to require secure communications for all connections. With this configuration comes the creation of a certificate authority (CA) certificate. That certificate is used to sign a server public key certificate and a server private key. That same certificate is also used on clients to generate client public key certificates and private keys. With clients storing their keys and servers configured appropriately, all connections are considered encrypted.

Best practices and common sense indicate that keys must not be stored where people can easily hijack and use them. This means that dynamic configuration might be used to directly load keys into an application's memory rather than storing them directly on a client's filesystem. There are better ways, though.

Securely stored secrets. Although securing a connection via SSL is a crucial first step, there are still vulnerabilities. After all, if an actor is able to acquire access to the client hosts, connections using those keys can be utilized to query data. Using a key management infrastructure secure service such as Hashicorp's Vault, Amazon's Key Management Service (KMS), or any other number of solutions allows for separation of key storage and management from those accessing the data.

Additionally, other pieces of information used to access the database such as username, password, IPs, and ports can be stored remotely in some of these services, ensuring that no credentials are stored on the filesystem where someone can acquire them and use them outside of application context.

Dynamically built database users. Building on the previous two stages, the natural evolution is using the same secure secrets service such as Vault to dynamically create ephemeral user accounts within the datastore. This allows an application host to register and request a user account that will be created at that moment. Using roles such as read-only facilitates various permissions being automatically applied, and these users can have limited lifetimes, ensuring that any access potentially hijacked lasts a limited time. Additionally, you have an ability to map users to specific application hosts now. This allows for auditing of queries and access that would have proved challenging in an environment that utilized shared usernames for a pool of servers.

Using a combination of SSL and VPN technology, all communication paths should be able to be encrypted based on the needs of the data being stored. Additionally, we can take advantage of secret management services to reduce the attack vectors of configuration files and keys sitting on filesystems for anyone with enough OS privilege to read and abuse. This is the concept of protecting data in flight. Now, let's move on to reviewing data at rest. We begin with data in the database itself.

Data in the Database

Also known as "Data in Use," data in the database must be accessible to applications, analysts, and consumer processes. This means that any encryption solution must allow for accessing of data by those authenticated to do so while preventing anyone who wishes to maliciously access data from doing so. If a user manages to authenticate into a database, he is generally able to read any data for which he has appropriate database read permissions.

A potential attacker can be broken into one of three categories:

- Intruder

- Insider
- Administrator

Intruders gain access to a database or its server to extract valuable information. Insiders belong to trusted groups with privileges in the database or OS and attempt to get information beyond their granted privileges. Administrators are people who have administration-level privileges at the database and/or OS level and use those to get valuable information.

Much of the data listed at the beginning of this section requires even further encryption to ensure that only appropriate users can read it. Let's review the options available to us and their features and potential drawbacks. We'd also like to remind you that encryption standards and best practices hold just as they do in SSL encryption, as we discussed earlier.

Application-level security

In this approach, specific tables or columns are identified as requiring encryption during threat modeling. Utilizing encryption libraries, the application encrypts data before submitting it to the application for storage. The data is then submitted just as any other string or binary data would be. Data is also retrieved similarly, and the application knows to decrypt it before presenting it for use. This encryption and decryption can be done with libraries such as Bouncy Castle and OpenSSL.

Using libraries at the application level provides database portability. Even if the backend changes, you can still perform encryption and decryption just as before. It also allows for control of encryption libraries. InfoSec can place these shared libraries in version control for anyone to use, and there is no further need for compliance auditing of that code because it is approved and used across the organization. Finally, this method allows for selective encryption, leaving other columns and tables unencrypted for easier reporting, indexing, and querying.

The primary disadvantage of this approach is that it is not a blanket approach that is applied to all data in the database. Thus, when new data is modeled and introduced into the application, developers must remember to consider if this new piece of data requires encryption and then to actually implement it. This approach also requires all other clients in the data pipeline who require reading of this data to utilize de-encryption libraries.

Application-level encryption provides the most flexibility at the cost of development velocity.

Database plug-in encryption

Plug-in encryption utilizes an encryption package installed in the database itself. This method is independent of the application, requiring less custom coding. Depending on the plug-in, selective encryption at the column level, access control features, and auditing of access are often features also.

Encrypting the database completely with one key is generally not recommended because a user can potentially exploit vulnerabilities and gain access greater than necessary to read data anywhere using that key. For example, an internal user with encryption key access could gain access to an elevated user and access data beyond her security group. Encrypting tables from different security groups using different keys ensures that users can decrypt only those objects within their security group. This means that any plug-ins you look to utilize should have selective encryption and access control features to be considered effective.

Unlike application-level encryption, this does create portability issues between databases. Thus, if you are working in a startup or an environment with frequently changing requirements, this can prove to be too inflexible of a solution.

Transparent database encryption

There are some security appliances that will encrypt/decrypt all communications through the database. This is a relatively easy approach that can make it easier to ensure that data is encrypted, but it does enforce the overhead of encryption for all data. That being said, the universality and low-level approach minimizes this overhead.

Query performance considerations

Even though encrypting data is a relatively trivial activity, querying that data can prove to be nonperformant and will affect schema and query design. Data encryption at the column or table level does not easily support range queries or string searches. Thus, queries must take into consideration how data will be filtered and sorted.

Most encryption functions do not preserve order, so you cannot use a *B-Tree index*, which is very standard for indexing ranges on encrypted data. You can often use unencrypted fields for filtering in a performant manner. For instance, you can use date range filters to reduce the dataset you need to scan for an encrypted value. To support more efficient querying of encrypted data, you can store a keyed-hash message authentication code (HMAC) of an encrypted field in your schema, and you can supply a key for the hash function. Subsequent queries of protected fields that contain the HMAC of the data being sought would not disclose the plain-text values in the query. This allows the database to perform a query against the encrypted data in your database without disclosing the plain-text values in the query. This also protects against data manipulation in the database by users who do not have the data needed to create an HMAC (*http://bit.ly/2zzUoUe*).

With indexes on these hashed fields, you get equality performance, but information about frequency and cardinality of indexed values is revealed. Similarly, a bad actor might be able to infer information about an encrypted database value by its position in an index or even search for other occurrences of the hash. With long-term access, information about the data can be gained by observing and analyzing changes over time. For instance, after data is inserted, a knowledgeable user could infer potential values by events and position in the index.

Thus, depending on the value of the data, you can potentially add obfuscation techniques to reduce the chance that an observer can infer linkage or values based on the hash, its relation to other hashes, and the values of new inserts. This can include adding dummy data with every insert, or batching inserts to not allow incremental observations on atomic inserts.

Although this is a very high-level overview of schema considerations for performance and security, we felt it important to bring up the concerns and a few sample approaches to mitigation so that database encryption is not considered to be a trivial matter during the planning phase.

Data that is stored within the database still ultimately sits on the filesystem. Similarly, logs, data dumps, and backups are all places on the filesystem that must be considered when protecting data. So, let's look at the encryption of data at rest from the filesystem level.

Data in the Filesystem

Through encryption of data in flight and data in use, we've provided significant levels of protection. Still, there is an opportunity for data to be accessed directly from disk, tape, or other media. Like all other mitigation techniques, there are multiple approaches to this. When considering a solution, it is important to consider how much data is stored, CPU, and latency impacts of reads and writes and how often the data must be accessed.

Attackers can use direct or indirect attack strategies against data in the filesystem. In direct storage attacks, the bad actor accesses database files directly, outside of the database software. This can include copying datafiles off of the server over the network by physical removal of storage devices or by getting data from the backup infrastructure. With indirect attacks, the bad actor can get schema information, log data, and metadata from files used by the database.

In addition to standard network and access-control strategies, encryption of filesystem data is required to ensure that anyone bypassing those steps can't access our tasty data. When considering storage encryption, there are multiple layers that must be considered. These are the data sitting on a filesystem, the filesystem, and the device.

Data encryption above the filesystem

When data is laid down on a filesystem, it can be encrypted automatically. This has similar considerations as discussed in "Data in the Database" on page 174. This generally would apply to data being uploaded to a filesystem, such as a backup or a datafile for importing. By encrypting at this layer, you can always know the encryption status of critical files.

Additionally, this data can be broken into chunks for distribution across multiple storage devices. This is a great option for sensitive data backups and large data dumps as it prevents a person accessing one storage device from getting a full dataset. Such chunking also can allow for parallelization of read and write operations, allowing for faster recovery. The trade-off is typically going to be the development and maintenance time of such a storage gateway.

Filesystem encryption

Because most datastores create their own files for metadata, logs, and data storage. A system must be in place for encrypting at the filesystem layer. You can do this on top of the filesystem with a stacked encrypted filesystem, directly in the filesystem via built-in encryption mechanisms, or below the filesystem at the block layer.

Stacking an encrypted filesystem on top of an existing filesystem allows for use of any filesystem underneath. This is a quite flexible option because you can use it for specific directories rather than encryption of the entire volume. Examples of Linux-based options include eCryptfs and EncFs. These do require keys to be provided manually or via a Key Management Interface (KMI). Many filesystems such as ZFS and BTRFS also have encryption options, though it is critical to see if they expose unencrypted metadata.

Block-level encryption systems operate below the filesystem, encrypting one disk block at a time. Some options for this in Linux include Loop-AES, dm-crypt, and Vera. Each of these operates below the filesystem layer using kernel space device drivers. These tools are useful when you want all data written to a volume to be encrypted regardless of what directory the data is stored in.

All of these solutions do have performance impacts that must be weighed with security requirements. It makes sense to put logs, metadata, and other similar files on encrypted filesystems. But, what about data files being accessed from the database itself? Many users find that application-level or column-level encryption of key data gives the necessary encryption within the database. This allows the database files themselves to stay unencrypted for performance reasons. Combining this solution with filesystem encryption of logs, metadata files, and other system-level files creates an effective multilayered solution that does not compromise on performance.

Device-level encryption

You can also utilize storage media that has built-in decryption. This increases storage costs and is of questionable value given that there are many known vulnerabilities. The point here was that this layer definitely adds to a defense-in-depth approach to data security.

As you can see by the broad level of discussion, data encryption merits significant engineering cycles for design, implementation, and auditing. In this section, we discussed the protection via encryption of data in transit, data in the database, and data at rest on filesystems. Data encryption is a last bastion of safety to provide protection when access controls, code hardening, and regular patching fail. Recognizing the criticality of this is also a recognition that every layer in security is vulnerable and that the protection of data must be considered at every level to create a reasonable amount of protection. When continuing along the path of encryption, regardless of which level, you can always be sure that you need to consider the following checklist:

- Has all data been classified according to sensitivity?
- Is there a standard on cipher suites, and is it audited for compliance?
- Are new reports of vulnerabilities and exploits being tracked and considered?
- Are new hires in SWE, SRE, Ops, and DBRE aware of centralized libraries and encryption standards?
- Are keys being managed effectively, including rotation, removal, and testing?
- Are you performing regular, automated penetration testing of key components including logs, backups, critical tables, and database connections?

Like any automated and manual testing, it is important to recognize that you will not be able to test everything. This is why focusing on high risk and easy exploitability allows for focus, prioritization, and tight feedback loops in a continuous process of testing and improvement.

Wrapping Up

You now have a deeper understanding not only of the nuanced layers of database security, but also of how to be an effective security champion in your organization. As with much in this book, the DBRE cannot be solely responsible for this function. That DBA thinking simply doesn't work in high velocity, dynamic environments that require DBRE mentality. Instead, you should be actively partnering with every group mentioned in this chapter to provide your own depth of knowledge to the creation of self-service platforms, shared libraries, and team processes.

In this, as in the preceding eight chapters, we have strived to create a solid foundation of not only operations, but also of effective collaboration and support of the other technical organizations that rely on you as a DBRE. Now, we will focus on helping you understand the wide range of database persistence options out there and how they implement key technologies to provide resilient, scalable, and performant data storage and retrieval. Throughout the next section, we will be referring back to the foundation laid out up to now.

CHAPTER 10

Data Storage, Indexing, and Replication

We've been talking about operations for much of this book in preparation for diving into datastores. The most critical thing every datastore has in common with one another is that they...wait for it...store data. In this chapter, we explain the ways a single node structures its data storage, how large datasets are partitioned, and how nodes replicate data between one another. It's going to be quite the chapter!

This book's scope is focused predominantly on reliability and operations, so we will be working on understanding storage and access patterns to facilitate infrastructure choices, to understand performance characteristics, and to make sure that you, as the database reliability engineer (DBRE), have the information required to help engineering teams choose the appropriate datastores for their services. For a much more detailed and nuanced review of this, we strongly suggest that you read Martin Kleppmann's book *Designing Data-Intensive Applications* (O'Reilly).

Data Structure Storage

Databases traditionally have stored data in a combination of tables and indexes. A table is the main storage mechanism, and an index is an optimized subset of data ordered to improve access times. With the proliferation of datastores now, this has evolved significantly. Understanding how data is written to and read from storage is crucial to being able to configure and optimize your storage subsystems and databases.

When understanding how a database stores data, you actually need to evaluate not only how the raw data is stored, but also how it is retrieved. In large datasets, accessing specific subsets of data at any reasonable level of latency will often require specialized storage structures, called indexes, to accelerate the finding and retrieval of that data. Thus, when looking at storage, we must take into account the storage and Input/

Output (I/O) requirements for putting data onto disk and into indexes as well as the I/O requirements for retrieving that data.

Database Row Storage

Much of the data here is applicable to more traditional relational systems. We will begin with this, and then we'll discuss some of the more prevalent alternative storage options. In relational databases, data is stored in containers called *blocks* or *pages* that correspond to a specific number of bytes on disk. Different databases will use blocks or pages in their terminology. In this book, we use blocks to refer to both. Blocks are the finest level of granularity for storing records. Oracle Database stores data in data blocks. A page is a fixed size called a block, just like blocks on disks. Blocks are the smallest size that can be read or written to access data. This means that if a row is 1 K and the block size is 16 K, you will still incur a 16 K read operation. If a database block size is smaller than the filesystem block size, you will be wasting I/O for operations that require multiple pages. This can be visualized in Figure 10-1.

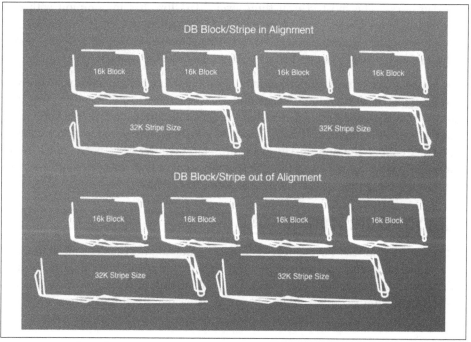

Figure 10-1. Aligned versus nonaligned block/stripe configurations.

A block requires some metadata to be stored, as well, usually in the form of a header and trailer or footer. This will include disk address information, information about the object the block belongs to, and information about the rows and activity that have occurred within that block. In Oracle, as of version 11g, Release 2, block overhead totals 84 to 107 bytes. In MySQL's InnoDB, as of version 5.7, header and trailer use 46 bytes. Additionally, each row of data will require its own metadata, including information about columns, links to other blocks that the row is spread across, and a unique identifier for the row.[1]

Data blocks are often organized into a larger container called an extent. For efficiency reasons, an extent is often the allocation unit when new blocks are required within a tablespace. A tablespace is typically the largest data structure, mapped to one or more physical files that can be laid out as required on disk. On systems mapped directly to physical disks, tablespace files can be laid out across different disks to reduce I/O contention. In the paradigms we focus on in this book, such curation of I/O is not necessarily an option. Large, generic RAID structures of stripes and potentially mirrored stripes can maximize I/O without significant time spent on microtuning. Otherwise, assuming rapid recovery and failover are available, focusing on simple volumes or even ephemeral storage provides ease of management and minimal overhead.

B-tree structures

Most databases structure their data in a binary tree format, also known as *B-tree*. A B-tree is a data structure that self-balances while keeping data sorted. The B-tree is optimized for the reading and writing of blocks of data, which is why B-trees are commonly found in databases and filesystems.

You can imagine a B-tree table or index as an upside-down tree. There is a root page, which is the start of the index that is built on a key. The key is one or more columns. Most relational database tables are stored on a primary key, which can be explicitly or implicitly defined. For instance, a primary key can be an integer. If an application is looking for data that maps to a specific ID or a range of IDs, this key will be used to find it. In addition to the primary key B-tree, secondary indexes on other columns or sets of columns can be defined. Unlike the original B-tree, these indexes store only the data that is indexed rather than the entire row. This means that these indexes are much smaller and can fit in memory much more easily.

A B-tree is called a tree because when you navigate through the tree, you can choose from two or more child pages to get to the data you want. As just discussed, a page contains rows of data and metadata. This metadata includes pointers to the pages below it, also known as *child pages*. The root page has two or more pages below it, also known as *children*. A child page, or node, can be an internal node or a leaf node. Internal nodes store pivot keys and child pointers and are used to direct reads through the index to one node or another. Leaf nodes contain key data. This structure creates a self-balancing tree that can be searched within only a few levels, which

---

1 Cole, Jeremy, "The physical structure of records in InnoDB" (*http://bit.ly/2zykQ0j*).

allows for only a few disk seeks to find the pointers to the rows that are needed. If the data needed is within the key itself, you don't even need to follow the pointer to the row.

Binary tree writes.   When inserting data to a B-tree, the correct leaf node is found via search. Nodes are created with room for additional inserts, rather than packing them in. If the node has room, the data is inserted in order in the node. If the node is full, a split has to occur. In a split, a new median is determined and a new node is created. Records are then redistributed accordingly. The data about this median is then inserted into the parent node, which can cause additional splits all the way up to the root node. Updates and deletes also begin with finding the correct leaf node via search, followed by the update or delete. Updates can cause splits if they increase data size to the point where it overflows a node. Deletes can cause rebalancing, as well.

Greenfield (new) databases begin with primarily sequential writes and reads. This shows as low latency writes and reads. As the database grows, splits will cause I/O to become random. This results in longer latency reads and writes. This is why we must insist on realistic datasets during testing to ensure that long-term performance characteristics will exhibit rather than these naive, early exhibitors.

Single-row writes require a page to be completely rewritten, at minimum. If there are splits, there can be many pages that must be written. This complex operation requires atomicity yet allows opportunities for corruption and orphaned pages if there is a crash. When evaluating a datastore, it is vital to understand what mechanisms are put in place to prevent this. Examples of such mechanisms include the following:

- Logs of write operations that are written to before the more complex operations of writing to disk, also known as Write Ahead Logs (WAL)
- Event logs for reconstruction
- Redo logs with before and after images of the mutated data

With all of this in mind, a crucial variable in configuring your databases for underlying storage is the database block size. We've discussed the importance of aligning database block sizes with the underlying disk block sizes, but that is not enough. If you are using Solid-State Drives (SSDs), for instance, you might find smaller block sizes provide much better performance while traversing B-trees. An SSD can experience a 30% to 40% latency penalty on larger blocks versus performance on Hard Disk Drives (HDDs). Because reads and writes are required in B-tree structures, this must be taken into account.

The following is a summary of the attributes and benefits of B-trees:

- Excellent performance for range-based queries.
- Not the most ideal model for single-row lookups.

- Keys exist in sorted order for efficient key lookups and range scans.

- Structure minimizes page reads for large datasets.

- By not packing keys into each page, deletes and inserts are efficient, with only occasional splits and merges being needed.

- Perform much better if the entire structure can fit within memory.

When indexing data, there are other options as well. The most predominant one is the hash index.

As we mentioned earlier, the B-tree tends to be fairly ubiquitous in relational databases. If you've worked in those environments, you've probably worked with them already. There are other options for data storage, however, and they are moving from experimental to mature. Let's look next at append-only log structures (*http://bit.ly/2zyttIz*).

Sorted-String Tables and Log-Structured Merge Trees

BigTable, Cassandra, RocksDB (which is available in MySQL via MyRocks and MongoDB), and LevelDB are all examples of databases that use sorted-string tables (SSTs) for primary storage. The terms SSTable and Memtable originally appeared in the Google BigTable paper (*https://research.google.com/archive/bigtable-osdi06.pdf*) that has been a source of inspiration for a number of database management systems (DBMS's) since then.

In an SST storage engine, there are a number of files, each with a set of sorted key–value pairs inside. Unlike in the block storage discussed earlier, there is no need for the metadata overhead at the block or row level. Keys and their values are opaque to the DBMS and stored as arbitrary binary large objects (BLOBs). Because they are stored in a sorted fashion, they can be read sequentially and treated as an index on the key by which they are sorted.

There is an algorithm that combines in-memory tables, batch flushing, and periodic compaction in SST storage engines. This algorithm is referred to a log-structured merge (LSM) tree architecture (see Figure 10-2). This was described by Patrick O'Neill in his paper (*http://nosqlsummer.org/paper/lsm-tree*).

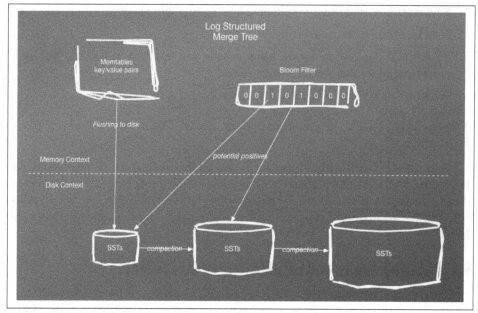

Figure 10-2. Log-structured merge tree structure with a bloom filter

With an LSM, SSTs are written to by periodic flushes of data that has been stored in memory. After data is flushed, sorted, and written to disk, it is immutable. Items cannot be added or removed from the map of key–value pairs. This is effective for read-only datasets because you can map an SST into memory for rapid access. Even if the SST does not fully fit in memory, random reads require a minimal amount of disk seeks.

To support fast writes, more is required. Opposite to writes on disk, writes on a dataset in memory are trivial because you are just changing pointers. An in-memory table can take writes and remain balanced. This is also referred to as a *memtable*. The memtable can also act as the first query point for reads before falling back to the newest SST on disk, followed by the next oldest, and then the next, until the data is found. After a certain threshold is reached, which can be time, number of transactions, or size, the memtable will be sorted and flushed to disk.

When deletes are done on data that is already stored in an SST, a logical delete must be recorded. This is also known as a *tombstone*. Periodically, SST's are merged together, allowing elimination of tombstones and saving of space. This merge and compaction process can be very I/O intensive and often requires significantly more space available than the actual working set. Until operations teams are used to these new capacity models, there might be impacts to availability Service-Level Objectives (SLOs).

There are data-loss possibilities that must be assumed during failure scenarios. Until memtables are flushed to disk, they are vulnerable to crashes. Unsurprisingly, there are similar solutions in SST storage engines as in B-tree based ones, including event logs, redo logs, and write ahead logs.

Bloom filters

You might imagine that having to search through a memtable and a large number of SSTables to find a record key that doesn't exist could be expensive and slow. You'd be right! An implementation detail to assist with this is a *bloom filter*. A bloom filter is a data structure that you can use to evaluate whether a record key is present in a given set, which, in this case, is an SSTable.

A datastore such as Cassandra uses bloom filters to evaluate which SSTable, if any, might contain the record key requested. It is designed for speed, and thus there might be some false positives. But, the overall effect is a significant reduction in read I/O. Inversely, if a bloom filter says that a record key does not exist in an SSTable, that is a certainty. Bloom filters are updated when memtables are flushed to disk. The more memory that can be allocated to the filter, the less likely a false positive will occur.

Implementations

There a number of datastores that utilize the LSM structure with SSTables as a storage engine:

- Apache Cassandra
- Google Bigtable
- HBase
- LevelDB
- Lucene
- Riak
- RocksDB
- WiredTiger

Implementation details will vary for each datastore, but the proliferation and growing maturity of this storage engine has put it into an important storage implementation for any team working with large datasets to understand.

While reviewing and enumerating data storage structures, we've mentioned logs multiple times as critical for data durability in the case of failures. We also discuss them in (Chapter 7). They are also critical for replicating data in distributed datastores. Let's dig deeper into logs and their usage in replication.

Indexing

We have already discussed one of the most ubiquitous of indexing structures, the B-tree. SSTs are also inherently indexed. There are some other index structures that you will find out in the database wild.

Hash indexes

One of the simplest index implementations is that of a *hash map*. A hash map is a collection of buckets that contain the results of a hash function applied to a key. That hash points to the location where the records can be found. A hash map is only viable for single-key lookups because a range scan would be prohibitively expensive. Additionally, the hash must fit in memory to ensure performance. With these caveats, hash maps provide excellent access for the specific use cases for which it works.

Bitmap indexes

A bitmap index stores its data as bit arrays (bitmaps). When you traverse the index, it is done by performing bitwise logical operations on the bitmaps. In B-trees, the index performs the best on values that are not repeated often. This is also known as *high cardinality*. The bitmap index functions much better when there are a small number of values being indexed.

Permutations of B-trees

There are permutations of the traditional B-tree index. These are often designed for very specific use cases, including the following:

Function Based
> An index based on the results of a function applied to the index.

Reverse Index
> Indexing values from the end of that value to the beginning to allow for reverse sorting.

Clustered Index
> Requires the table records to be physically stored in indexed order to optimize I/O access. The leaf nodes of clustered index contain the data pages.

Spatial Index
> There are a number of different mechanisms for indexing spatial data. Standard index types cannot handle spatial queries efficiently.

Search Index
> These indexes allow for searching of subsets of data within the columns. Most indexes cannot search within the indexed value. There are some indexes

designed for this, however, and some entire datastores, such as ElasticSearch, are built for this operation.

Each datastore will have its own series of specialized indices that are available, often to optimize the typical use cases within that datastore.

Indexes are tremendously critical for rapid access of subsets of data. When evaluating bleeding-edge datastores, understanding the limitations in terms of indexes, such as the ability to have more than one index or how many columns can be indexed or even how those indexes are maintained in the background, is crucial to understand.

Logs and Databases

Logs began as a way to maintain durability in database systems. They evolved to the mechanism used to replicate data from primary to replica servers for availability and scalability reasons. Eventually, services were built to use these logs to migrate data between different database engines with a transformation layer between them. This then evolved into a full messaging system with logs becoming events that a subscribing service could use to perform discreet pieces of work for downstream services.

With opportunities of so many use cases for logs, we'd like to focus specifically on replication in this chapter. Having discussed how data can be stored and indexed on a local server, we now will move on to how that data can be distributed to other servers.

Data Replication

For this entire book, we have been working under the assumption that you will be working primarily on distributed datastores. This means that there must be a way for data that is written on one node to be moved around between nodes. There are entire books written on this topic alone,[2] so we will focus on well-known and utilized examples rather than more theoretical ones. Our goal for you as a DBRE is for you and the engineers you support to be able to look at replication methods offered and to understand how they work. Knowing the pros and cons and patterns and antipatterns that are associated with replication options is crucial for a DBRE, an architect, a software engineer, or an operations person to do their jobs well.

There are some high-level distinctions in replication architectures that can be used for an initial enumeration. When discussing replication here, we are referring to leaders as nodes that take writes from applications and followers as nodes that receive replicated events to apply to their own datasets. Finally, readers are nodes that applications read data from.

---

2 See the book *Replication Techniques in Distributed Systems* (Advances in Database Systems, 1996).

Single Leader
    Data is always sent to one specific leader.

Multiple Leader
    There can be multiple nodes with a leader role, and each leader must persist data across the cluster.

No Leader
    All nodes are expected to be able to take writes.

We will begin with the simplest replication method, single-leader, and build on from there.

Single-Leader

As the title implies, in this replication model all writes go to a single leader and are replicated from there. Thus, you have one node out of N nodes that is designated as the leader, and the others are replicas. Data flows from the leader out. This method is widely utilized for its simplicity, and you can make a few guarantees. These guarantees include:

- There will be no consistency conflicts because all writes occur against one node.
- Assuming that all operations are deterministic, you can guarantee that they will result in the same outputs on each node.

There are some permutations here, such as one leader replicating to a few relay replicas that then have their own replicas. Regardless, there is one leader taking writes, which is the key attribute of this architecture. There are a few different approaches to replication in single leader. Each approach trades off some level of consistency, latency, and availability. Thus, the appropriate choice will vary based on the applications and how they use database clusters.

Replication models

When replicating data in single-leader fashion, there are three different models that you can be use:

Asynchronous
    optimize latency over durability

Synchronous
    optimize durability over latency

Semi-synchronous
    compromise latency and durability

In *asynchronous replication* models, a transaction is written to a log on the leader and then committed and flushed to disk. A separate process is responsible for shipping those logs to the followers, where they are applied as soon as possible. In asynchronous replication models, there is always some lag between what is committed on the leader and what is committed on the followers. Additionally, there is no guarantee that the commit point on one follower is the same as the others. In practice, the time gap between commit points might be too small to notice. It is just as easy to find clusters using asynchronous replication for which there is a time gap of seconds, minutes, or hours between leaders and followers.

In *synchronous replication* models, a transaction that is written to a log on the leader is shipped immediately over the network to the followers. The leader *will not commit the transaction* until the followers have confirmed that they have recorded the write. This ensures that every node in the cluster is at the same commit point. This means that reads will be consistent regardless of what node they come from, and any node can take over as a leader without risk of data loss if the current leader fails. On the other hand, network latency or degraded nodes can all cause write latency for the transaction on the leader.

Because synchronous replication can have a significant impact on latency, particularly if there are many nodes, *semi-synchronous* replication can be put in place as a compromise. In this algorithm, only one node is required to confirm to the leader that they have recorded the write. This reduces the risk of latency impacts when one or more nodes are functioning in degraded states while guaranteeing that at least two nodes on the cluster are at the same commit point. In this mode, there is no longer a guarantee that all nodes in the cluster will return the same data if a read is issued on any reader. There is, however, still a guarantee that you can promote at least one node in the cluster to leader status, if needed, without data loss.

Replication log formats

To achieve single-leader replication, you must use a log of transactions. There are a number of approaches to how these logs are implemented. Each one has benefits and trade-offs, and many datastores might implement more than one to allow you to choose what works best. Let's review them here.

Statement-based logs. In statement-based replication, the actual SQL or data write statement used to execute the write is recorded and shipped from the leader to followers. This means that the entire statement will be executed on each follower.

Pros:

- A statement can execute hundreds or thousands of records. That's a lot of data to ship. The statement is usually much smaller. This can be optimal when replicating across datacenters where network bandwidth is scarce.

- This approach is very portable. Most SQL statements will result in the same outputs even on different versions of the database. This allows you to upgrade followers before upgrading leaders. This is a critical piece of high-availability approaches to upgrades in production. Without backward-compatible replication, version upgrades can require significant downtime while an entire cluster is upgraded.

- You can also use log files as audits and for data integration because they contain entire statements.

Cons:

- A statement might require significant processing time if it is using aggregation and calculation functions on a selected dataset to determine what it will write. Running the statement can take much longer than simply changing the records or bits on disk. This can cause replication delay in serialized apply processes.

- Some statements might not be deterministic and can create different outputs to the dataset if run on different nodes.

MySQL statement-based replication is an example of this.

Deterministic Transactions

Deterministic means that the processing output of a statement is not dependent on time and cannot be influenced by external factors. If a statement is run on the same dataset and in the same sequence, regardless of which node it is on, it should create the same output. Examples of nondeterministic statements include the use of local time functions, such as `now()` or `sysdate()`, or that use random ordering, such as order by `rand()`.

Similarly, stored code such as user-defined functions, stored procedures, and triggers can cause a statement to be nondeterministic and thus not safe for statement-based replication.

Write-ahead logs. A write-ahead log (WAL), also known as a redo log, contains a series of events, each event mapped to a transaction or write. In the log are all of the bytes required to apply a transaction to disk. In systems, such as PostgreSQL, that use this method, the same log is shipped directly to the followers for application to disk.

Pros:

- Very fast as the parsing and execution of the statement has already occurred. All that is left is to apply the changes to disk.

- Not at risk of impacts from nondeterministic SQL.

Cons:

- Can consume significant bandwidth in high-write environments.
- Not very portable because the format is closely tied to the database storage engine. This can make it challenging to perform rolling upgrades that allow for minimization of downtime.
- Not very auditable.

WALs will often use the same logs built for durability and just bolt on a log shipping process for replication. This is what gives us the efficiency of this format, but also its lack of portability and flexibility.

Row-based replication.   In row-based replication (also called logical), writes are written to replication logs on the leader as events indicating how individual table rows are changed. Columns with new data are indicated, columns with updated information show before/after images, and deletes of rows are indicated as well. Replicas use this data to directly modify the row rather than needing to execute the original statement.

Pros:

- Not at risk of impacts from nondeterministic SQL.
- A compromise on speed between the two previous algorithms. Logical translation to physical is still required, but entire statements do not need to run.
- A compromise on portability between the two pervious algorithms. Not very human readable but can be used for integrations and inspection.

Cons:

- Can consume significant bandwidth in high-write environments.
- Not very auditable.

This method has also been called *change data capture* (CDC). It exists in SQL Server and MySQL and is also used in data warehouse environments.

Block-level replication.   So far, we have been speaking about replication methods using native database mechanisms. In contrast, block-device replication is an external approach to the problem. A predominant implementation of this is Distributed Replicated Block Device (DRBD) for Linux. DRBD functions a layer above block devices and propagates writes not only to the local block device, but also to the replicated block device on another node.

Block-level replication is synchronous and eliminates significant overhead in the replicated write. However, you cannot have a running database instance on the secondary node. So, when a failover occurs, a database instance must be started. If the former master failed without a clean database shutdown, this instance will need to perform recovery just as if the instance had been restarted on the same node.

So, what we have with block-level replication is synchronous replication with very low latencies, but we lose the ability to use the replicas for scalability or workload distribution. Happily for us, using an external replication method, such as block-level replication, can be combined with native replication, such as statement-based or row-level replication. This can give a combination of zero-data-loss replication along with the flexibility of asynchronous replication.

Other methods. There are other methods for replication that are decoupled from the database logs. Extraction, Transform, and Load (ETL) jobs used to move data between services will often look for indicators of new or changed rows such as IDs or timestamps. With these indicators, they will pull out data for loading elsewhere.

Triggers that are on tables can also load a table with changes for an external process to listen on. These triggers can simply list out IDs for changes or give full change data capture information just like a row-based replication approach will.

When evaluating options for replication, you will need a combination of options depending on your source datastore, target datastore, and the infrastructure that exists between the two datastores. We will discuss this more in the next section on replication uses.

Single-leader replication uses

At this point in datastore maturity, replication is more often than not a requirement rather than an option. But, there are still a variety of reasons to implement replication that can affect architecture and configuration. In single-leader architectures, most of these can be enumerated as availability, scalability, locality, and portability.

Availability. It goes without saying that if a database leader fails, you want to have the fastest recovery option possible to which to point application traffic. Having a live database with a fully up-to-date copy of data is far preferable to a backup that must be recovered and then rolled forward to the failure point. This means that mean time to recover (MTTR) requirements and data-loss requirements must be kept at the forefront when making choices about replication. Synchronous and semi-synchronous replication gives the best options for no data loss with a low MTTR, but they do affect latency. Finding the elusive trifecta of low MTTR, low latency, and no data loss via replication alone is not possible without some external support, such as a messaging system that you can write to in addition to the datastore to allow for recovery of data that might be lost in a leader failover in an asynchronously replicated environment.

Scalability. A single leader creates a boundary on write I/O, but the followers allow for reads of data to scale based on the number of reads provided. For read-intensive applications that experience a relatively small amount of writes, multiple replicas do create an opportunity for creating more capacity in the cluster. This capacity is bounded, as replication overhead does not allow for linear scalability. Still, this does create an opportunity for increasing runway. To support scalability, the data on replicas must be recent enough to support business requirements. For some organizations, the replication delay inherent in asynchronously replicated systems is acceptable. However, for other requirements, synchronous replication is absolutely required, regardless of the impact to write latency.

Locality. Replication is also a way to keep datasets in various locations that are closer to consumers to minimize latency. If you have customers across countries or even on different coasts, the impact of long-distance queries can be significant. Large datasets are not very portable in their entirety, but incremental application of changes keeps those datasets up to date. As we mentioned previously, long-distance replication over bandwidth-starved networks often requires statement-based replication if compression is not enough to manage row-based or WAL entries. Modern networks and compression often alleviate this. Also, semi-synchronous or synchronous algorithms are generally not feasible with long-distance latencies, leading to the choice of asynchronous replication.

Portability. There are a number of opportunities in other datastores for the data residing in your leader. You can use replication logs to push into data warehouses as events for consumers in a data pipeline or for transformation into other datastores with more appropriate query and indexing patterns. Utilizing the same replication streams as replicas that are in place for availability and scale ensures that the datasets streaming from the leader are the same. That being said, more custom solutions such as query-based ETL and trigger-based approaches provide filtering of the appropriate subsets of data rather than the entire transaction stream coming out of the replication logs. These jobs also often have significant leeway in the freshness requirements of data, which allows for choices that have less of an impact on latency than other approaches.

Based on these needs, you and your engineering teams should be able to select one or more choices for replication. Regardless of which choices you make, there are a number of challenges that can come up in these replicated environments.

Single leader replication challenges

There a number of opportunities for challenges in any replicated environment. Even though single-leader is the simplest of replicated environments, that does not by any means indicate simplicity or ease. In this section, we walk through the most common of these challenges.

Building replicas.   With large datasets, the portability of your data can be reduced significantly. We reviewed this in (Chapter 7). As the dataset increases, the MTTR also increases, which can lead to a need for a larger number of replicas or a new backup strategy that can keep the MTTR within acceptable levels. Other options include reducing the dataset size in one group of server by breaking out one dataset into multiple smaller datasets. This is also called *sharding*. We discuss this further in Chapter 12.

Keeping replicas synchronized.   Building a replica is only the first step in a replicated environment. While using asynchronous replication, keeping that replica caught up proves to be its own challenge in environments characterized by frequent or large changes to the dataset. As we discussed in "Replication log formats" on page 191, changes must be logged, logs must be shipped, and changes must be applied.

Relational databases, by design, typically translate writes to a linearized series of transactions that must be followed strictly to ensure dataset consistency between replicas and leaders. This generally translates into the need for serialized processes applying one change at a time on the replicas. These serialized apply processes on replicas often are unable to catch up or stay caught up with the leader for a number of reasons, including the following:

- Lack of concurrency and parallelism as compared to the leader. I/O resources are often wasted on the replicas.

- Blocks to be read in transactions are not in memory on replicas if read traffic is not common.

- When distributing writes to leaders and reads to replicas, read traffic concurrency can affect write latency on replicas.

Regardless of the reason, the end result is often called *replica lag*. In some environments, replica lag might be an infrequent and ephemeral problem that resolves itself frequently, and within SLOs. In other environments, these issues become pervasive and can lead to replicas being unusable for their original purposes. If this occurs, there is an indication that the workload for your datastore has grown too large and must be redistributed via one or more techniques. We discuss these techniques in more detail in Chapter 12. In brief, they are as follows:

Short Term
> Increase capacity on the cluster so that the current workload fits within the clusters capacity.

Medium Term
> Break out functions of the database into their own clusters to guaranty workload bounds fit within the cluster capacity. Also known as *functional partitioning or sharding*.

Long Term

Break out your dataset into multiple clusters, allowing you to maintain workload bounds so that they fit within the cluster's capacity. Also known as *dataset partitioning or sharding.*

Long Term

Choose a database management system whose storage, consistency, and durability requirements make more sense for your workload and SLOs and that will not have the same scaling problems.

As you can see in the choices described, none of these will work for continued growth. In other words, they do not scale linearly with workload. Some, like capacity increases of functional partitioning, have shorter runways than others, like dataset partitioning. But even dataset partitioning will eventually find limits in how far it can be solved. This means that other things must be evaluated to ensure that the bounds never increase to the point of diminishing returns that render the solution obsolete.

If you are experiencing replication lag and must mitigate impacts while a longer-term solution is put in place, there are some short-term tactics that can be employed. These include:

- Preloading active replica datasets into memory to reduce disk IO.
- Relaxing durability on the replicas to reduce write latency.
- Parallelizing replication based on schemas if there are no transactions that cross schemas.

These are all short term tactics that can allow for breathing room, but they all also have tradeoffs in terms of fragility, high maintenance costs, and potential data issues so they must be scrutinized very carefully and only in great need.

Single leader failovers. One of the greatest values of replication is the existence of other datasets that are caught up and can be used as leaders in the case of a failure or because of the need to move traffic off of the original leader. This is not a trivial operation, however, and there are a number of steps that occur. In a planned failover, these steps include the following:

- Identification of the replica that you want to promote to the new leader.
- Depending on the topology, a preliminary partial reconfiguration of the cluster can be performed, to move all replicas to replicate from the candidate leader.
- If asynchronous replication is used, a pause in application traffic to allow the candidate leader to catch up.
- Reconfiguration of all application clients to point to the new replica.

In a clean, planned failover, this all can appear to be quite trivial if you've effectively scripted and automated certain steps. However, relying on these failovers during failure scenarios can create lots of opportunity for problems. An unplanned failover might look something like this:

1. Leader database instance becomes unresponsive.
2. A monitoring heartbeat process attempts to connect to the database leader.
3. After 30 seconds of hanging, the heartbeat triggers a failover algorithm.
4. The failover algorithm does the following:

    • Identifies the replica with the latest commit level as the promotion candidate
    • Reattaches the other replicas at the appropriate point in the log stream to the promotion candidate
    • Monitors until the cluster replicas are caught up
    • Reconfigures application configurations via file or a service and pushes
    • Instantiates rebuilding of a new replica

Within this, there are numerous inflection points. We discuss these further in Chapter 12.

Despite these challenges, replication remains one of the most commonly implemented features of databases and thus becomes a critical part of the database infrastructure. This means that it must be incorporated into the rest of your reliability infrastructure.

Single leader replication monitoring

Effective management of replication requires effective monitoring and operational visibility. There are a number of metrics that must be collected and presented to ensure that replicas are effective in supporting the organization's SLOs. Critical areas to monitor include the following:

• Replication lag
• Latency impacts to writes
• Replica availability
• Replication consistency
• Operational processes

This is touched upon somewhat in Chapter 4, but is worth mentioning again here.

Replication lag and latency.   To understand replication flows, we must understand the relative time it takes to perform replicated operations. In asynchronous environments, this means understanding the amount of time that has lapsed between an operation occurring on the master and the time when that write has been applied to the replica. This time can vary wildly from second to second, but the data is crucial. There are a number of ways that you can measure this.

Like any distributed system, these measurements rely at some level on the local machine time. Should system clocks or Network Time Protocol (NTP) drift apart from one another, the information can be skewed. There is simply no way to rely on local time on two machines and assume that they are synchronized. For most distributed databases relying on asynchronous replication, this is not an issue. Times are very close, and this will suffice. But, even in these situations, remembering the fact that time is a very relative concept on each node can assist in forensics on some troubling issues.

One common approach to measuring the time from insert on a leader to insert on a replica is to insert a heartbeat row of data and then to measure when that time appears on the replica. For example, if you insert data at 12:00:00 and you regularly poll the replica and see that it has not received that value, you can assume that replication is stalled. If you query at 12:01:00 and the data for 11:59:00 does exist, but 12:00:00 and beyond doesn't, you know replication is one second behind at 12:01:00. Eventually, this row will commit, and you can use the next row to measure how far beyond the database is currently.

In the case of semi- or fully synchronous replication, you will want to know the impact of these configurations on writes. This can and will be measured as part of your overall latency metrics, but you will also want to measure the time the network hops from the leader to the replica takes because this will be the cost of synchronous writes over the network.

The following are critical metrics that you must ensure are being gathered:

- Delay in time from leader to replica in asynchronous replication
- Network latency between leader and replicas
- Write latency impact in synchronous replication

These metrics are invaluable for any service. Proxy infrastructures can use replication lag information to validate which database replicas are caught up enough to take production read traffic. A proxy layer that can take nodes out of service not only assists in guaranteeing that stale reads do not occur, but also allows replicas that are behind to catch up without the burden of supporting read traffic. Of course this algorithm must take into account what happens if all replicas are delayed. Do you serve from the leader? Do you shed load at the frontend until enough replicas are caught up? Do you put the system in read-only mode? All of these are potentially effective options if planned for.

Additionally, engineers can use replica lag and latency information to troubleshoot data consistency issues, performance degradations, and other complaints that can result from replication delays.

Now, let's look at the next set of metrics: on availability and capacity.

Replication availability and capacity. If you are working with a datastore such as Cassandra that distributes data synchronously based on a replication factor, you also need to monitor and be aware of the number of copies that are available to satisfy a quorum read. For instance, suppose that we have a cluster with a replication factor of 3, which means that a write must be replicated to three nodes. Our application requires that 2/3 of the nodes with this data must be able to return results during a query. This means that if we have two failures, we will no longer be able to satisfy our applications queries. Monitoring replica availability proactively lets you know when you are in danger of failing this.

Similarly, even in environments without replication factor and quorum requirements, database clusters are still designed with an eye toward how many nodes must be available in order to satisfy SLOs. Monitoring how cluster size matches these expectations is critical.

Finally, it is important to recognize when replication has broken completely. Although monitoring replication lag with heartbeats will inform you that replication is falling behind, it will not alert you that something has occurred and the replication stream is broken. There are a number of reasons that replication might break:

- Network partitions
- Inability to execute Data Manipulation Language (DML) in statement-based replication, including:
  - Schema mismatch
  - Nondeterministic SQL causing dataset drift that violates a constraint
  - Writes that went accidentally to the replica causing dataset drift
- Permissions/security changes
- Storage space starvation on replica
- Corruption on replica

The following are examples of metrics to gather:

- Actual number of available copies of data versus expected number
- Replication breakage requiring repair of replicas

- Network metrics between the leaders and replicas
- Change logs for the database schemas and user/permissions
- Metrics on how much storage is being consumed by replication logs
- Database logs that provide more information about issues such as replication errors and corruption

With this information, automation can use replica availability metrics to deploy new replicas when you are underprovisioned. Operators can also more quickly identify the root cause of breakage to determine if they should repair or simply replace a replica or if there is a more systemic issue that must be addressed.

Replication consistency. As we discussed earlier, there are possible scenarios that can occur that will cause your datasets to be inconsistent between leader and replica. Sometimes, if this causes a replication event to fail during the apply phase, you will be alerted to this via replication breaking. What is even worse though, is silent corruption of data that you do not detect for quite a long time.

You will recall from Chapter 7 that we discussed the importance of a validation pipeline for maintaining consistency of datasets with business rules and constraints. You can utilize a similar pipeline to ensure that data is identical across replicas. Like data validation pipelines for consistency, this is often neither simple nor inexpensive in terms of resources. This means that you must be selective in determining which data objects are reviewed and how often.

Data that is append-only, such as SSTs or even insert-only tables in B-tree structures, is easier to manage because you can create checksums on a set of rows based on a primary key or date range and compare these checksums across replicas. As long as you let this run frequently enough that you don't fall behind, you can be relatively sure that this data is consistent.

For data that allows for mutations, this can prove more challenging. One approach is to run and store a database-level hashing function on the data after a transaction is completed in the application. When incorporated into the replication stream, a hash will create identical values in each replica if the data replicated appropriately. If it didn't, the hashes will be different. An asynchronous job that compares hashes on recent transactions can then alert if there is a difference.

These are just a few ways to monitor replication consistency. Creating patterns for your software engineers (SWEs) to use, as well as a classification system of data objects to help them determine if a table requires a place in a validation pipeline, will help to ensure that you don't use too many precious resources. Sampling or just doing recent time windows may also be effective depending on the type of data that you are storing.[3]

Operational processes.   Finally, it is important to monitor the time and resources required to perform operational processes critical to replication. Over time, as datasets and concurrency grow, these processes can grow more burdensome on a number of dimensions. If you exceed certain thresholds, you might be at risk of being able to maintain replication freshness or to keep an appropriate number of replicas online at any time to support traffic. Some of these metrics include:

- Dataset size
- Backup duration
- Replica recovery duration
- Network throughput used during backup and recovery
- Time to synchronize after recovery
- Impact to production nodes during backups

By sending events with appropriate metrics every time a backup, recovery, or synchronization occurs, you can create reports to evaluate and potentially predict when your dataset and concurrency will cause your operational processes to become unusable. You can also utilize some basic predictive evaluations on how durations or consumption of resources can change based on changes in dataset size or concurrency.

Outside of predictive automation, regular reviews and tests can help operations staff to evaluate when their operational processes are no longer scaling. This will allow you to either provision more capacity, to redesign systems or processes, or to rebalance dataset distributions to maintain effective times that support availability and latency SLOs.

Although there will inevitably be other metrics or indicators that you want to measure with respect to your data replication, these are a good working set to ensure that your replication is working effectively and is supporting the SLOs against which you designed it.

Single-leader replication is by far the most common implementation of replication due to its relative simplicity. Still, there are times when availability and locality needs are not met by this approach. By allowing writes into a database cluster from more than one leader, the effects of leader failovers can be reduced, and leaders can be put

---

3 Download the paper "Replication, Consistency, and Practicality: Are These Mutually Exclusive?" (*https://www.eng.tau.ac.il/~yash/sigmod98.ps*).

in different zones and regions to allow for better performance. Let's now review the approaches and challenges of this requirement.

Multi-Leader Replication

There are really two different approaches to breaking free from the single-leader paradigm of replication. The first method is what we can call multi-directional replication, or traditional multileader. In this approach, the concept of a leader role still exists, and leaders are designed to take and propagate writes to replicas as well as to the other leader. Typically, there will be two leaders distributed into different datacenters. The second approach is write-anywhere, meaning that any node in the database cluster can effectively take reads or writes at any time. Writes are then propagated to all other nodes.

Regardless of which solution is attempted here, the end result is more complex because you must add a layer of conflict resolution. When all writes are going to one leader you are working with a premise that there can be no chance of conflicting writes going to different nodes. But, if you allow writes to multiple nodes, there is a chance that conflicts can occur. This must be planned for appropriately, causing increased application complexity.

Multileader use cases

If the end result of multileader replication is complexity, what requirements could be worth that cost and risk? Let's look at them here.

Availability.   When a leader failover occurs in single-leader asynchronous replication, there is generally an impact to the application of anywhere between 30 seconds on the low end and 30 minutes or even one or more hours on the high end, depending on how the system is designed. This is due to the need for replication consistency checks, crash recovery, or any of a number of other steps.

In some cases, this disruption to service might simply be unacceptable, and there are not resources or ability to change the application to tolerate the failovers more transparently. In this case, the ability to load balance writes across nodes becomes potentially worth the inevitable complications.

Locality.   A business might need to run active sites in two different regions to ensure low latency for a global or distributed customer base. In a read-heavy application, you can still often do this via single-leader replication over a long-distance network. However, if the application is write intensive, the latency impact of sending writes across those long-distance networks might be too great. If this is the case, putting a leader in each datacenter and managing conflict resolution can prove to be the best approach.

Disaster recovery. Similar to locality and availability, there are times when an application is so critical that it must be separated across datacenters to ensure availability in the infrequent case of a failure at the datacenter layer. You can still accomplish this goal with single-leader replication but only if the secondary region is used for reads only, as discussed earlier, or if it is used only for redundancy. Few businesses can afford to spin up an entire datacenter without using it, however, so multileader replication is often chosen to allow both datacenters to actively take traffic and support customers.

With a greater percentage of infrastructures running in cloud services, or with global distribution requirements, it is almost an inevitability that you will need to evaluate multileader replication eventually for one of the aforementioned reasons. Often, the physical implementation of the multileader replication can be supported natively or with a third party piece of software. The challenge comes in managing the inevitable conflicts that will occur.

Conflict resolution in traditional multidirectional replication

Traditional multidirectional replication bears the closest resemblance to single leader. Essentially, it just pushes the writes both directions as you allow writes to go to more than one leader. It sounds good and meets all of the use cases we just discussed. But if you are using asynchronous replication, which is the only feasible approach in an environment incorporating multiple datacenters and slow network connections, there can and will be problems. During times of replication latency or partitioned networks, applications that rely on the stored state in the database will be using stale state. On repair of the replication lag or the network partition, the writes that have been built using different versions of state must be resolved. So how do you and your SWEs manage the problem of conflicting writes in a multileader replication architecture? Very carefully. As with most problems, we can work on this with a few approaches.

Eliminate conflicts. The path of least resistance is always avoidance. There are times when you can perform writes or direct traffic in such a way that there simply are no conflicts. Here are a few examples:

- Give each leader a subset of primary keys that can be generated only on that specific leader. This works well for insert/append-only applications. At its simplest, this might look like one leader writing odd number incrementing keys and the other leader writing even number ones.

- Affinity approaches in which a specific customer is always routed to a specific leader. You can do this by region, unique ID, or any number of ways.

- Use a secondary leader for failover purposes only, effectively writing to only one leader at a time but maintaining a multileader topology for ease of use.

- Shard at the application layer, putting full application stacks in each region to eliminate the need for active/active cross region replication.

Of course, just because you configure things this way doesn't mean it will always work. Configuration mistakes, load balancer mistakes, and human errors are all possible and can cause replication to break or data to be corrupted. Thus, you still need to be prepared for accidental conflicts even if they are rare. And as we've discussed before, the rarer the error, the more dangerous it can be.

Last write wins.   For the case in which you will not be able to avoid potential write conflicts, you need to decide how you want to manage them when they occur. One of the more common algorithms provided natively in datastores is Last Write Wins (LWW). In LWW, when two writes conflict, the write with the latest timestamp wins. This seems pretty straightforward, but there are a number of issues with timestamps.

Timestamps—Sweet Little Lies

Most server clocks use wall clock time, which relies on `gettimeof day()`. This data is provided by hardware and NTP. Time can flow backward instead of forward for many reasons, such as the following:

- Hardware issues
- Virtualization issues
- NTP not being enabled, or upstream servers might be wrong
- Leap seconds

Leap seconds are rather horrifying. POSIX days are defined as 86,400 seconds in length. Real days are not always 86,400 seconds, however. Leap seconds are scheduled to keep days in line, by skipping or double-counting seconds. This can cause tremendous problems, and Google spreads out the time over a day to keep time monotomic (*http://bit.ly/2zzUTO6*).

There are times when LWW is relatively safe. If you can perform immutable writes because you know the correct state of your data at the time of write, using LWW can work. But, if you are relying on state you've read in the transaction to perform a write, you are at significant risk of data loss in the case of a network partition.

Cassandra and Riak are examples of datastores with LWW implementations. In fact, in the Dynamo paper (*http://bit.ly/2zyOVwP*), LWW is one of the two options described for handling update conflicts.

Custom resolution options. Due to the constraints of basic algorithms that rely on timestamps, more custom options must often be taken into account. Many replicators will allow for custom code to be executed when a conflict is detected after a write. The logic required to automatically resolve write conflicts can be quite extensive, and even so, there can be opportunities for making mistakes.

Using optimistic replication, which allows for all mutations to be written and replicated, you can allow background processes, the application, or even users to determine what to do to resolve those conflicts. This can be as simple as choosing one version or another of the data object. Alternatively, you could do a full merge of the data.

Conflict-free replicated datatypes. Due to the complexity of logic in custom code for conflict resolution, many organizations might balk at the work and the risks. There is a class of data structures, however, that are built to effectively manage writes from multiple replicas that might have timestamp or network issues. These are called *conflict free, replicated datatypes* (CRDTs). CRDTs provide strong, eventual consistency as they are always able to be merged or resolved without conflicts. CRDTs are effectively implemented in Riak as of this writing and utilized in very large implementations of online chat and online betting.

As we can see here, conflict resolution in multi-leader environments is absolutely possible but not a simple problem. The complexity involved in distributed systems is very real and requires a significant amount of engineering time and effort. Additionally, mature implementations of these approaches might not be available in the datastores at which you and your organization work most effectively. So, be very careful before going down the rabbit hole of multileader replication.

Write-anywhere replication

There is an alternate paradigm to the traditional multidirectional replication. In a write-anywhere approach, there are no leaders. Any node can take reads or writes. Dynamo-based systems, such as Riak, Cassandra, and Voldemort are examples of this approach to replication. There are certain attributes of these systems that we will go over in more detail now:

- Eventual consistency
- Read and write quorums
- Sloppy quorums
- Anti entropy

Different systems will vary on their implementations of these, but together they form an approach to leaderless replication as long as your application can tolerate unordered writes. There are usually tunables that help modify the behavior of these systems to better match your needs, but the presence of unordered writes is an inevitability.

Eventual consistency. The phrase "eventual consistency," is often touted in relation to a class of datastores known as NoSQL. In distributed systems, server or network issues will fail. These systems are distributed to allow for continued availability but at a cost in data consistency. With a node down for minutes, hours, or even days, nodes easily diverge in terms of the data stored within them[4]

When systems come back up, they will resolve using the methods discussed in the previous section on conflict resolution, including the following:

- LWW via timestamps or vector clocks[5]
- Custom code
- Conflict free replicated datatypes

Although there is no guarantee that data is consistent across all nodes at any time, that data will eventually converge. When you build the datastores, you configure how many copies of the data must be written to provide quorum during failures.

That being said, eventual consistency still must be proven to work. There are plenty of opportunities for data loss, whether through misunderstanding of the conflict resolution techniques used and the results of their application or through bugs. Jepsen is a great test suite that shows how to effectively test data integrity in a distributed datastore. You can find some additional reading at the following:

- Jepsen's Distributed Systems Safety Research (*https://jepsen.io*)
- Martin Fowler's "Eventual Consistency" (*http://bit.ly/2zxs6JS*)
- Peter Bailis and Ali Ghodsi's "Eventual Consistency Today: Limitations, Extensions, and Beyond" (*http://queue.acm.org/detail.cfm?id=2462076*)

Read and write quorums. One key factor in write anywhere replication is an understanding of how many nodes must be available to deliver or accept data to maintain consistency. At the client or database levels, there is generally an ability to define quorum. Historically, a quorum is the minimum number of members of a assembly necessary to conduct the business of that group. In the case of distributed systems, this means the minimum number of readers or writers necessary to guarantee consistency of data.

---

4 Vogels, Werner, "Eventually Consistent" (*http://stanford.io/2zxRXBu*), *practice.*

5 Baldoni, Roberto and Raynal, Michel, "Fundamentals of Distributed Computing: A Practical Tour of Vector Clock Systems" (*http://bit.ly/2zylMll*), *Distributed Systems Online.*

For instance, in a cluster of three nodes, you might want to tolerate one node's failure. This means you require a quorum of two for reads and writes. When making decisions about quorums, there is an easy formula. N is the number of nodes in a cluster. R is the number of read nodes available, and W is the number of write nodes. If $R + W$ is greater than N, you have an effective quorum to guarantee at least one good read after a write.

In our example of three nodes, this means that you need at least two readers and two writers given that $2 + 2 > 3$. If you lose two nodes, you have only $1 + 1$, or 2. That is less than 3, and thus you don't have quorum, and the cluster should not return data on read. If on reading two nodes, the application receives two different results (either missing data on one node or divergent data), repair will be done using the defined conflict resolution methods. This is called a *read repair*.

There is a lot more to understanding quorums and all of the theory and practice of distributed systems. For more reading, we recommend the following:

- The Load, Capacity, and Availability of Quorum Systems (*http://bit.ly/2xjZNRZ*)
- *Quorum Systems: With Applications to Storage and Consensus*

Sloppy quorums.   There will be times when you have nodes up, but they do not have the data needed to meet quorum. Perhaps *N1*, *N2*, and *N3* are configured to take writes, and *N2* and *N3* are down, but *N1*, *N4*, and *N5* are available. At this point, the system should stop allowing writes for that data until a node can be reintroduced into the cluster and quorum is resumed. However, if it is more important to continue receiving writes, you can allow a sloppy quorum for writes. This means that another node can begin receiving writes to get quorum met. Once *N2* or *N3* are brought back into the cluster, the data can be propagated back to them via a process called a *hinted hand-off*.

Quorums are trade-offs between consistency and availability. It is absolutely crucial that you understand how your datastore actually implements quorums. You must understand when sloppy quorum is allowed and what quorums can lead to strong consistency. Documentation can be misleading, so testing the realities of the implementations is part of your job.

Anti-entropy.   Another tool in maintaining eventual consistency is anti-entropy. Between read repairs and hinted hand-offs, a Dynamo-based datastore can maintain eventual consistency quite effectively. However, if data is not read very often, inconsistencies can last for a very long time. This can put the application at risk for receiving stale data in the case of future failovers. Thus, there needs to be a mechanism for synchronizing data outside of these mechanisms. This process is called anti-entropy.

An example of anti-entropy is the Merkle tree, which you can find implemented in Riak, Cassandra, and Voldemort. The Merkle tree is a balanced tree of object hashes. By building hierarchical trees, the anti-entropy background process can rapidly identify different values between nodes and repair them. These hash trees are modified on write, and are regularly cleared and regenerated to minimize risk of missing inconsistent data.

Anti-entropy is critical for datastores that store a lot of cold, or infrequently accessed, data. It is a good complement to hinted hand-offs and read repair. Making sure that anti-entropy is in place for these datastores will help to provide as much consistency as possible in your distributed datastore.

Although there is a significant difference in implementation details of these systems, the recipes come down to the components discussed earlier. Assuming that your application can tolerate unordered writes and stale reads, the leaderless replication system can provide excellent fault tolerance and scale.

Having reviewed the three most common approaches to replicated datastores, you and your supported teams should have a solid high-level understanding of the approaches taken to distributing your data across multiple systems. This allows you to design systems that meet your organization's needs based on your team's experience and comfort zones, needs for availability, scale, performance, and data locality.

Wrapping Up

This chapter was a crash course in data storage. We've looked at storage from how we lay data down on disk to how we push it around clusters and datacenters. This is the foundation for database architecture, and armed with the knowledge, albeit at a high level, we will dive even more deeply into the attributes of datastores to help you and your teams choose the appropriate architectures for your organizations needs.

CHAPTER 11

Datastore Field Guide

Technically, a datastore is just that—storage of data and the associated software and structure to allow it to be stored, modified, and accessed. But we are specifically speaking of datastores that today's organizations would use to fulfill these purposes with nontrivial amounts of users accessing nontrival amounts of data at nontrivial levels of concurrency.

A field guide is traditionally carried by a reader looking to identify flora, fauna, or other objects in nature. Carried out into the field, it helps the user distinguish between a wide range of similar objects. Our goal in this chapter is to help you understand the identifying characteristics of various datastores. Armed with this information we hope that you can go into the world understanding the best use cases for these datastores—as well as appropriate care and feeding.

In this chapter, we begin by defining attributes and categories of a datastore that are pertinent to the developers of applications that write and consume data. After this, we dive into the categories that would be of greater interest to architects and operators of datastores. Although we believe anyone developing, designing, or operating datastores should be aware of all of the attributes of that datastore, we recognize that people often evaluate these things from their specific job roles. Our goal is not to be comprehensive here, because there are any number of datastores out there in use. Instead, we hope to familiarize you with a good sampling and to give you the tools to do further investigation based on your own needs and objectives.

Conceptual Attributes of a Datastore

There are numerous ways to categorize a datastore. How you do so really depends on your job and how you might interact with the datastore. *Do you build features in applications that query, store, and modify data? Do you query and analyze data for decision making? Do you design the systems on which the database will run? Do you administer, tune, or monitor the database?* Each role has a certain view of the database and the data within.

In the world of ORMs and serverless architectures exposing APIs, there has been a movement toward abstracting away the datastores from the consumers who use them. We don't agree with this. Understanding each attribute and the (implications thereof) of the datastore you (or someone else) are choosing is critical to doing your job well. There is no such thing as a free lunch, and each attractive feature will come with a trade-off or caveat. Ensuring that the teams working with these datastores are fully educated about this is a crucial function.

The Data Model

For most software engineers (SWEs), the data model is one of the most important categorizations. How the data is structured and how relationships are managed is crucial to those building applications on top of it. This also significantly affects how you manage database changes and migrations, as the different models often manage such changes very differently.

There are four prevalent permutations of data models in this section: relational, key–value, document, and navigational, or graph models. Each has its own uses, limitations, and quirks. The relational model has historically been the most prevalent. With significant time in production in a huge number of shops, it can be considered the most well understood, the most stable, and the least risky of the choices available.

The relational model

The relational model has been around since its initial proposal by E.F. Codd, who issued his paper "A Relational Model of Data for Large Shared Data Banks" (*https:// en.wikipedia.org/wiki/Edgar_F._Codd#cite_note-relationalmodel-4*) in 1970 after an internal IBM paper one year earlier. Because the purpose of this guide is not to give you a full background but rather to help you to understand systems you encounter today, we will focus on relational systems in modern organizations.

The basic premise of relational database models, is that data is represented as a series of relationships, based around unique keys that are the core identifiers for a piece of data. The relational model creates consistency of data across tables with constraints on relationships, cardinality, values, and the requirements for certain attributes to exist or not. The relational model is formalized and includes various levels of strictness, also known as *normalization*. The reality is that many of these theoretical requirements fall by the wayside as performance and concurrency come into play.[1]

Well-known relational databases include *Oracle, MySQL, PostgreSQL, DB2, SQL Server*, and *Sybase*. More alternative players in field include *Google Spanner, Amazon RedShift, NuoDB*, and *Firebird*. Many of these alternative systems are classifed as NewSQL. These are considered to be a subclass of relational database management systems that seek to break some of the barriers of concurrency and scale while maintaining consistency guarantees. This will be discussed further in this chapter.[2]

The relational model provides a very well-known approach to data retrieval. By supporting joins, one-to-many, and many-to-many relationships, developers have a high level of flexibility in how they define their data model. This can also lead to much more challenging approaches to schema evolution, as the addition, modification or removal of tables, relationships, and attributes all can require a large amount of coordination and moving parts in order to be accomplished. This can lead to expensive and risky changes, as discussed in Chapter 8.

Many software teams choose to operate an object relational management (ORM) layer to facilitate work by mapping the relational model to the object model defined at the software layer. Such ORMs can be great tools for developer velocity, but they can prove problematic to the database reliability engineer (DBRE) team in multiple ways.

ORMs and You

ORMs have matured greatly over the past decade, and as a DBRE, you don't need to be as leery of them as you used to be. Still, there are some gotchas that you will need to consider.

- ORMs tie reads and writes to tables. This makes any number of optimizations for one part of the workload more challenging because it affects the entire workload.
- ORMs can hold transactions much longer than necessary, causing significant impact to finite resources because snapshots are maintained excessively.
- ORMs can create a huge number of unnecessary queries.
- ORMs can create convoluted and poorly performing queries.

---

1 Codd, E.F., "The relational model for database management: version 2" (*http://dl.acm.org/citation.cfm?id=77708*), ACM Digital Library.

2 Ibid.

Beyond these obvious issues, one of the greater challenges is that the ORM abstracts the database away, which eliminates the collaboration needed to scale an organization past the physical number of database administrators (DBAs) who work for them. The ORM allows constraints to be ignored, logic to be obfuscated, and creates barriers for DBREs to understand the application's interactions with the datastores.[3]

All of this leads many software engineers and architects to think of relational systems as unflexible and an impedance to developer velocity. This is far from accurate, however, and later in this chapter we present a more accurate list of pros and cons and bust some of the myths prevalent in many such lists.

The key–value model

A key–value model stores data as a dictionary or hash. A dictionary is analogous to a table and contains any number of objects. Each object can store any number of attributes or fields within it. Like a relational database, these records are uniquely identified with a key. Unlike relational databases, there is no way to create mappings between objects based on those keys.

The key–value datastore sees an object as a blob of data. It isn't inherently aware of the data it holds, and thus each object can have different fields, nested objects, and an infinite amount of variety. This variety comes at a cost, including the potential for inconsistency because rules are not enforced at the common storage layer. Similarly, efficiencies in datatypes and indexing are unavailable. On the other hand, a lot of the overhead inherent to managing various datatypes, constraints, and relationships are gone. If the application doesn't need this, efficiencies can be realized.

Examples of key–value stores can be quite varied. One example is Dynamo. In 2007, Amazon published the Dynamo paper as a set of techniques to build a highly available, distributed datastore. As soon as we've gone over all of the attributes, we will discuss Dynamo in more detail. Dynamo-based systems include *Aerospike* (*http://bit.ly/2zy49Ch*), *Cassandra* (*http://bit.ly/2zyAucm*), *Riak* (*http://bit.ly/2zxKUsJ*), and *Voldemort* (*http://stanford.io/2zxtrk3*). Other key–value implementations include *Redis, Oracle NoSQL Database*, and *Tokyo Cabinet*.

The document model

The document model is technically a subset of the key–value model. The difference with the document model is that the database maintains metadata about the structure of the document. This allows for datatype optimization, secondary indexing, and

---

3 Ireland, Christopher, et. al, "A Classification of Object-Relational Impedance Mismatch" (*http://bit.ly/2zymmQ3*), IEEE Xplore.

other optimizations. Document stores store all information about the object together, rather than across tables. This allows for all data to be retrieved from one call, rather than requiring joins, which, although declaratively easy, can consume significantly more resources. This also typically eliminates the need for an ORM layer.

On the other hand, this means that document stores inherently require denormalization if there are different views of the object required. This can cause bloat and create consistency issues. Additionally, external tools are required to enforce data governance, as the schema no longer exists as a self-documenting system.[4]

Data Governance

Data governance is the management of the availability, integrity, and security of the data that an organization saves and uses. Introduction of new data attributes is something that should be considered carefully and documented. The use of JSON for data storage allows new data attributes to be introduced too easily and even accidentally.

The navigational model

Navigational models began with hierarchical and network databases. Today, when referring to navigation models, we are almost always discussing the graph data model. A graph database uses nodes, edges, and properties to represent and store data and the connections between objects. The node holds the data about a specific object, the edge is the relationship to another object, and properties allow additional data about the node to be added. Because relationships are directly stored as part of the data, links can easily be followed. Often, an entire graph can be retrieved in one call.

Graph stores, like document stores, often map more directly to the structure of object-oriented applications. They also eliminate the need for joins and can prove to have more flexibility in terms of data model evolution. Of course, this works only for data that is ideal for graph-appropriate queries. Traditional queries can prove to be far less performant.[5]

Each of these models has its place in a certain subset of applications. We will summarize the options and trade-offs within. First, let's look at transactional support and implementation attributes.

---

4 Vera, Harley, et al., "Data Modeling for NoSQL Document-Oriented Databases" (*http://ceur-ws.org/Vol-1478/paper17.pdf*).

5 Stonebraker, Micheal and Held, Gerald, "Networks, Hierarchies and Relations in Data Base Management Systems" (*http://bit.ly/2zxrbcq*).

Transactions

How a datastore handles transactions is also a considerably important attribute to understand and consider. A transaction is effectively a logical unit of work within a database that can be considered to be indivisible. All of the operations in the transaction must be executed, or rolled back, to maintain consistency within the datastore. Being able to trust that all aspects of a transaction will be committed or rolled back greatly simplifies error handling logic in database-driven applications. These guarantees of the transactional model allow developers to ignore certain aspects of failure and concurrency that would consume significant developer cycles and resources.

If you've worked predominantly with traditional relational datastores, you probably take the existence of transactions for granted. This is because almost all of these datastores are built on the ACID model, explained next, introduced by IBM in 1975. All reads and writes are considered to be transactions, and they utilize the underlying architecture of database concurrency to achieve this.

ACID

An ACID database provides a set of guarantees that, when put together, create the acronym ACID. These guarantees are *(A)tomicity, (C)onsistency, (I)solation,* and *(D)urability*. In 1983, Andreas Reuter and Theo Härder coined the acronym (*https:// en.wikipedia.org/wiki/ACID#cite_note-2*), building on work by Jim Gray (*https:// en.wikipedia.org/wiki/Jim_Gray_(computer_scientist)*), who enumerated Atomicity, Consistency, and Durability but left out Isolation. These four properties describe the major guarantees of the transaction paradigm, which has influenced many aspects of development in database systems.

It is of the utmost importance when working with a datastore to understand how it defines and implements these concepts because there can be a significant amount of ambiguity and diversity. With this in mind, it behooves us to consider each property and to understand the variations to be found in the wild.[6]

Atomicity

Atomicity refers to the guarantee that an entire transaction will be committed, or written, to the datastore or that the entire transaction will be rolled back. There is no such thing as a partial write or rollback in an atomic database. Atomicity, in this context, does not refer to atomic operations as you might find in software engineering. That term refers to the guarantee of isolation from concurrent processes seeing work *in progress* rather than only the before and after results.

---

6 Vieira, Marco, et al., "Timely ACID Transactions in DBMS" (*http://bit.ly/2zyR2Rh*).

There are many reasons that a transaction might fail and require rollback. The client process might terminate mid-transaction, or perhaps a network fault could terminate the connection. Similarly, database crashes, server faults, and numerous other operations could require a partially completed transaction to be rolled back.

PostgreSQL implements this by using `pg_log`. Transactions are written in `pg_log` and given a state of *in progress*, *committed*, or *aborted*. Should a client abandon or rollback a transaction, it will be marked as aborted. Backend processes will also periodically mark transactions as aborted if there are no backends mapped to it.

It is important to note that you can consider writes atomic only if the underlying disk page writes are atomic. There is significant disagreement on the atomicity of sector writes. Most modern disks will channel power to writing a sector even during a disk failure. But depending on the layers of abstraction between the physical drive and the actual writes being flushed to disk, there are still plenty of opportunities for data loss.

Consistency

The guarantee of consistency is a guarantee that any transaction will bring the database from one valid state to another. A transaction being written can assume to not be able to violate defined rules. Technically, consistency is defined at the application level rather than the database. Traditional databases do, however, give the developer tools to enforce this consistency. Those tools can be guaranteed effective and include constraints and triggers. Constraints can include foreign keys with cascading, not null, uniqueness constraints, datatypes and lengths, and even specific values being allowed in a specific field.

It is interesting and frustrating that consistency is used elsewhere in the realms of databases and software. The CAP theorem uses the term consistency also but in a very different way. Similarly, you will hear this term when discussing hashing and replication.

Isolation

The isolation guarantee is a promise that the concurrent execution of transactions results in the same state that would occur if you were to run those transactions serially and sequentially. ACID databases do this via a combination of techniques that can include write locks, read locks, and snapshots. Collectively this is called *concurrency control*. In practice, there are multiple types of concurrency control that can lead to different behaviors in the database. Stricter versions can significantly impact performance of concurrent transactions, whereas more relaxed ones might lead to better performance at the cost of less isolation. [7]

---

7 Adya, Atul et al., "Generalized Isolation Level Definitions" (*http://pmg.csail.mit.edu/papers/icde00.pdf*).

The ANSI/ISO SQL standard defines four possible levels of transaction isolation. Each level would potentially provide a different outcome for the same transaction. These levels are defined in terms of three potential occurrences that are permitted or not at each isolation level:

Dirty read
> With a dirty read, you can potentially read uncommitted, or dirty, data that is being written in another transaction from another client.

Nonrepeatable read
> With a nonrepeatable read, within the context of a transaction, if you perform the same read twice, you could potentially get different results based on other concurrent activities in the database.

Phantom read
> With a phantom read, within the context of a transaction, you perform the same read twice, and the data returned the second time is different from the first. This is different from a nonrepeatable read because with a phantom read, data you have already queried does not change, but more data is returned by your query than before.

To avoid these phenomena, there are four potential isolation levels that can be utilized:

Read Uncommitted
> This is the lowest isolation level. Here, dirty reads, dirty writes, and nonrepeatable and phantom reads are all allowed.

Read Committed
> In this isolation level, the goal is to avoid dirty reads and dirty writes. In other words, you should not be able to read, or overwrite, uncommitted data. Some databases will avoid dirty writes via write locks acquired on selected data. Write locks are held until the data is committed, and read locks are released after select. Dirty reads are usually implemented by keeping two copies of the data being written in the transaction, one of older committed data to be used for reads from other transactions and one for the data that has been written but not committed.
>
> In *read committed* isolation, you can still experience nonrepeatable reads however. If uncommitted data is read once and then read again after it has been committed, you will see different values *within the context of your own transaction*.

Repeatable Reads
> To achieve read committed isolation level and to avoid nonrepeatable reads, you must implement additional controls. If a database is using locks to manage concurrency control, a client would need to keep read and write locks until the end of the transaction. This would not maintain a range lock, though, so it would be

possible to get phantom reads. As you can imagine, this lock-based approach is heavy handed and can lead to significant performance impact on highly concurrent systems.

The other way to accomplish this is via snapshot isolation. In snapshot isolation, after a transaction is started, the client will see an image of the database based on the current time. Additional writes will not show in the snapshot, allowing for long-running queries to have consistent, repeatable reads. Snapshot isolation uses write locks but not read locks. The goal is to ensure that reads do not block writers, and vice versa. Since this requires more than just two copies, it is referred to as *multiversion concurrency control* (MVCC).

In repeatable read snapshot isolation, write skew can still occur. In write skew, two writes can be allowed on the same column or columns in a row from two different writers who have read the columns they are updating. This results in rows that can have data from two transactions.

Serializable

This is the highest isolation level and is meant to avoid all of the aforementioned phenomena. Like in repeatable read, if locks are the focus of concurrency control, read and write locks are held for the duration of the transaction. There are additions, however, and the locking strategy is called 2-phase locking (2PL).

In 2PL, a lock can be shared or exclusive. Multiple readers can hold shared locks for reading. However, to get an exclusive lock for a write, all shared read locks must be released after a commit. Similarly, if a write is occurring, shared locks for reads cannot be acquired. In this mode, it can be quite common in high-concurrency environments for transactions to be stuck waiting for a lock. This is called a *deadlock*. Additionally, range-locks must also be acquired for queries using ranges in their WHERE clauses. Otherwise, phantom reads occur.

2PL can dramatically affect latency for transactions. When many transactions are waiting, system-wide latency can increase significantly. Thus, many systems do not truly implement serializability and stick to repeatable read.

The non-lock-based approach builds on snapshot isolation and is called *serial snapshot isolation* (SSI). This approach is an optimistic serialization, whereby the database waits until commit to see if any activities have occurred to cause a serializability issue, most often a write collision. This can significantly reduce latency in systems for which concurrency violations are few. However, if these are regular things, the constant rollback and retries can be quite significant.

Because each isolation level is stronger than those below in that no higher isolation level allows an action forbidden by a lower one, the standard permits a DBMS to run a transaction at an isolation level stronger than that requested (e.g., a "Read Committed" transaction may actually be performed at a "Repeatable Read" isolation level).

Variability in Isolation

As we mentioned, there are significant differences between datastores in their implementation of the ANSI isolation standards

- PostgreSQL: Has read committed, repeatable read, and serializable levels. Uses SSI for serializable.

- Oracle: Only has read-committed and serializable options. Serializable is closer to repeatable-read than actual serializable.

- MySQL w/InnoDB: Has read committed, repeatable read, and serializable levels. Uses 2PL for serializable but does not detect lost updates.[8]

We have only scratched the surface of isolation, isolation anomalies, and isolation implementations. We have a few delightful recommended reads for you for further dives at the end of the chapter.

Durability

The durability guarantee promises us that as soon as a transaction has been committed, it remains committed. Whether there is a power loss, database crash, hardware fault, or any other issue, the transaction stays durable. Obviously, the database cannot promise that the underlying hardware will support this durability. As discussed in Chapter 5, there are numerous opportunities for the database to believe it has synchronized to disk, when the reality is very different.

Durability is linked closely to atomicity, as durability is required for atomicity. Many databases implement a *write-ahead log* (WAL) to capture all writes before they are pushed to disk. This log is used to undo a transaction as well as to reapply it. If there is a failure, upon restarting, the database can check this log against the system to determine whether the transaction must be undone, completed, or ignored.

Much like isolation levels, there are times when durability can and should be relaxed to accommodate performance. For true durability, flush to disk must occur on every commit. This can become prohibitively expensive and is not required for all transactions and writes. For instance, in MySQL, you can tune the Innodb log flush to per-

---

8 See the post "If Eventual Consistency Seems Hard, Wait Till You Try MVCC" (*http://bit.ly/2zyNy1m*) on Baron Schwartz's blog.

form periodically rather than after each commit. Similarly, you can do this for replication logs.[9]

Even though we have stayed fairly high-level here, it should be apparent just how much detail is hidden and taken for granted in systems that support transactions. As a DBRE in an organization, it is critical for you to ensure familiarity with the implementation not only for yourself, but also for the development organization. Often the details of these implementations are not readily apparent from documentation, and further tests via such tools as Jepsen (*https://github.com/jepsen-io/jepsen*) and Hermitage (*https://github.com/ept/hermitage*) can assist you in this discovery process.

Similarly, this knowledge can help you in choosing appropriate configurations when there are options to relax durability or use weaker isolation. Alternatively, knowing when database defaults do not meet your applications needs can be just as important.

BASE

As engineers have looked to alternatives to traditional relational systems, the term *BASE* has begun to be used as a foil to ACID. BASE stands for *basically available, soft state,* and *eventual consistency.* This focuses on nontransactional systems that are distributed and might have fairly nontraditional replication and synchronization capabilities. Unlike ACID systems, there might not ever be a clear state while the system is up and taking traffic. Similarly, without concurrency control needs for transactions, write throughput and concurrency can be dramatically increased at the expense of atomicity, isolation, and consistency.[10]

Having looked at the data models and transactional models available to datastores, we've covered the conceptual attributes most relevant to developers. Still, there are numerous other attributes that must be considered when evaluating not only database choice but also the entire operational ecosystem and infrastructure around those databases (Table 11-1).

Table 11-1. Datastore conceptual attribute summary

Attribute	MySQL	Cassandra	MongoDB	Neo4J
Data model	Relational	Key–Value	Document	Navigational
Model maturity	Mature	2008	2007	2010
Object relationships	Foreign keys	None	DBRefs	Core to model
Atomicity	Supported	Partition level	Document level	Object level

---

9 Sears, Russell, and Brewer, Eric, "Segment-Based Recovery: Write-ahead loggin revisited" (*http://www.vldb.org/pvldb/2/vldb09-583.pdf*).

10 Roe, Charles, "The Question of Database Transaction Processing: An ACID, Base, NoSQL Primer" (*http://bit.ly/2zw5Obr*).

Attribute	MySQL	Cassandra	MongoDB	Neo4J
Consistency (node)	Supported	Unsupported	Unsupported	Strong consistency
Consistency (cluster)	Replication based	Eventual (tunable)	Eventual	XA transaction support
Isolation	MVCC	Serializable option	Read-uncommitted	Read committed
Durability	For DML, not DDL	Supported, tunable	Supported, tunable	Supported, WAL

Now, a lot of this is overly simplified, and a trusty skepticism of the functionality of a feature, supported with testing the efficacy of those claims, will help to clarify things as you evaluate a datastore for your application. Even with these caveats, there are some definite differences that will help to determine the appropriate choice for your application. The next step is to evaluate the internal attributes of a datastore to get the full picture.

Internal Attributes of a Datastore

There are numerous ways to describe and categorize a datastore. The data model and transactional structures are attributes that directly affect application architecture and logic. They tend to thus be a big focus of developers who are looking for velocity and flexibility. The internal, architectural implementations of these databases tend to be black boxes or at least, only features on a glossy marketing brochure. Still, they are crucial to choosing the appropriate datastore for the long term.

Storage

We went over storage in detail in Chapter 10. Each datastore will have one or more options for laying data down on disk that are available to it. This often comes in the form of storage engines. The storage engine manages the reading and writing of data, locking, concurrency access to data, and any processes needed to manage data structures, such as B-tree indexes, log structured merge (LSM) trees, and bloom filters.

Some databases, like MySQL and MongoDB, offer multiple storage engine options. For example, in MongoDB, you can use MMap, WiredTiger in MMap, or LSM structures or RocksDB, which is based on LSM trees. Storage engines implementations will vary significantly, but their attributes can generally be broken down to the following:

- Write performance
- Read performance
- Durability of writes
- Storage size

Evaluating storage engines based on these attributes will help to determine which to choose for your datastore. There are often tradeoffs between read and write performance as well as durability. There are also features that can be implemented to increase the effective durability of the storage engine. Understanding these and of course, benchmarking and testing the veracity of claims of durability are of the utmost importance.

The Ubiquitous CAP Theorem Section

Often, when people discuss these attributes, they will refer to Eric Brewer's CAP theorem (*http://bit.ly/2zxuOiw*) (see Figure 11-1). The CAP theorem states that any networked shared-data system can have at most two of three properties or guarantees: (C)onsistency, (A)vailability, or network (P)artition tolerance. As with the terms in ACID, these terms are overly generalized. Each one is not truly either/or and is, in fact, a continuum. Many will refer to a system as CP or AP, meaning that they are designed to encompass two specific properties while trading-off another. Yet, if you dive into those systems, you will find their implementations of each specific attribute to be incomplete, having only achieved a portion of Availability or Consistency.[11]

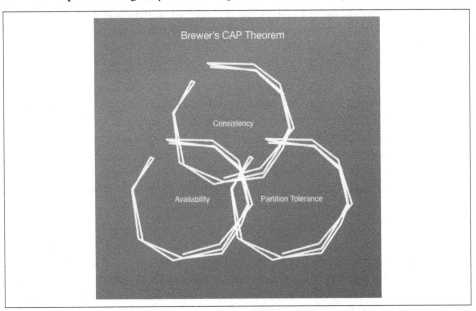

Figure 11-1. Brewer's CAP theorem: Consistency, Availability, and Partition tolerance

CAP is meant to help designers understand the trade-offs between consistency or availability. Network partitions in distributed systems are an inevitability. Networks are inherently unreliable. In the case of such, the node(s) on one side of a partition will inevitably lose consistency if they allow state to be updated. If consistency is pre-

---

11 See Martin Kleppmann's article "Please stop calling databases CP or AP" (*http://bit.ly/2zxUA6k*).

ferred, one side of the partition must become unavailable. Let's look at each term more carefully to understand what those attributes can potentially encompass.

Consistency

Recall that we discussed consistency in the section on transactions. It is the C in ACID. Annoyingly, ACID consistency is not the same as CAP consistency. In ACID, consistency means that a transaction preserves all database rules and constraints. In CAP, consistency means *linearizability*. Linearizability guarantees that a set of operations on an object in a distributed database will occur in real-time order. Because operations can be reads and writes, this means that these operations must appear as they occur to the rest of the users in the system. Linearizability is a guarantee of sequential consistency within real time.[12]

ACID consistency, like CAP consistency, cannot be maintained across a network partition. This means that ACID-based transactional datastores can guarantee consistency only by sacrificing availability in the face of a network partition.[13] BASE systems were developed, amongst other reasons, to be able to tolerate network partitions without sacrificing availability.

Availability

The availability aspect of the CAP theorem refers to the ability to process requests. Normally, most distributed systems can provide consistency and availability. But, in the face of a network partition where a subset of nodes is split off from another subset of nodes, the decision must be made to remain available at the expense of consistency. Of course, no system can maintain 100% availability over time, reflecting what we said before regarding availability as a continuum rather than either/or.

Partition tolerance

A network partition is a temporary or permanent disruption in connectivity that ends up disrupting communication between two subsets of the network infrastructure. In effect, this often will create two smaller clusters. Each of these clusters can believe it is the last cluster standing, allowing writes to continue. This leads to two divergent datasets and is also referred to as a *split brain*.

The CAP theorem was published to help people understand the trade-offs between consistency and availability in distributed datastores. In practice, network partitions encompass a small amount of time in the life cycle of a datastore. Consistency and availability can and should be delivered together. When partitions do occur, however,

---

12 See Peter Bailis's article "Linearizability versus Serializability" (*http://bit.ly/2v08Ymd*).

13 See Eric Brewer's post "CAP Twelve Years Later: How the 'Rules' Have Changed" (*http://bit.ly/2psQjuC*).

the system must be able to detect, manage, and recover to restore consistency and availability.

It is worth noting that the CAP theorem does not account for latency or performance at all. Latency can be as crucial as availability, and bad latency can also be a potential cause of consistency issues. Long enough latency can pass a boundary that forces a system to enter into the failure state associated with network partitions. There is a trade-off with regard to latency that is often made more explicitly than those of Consistency and Availability. In fact, the other important reason that BASE systems and the NoSQL movement came about was because of the requirements for increased performance at scale.

Now that we have familiarized ourselves with the CAP theorem, let's discuss how that might influence our database taxonomy. We could go with the concept of CP versus AP, but we've already discussed the oversimplification of such an approach. Rather, let's look at how distributed systems maintains both consistency and availability.

Consistency Latency Trade-offs

In a distributed system, the system is said to be strongly consistent if all nodes see all transactions in the same order in which they were written. In other words, the system is linearizable. The CAP theorem specifically discusses how the distributed datastore favors consistency or availability in the event of a network partition. Consistency is required throughout the life cycle of the datastore, however, and cannot be looked at just through the CAP paradigm.[14]

Everyone would like a strongly consistent distributed datastore, but few people are actually willing to accept the impacts to latency and availability that come with this. So, tradeoffs are made. In this section, we evaluate the trade-offs that are made and how they affect overall consistency in the cluster. This allows us to clearly evaluate a datastore to see if it meets our needs.

When writing data to a node in a distributed datastore, the data must be replicated to meet availability guarantees. As reviewed earlier, we can replicate this data in a few different ways:

- Send writes to all nodes at once, synchronously.
- Send writes to one node, the role of primary. Replication occurs asynchronously, semi-synchronously, or synchronously.

---

14 See Daniel Abadi's cover feature, "Consistency Tradeoffs in Modern Distributed Database System Design" (*http://bit.ly/2zxYLiH*).

- Send writes to any node, which functions as primary for that transaction only. Replication occurs asynchronously, semi-synchronously, or synchronously.

When writing to any node in a cluster, there is the opportunity for consistency to be broken without some coordinator process, such as Paxos, that can order the writes effectively. This inherently adds more latency to the transaction. This is one way in which strong consistency is maintained while latency impacts are traded off. Inversely, if latency is more crucial than ordering, consistency could be sacrificed at this stage. This is the *ordering-latency* trade-off.

When sending writes to one node that must propagate to other nodes, there is the possibility that the primary node accepting writes is unavailable due to it being shut down/crashed or due to it having unacceptable amounts of load that can lead to time-outs. Retries or waits increase latency. However, you can configure load balancers or proxies to send writes to another node after a timeout. Writes going to another node can cause consistency issues, however, as conflicts can occur if the original transaction processed but did not provide confirmation. The amount of retries or increased time-out windows impact latency, and eventually availability, while maintaining consistency. This is the *primary timeout retry* trade-off.

When reading from a node, you can also experience time-outs or unavailability. Sending reads to other nodes in asynchronously replicated environments can lead to stale reads and thus consistency issues. Increasing time-outs and retries reduces the risk of inconsistent results but at the cost of increased latency. This is the *reader time-out retry* trade-off.

When writing to all nodes synchronously, whether via ordered processor or replication, you also are incurring additional latency due to the overhead of all transactions being shipped to other nodes. If these nodes are on a congested network or are communicating across networks, this latency can be very high. This is the *synchronous replication-latency* trade-off. A compromise for this trade-off is semi-synchronous replication. This reduces potential latency impacts by reducing the number of nodes and network connections that might affect the replication. Semi-synchronous is a compromise, however, because by increasing latency, you have increased risk of data loss, trading off availability. This is the *semi-synchronous availability-latency* trade-off.

Each of these shows opportunities for tuning a system toward greater consistency or reduced latency. These trade-offs are crucial for the times when the systems are behaving outside of a network partition and are servicing requests.

Availability

Similarly to consistency and its relationship to latency, we have availability. There is availability in the face of a network partition as in the CAP theorem. But, there is also daily availability in the face of node-level, multinode, or entire cluster failures. When discussing availability in distributed systems, we find it useful to refer to *yield* and *harvest* rather than simply availability. Yield (*http://mauricio.github.io/pwl-harvest-yield/#/20*) refers to the ability to get an answer to your question. Harvest refers to the completeness of the dataset. Rather than simply considering whether a system is up or down, you can evaluate which approach is best—reducing yield or reducing harvest in the face of failures.

The first question to ask yourself in a distributed system is whether it is acceptable to reduce the harvest to maintain the yield. For example, is it acceptable to deliver 75% of the data in a query if 25% of your node capacity is down? If you are delivering a large amount of search results, this might be acceptable. If so, this allows a greater tolerance for failure, which could mean reducing replication factors in your Cassandra ring. Similarly, if your harvest must stay close to 100%, you need to distribute more copies of your data. This means not just more replicas but more availability zones within which replicas should exist.

You can also see this in the decomposition of applications into their own sub-applications. Whether you see this in functional partitioning or microservices, the result is that one failure can be isolated from the rest of the system. This will often require programming work, as well, but it is an example of reducing harvest to maintain yield.

Understanding the storage mechanisms and the way your datastore implements the trade-offs of consistency, availability, and latency give you the "under the covers" understanding of the datastore that complements the conceptual attributes we've already covered. The engineers and architects who are responsible for the performance and functionality of the application are most concerned with the conceptual attributes. Operational and database engineers are often focused on making sure that the internal attributes (see Table 11-2) meet the Service Level Objectives (SLOs) that have been set forth for them by the business.

Table 11-2. Datastore internal attribute summary

Attribute	MySQL	Cassandra	MongoDB	Neo4J
Storage engines	Plugins, B-tree primarily	LSM only	Plugins, B-tree, or LSM	Native graph storage
Distributed consistency	Focused on consistency	Eventual, secondary to availability	Focused on consistency	Focused on consistency
Distributed availability	Secondary to consistency	Focused on availability	Secondary to consistency	Secondary to consistency
Latency	Tunable based on durability	Optimized for writes	Tunable for consistency	Optimized for reads

Wrapping Up

Hopefully this field guide has given you a good list of attributes, and the variety therein, for the wild datastore. This should be useful to you whether you are considering a new application, learning an existing one, or evaluating the request by a developer team for the newest cool datastore. Now that we have climbed the ladder from storage to datastore, it's time to move on to data architectures and pipelines.

CHAPTER 12

A Data Architecture Sampler

Now that we've gone over storage engines and individual datastores, let's broaden our view to look at how those datastores can fit within multisystem architectures. Rare is the architecture that only involves one datastore. The reality is that there will be multiple ways to save data, multiple consumers of that data, and multiple producers of data. In this chapter, we present you a delightful little sampler of architectural components that are often used to enable our datastores followed by a few data-driven architectures that are found in the wild and the problems they attempt to solve.

Although this will be no where close to comprehensive, it should give you an excellent overview of the ecosystem and what to look for. This chapter will help you understand the effective uses for these components as well as the ways in which they can affect your data services, both positively and negatively.

Architectural Components

Each of these components falls within the purview of the day-to-day duties of the database reliability engineer (DBRE). Gone are the days when we can ignore all of the components around the data ecosystem. Each of these components has a definitive impact on overall data service availability, data integrity, and consistency. There is no way to ignore them when designing services and operational processes.

Frontend Datastores

The frontend database is the bread and butter of much of what we have been discussing throughout this book. Users of your applications typically query, insert, and modify data in these datastores through the data access layer. Historically, many applications are designed to function as if these databases were always available. This means that anytime these frontend datastores are down or so busy that they are slow enough to affect customer experience, the applications become unusable.

Historically, these systems have been referred to as OnLine Transactional Processing (OLTP) systems. They were characterized by a lot of quick transactions, and thus they were designed for very fast queries, data integrity in high concurrency, and scale based on the number of transactions they can handle concurrently. All data is expected to be real time with all of the necessary details to support the services using them. Each user or transaction is seeking a small subset of the data. This means query patterns tend to focus on finding and accessing a small, specific dataset within a large set. Effective indexing, isolation, and concurrency are critical for this, which is why it tends to be fulfilled by relational systems.

A frontend datastore is also characterized by the fact that its data is primarily populated by the users themselves. There are also user-facing datastores that are predominantly for analytics, often historically referred to as OnLine Analytics Processing (OLAP). These are discussed in the downstream analytics section.

We have already discussed the various attributes that most of these datastores employ: storage structure, data model, ACID/BASE paradigms, and trade-offs between availability, consistency, and latency. Additionally, we must consider overall operability and how they integrate with the rest of the ecosystem. Typical attributes required include the following:

- Low-latency writes and queries
- High availability
- Low Mean Time to Recover (MTTR)
- Ability to scale with application traffic
- Easy integration with application and operational services

As you might imagine, this is a pretty steep bar for any architecture all by itself. These requirements can rarely be met without help from other components in the infrastructure, which we will review.

Data Access Layer

An application is often broken into presentation and business logic tiers. Within the business logic tier is what is known as the data access layer (DAL). This layer provides a simplified access to the persistent datastores used for the read and write components of the application. This often exhibits as a set of objects with attributes and methods that refer to stored procedures or queries. This abstraction hides datastore complexity from software engineers (SWEs).

An example of a DAL is the use of data access objects (DAO). DAOs provide interfaces to the database by mapping application calls to database. By keeping this persistence logic in it own place, SWEs can test data access discretely. Similarly, you can provide stubs instead of databases, and the application can still be tested. The common thought regarding this approach is that it requires a lot more coding in Java Database Connectivity (JDBC) or other equivalents. Still, by staying closer to the database, it gives you the ability to code effectively when performance must be achieved via specific methods. The other negative often given is that it requires the developer to have a greater understanding of the schema. We happen to think that this is a positive thing and that the more developers understand the schema, the better for everyone involved.

Another example of a DAL is the Object-Relational Mapper (ORM). As we've made clear, we don't like ORMs for any number of reasons. There are some benefits, however. The ORM can provide a lot of features, including caching and auditing. It is critical to understand what your SWE teams are using, and what flexibility or constraints are introduced in data access coding and optimization.

Database Proxies

The database proxy layer sits between the application servers and the frontend datastores. Some proxies sit on Layer 4 (L4) of the networking transport layer and use the information available at that layer to decide how to distribute requests from application servers to the database servers. This includes the source and destination IP addresses and ports in the packet header. L4 functionality allows you to distribute traffic according to a specific algorithm but cannot take other factors like load or replication lag into account.

Layer 4 and 7

When we discuss layers, we are discussing layers of the Open Systems Interconnection (OSI) model. This model defines the standard for networking.

A Layer 7 (L7) proxy operates at the highest level of the networking transport layer. This is also known as the application, or in this case, the HTTP layer. At L7, the proxy has access to significantly more data from the TCP packet. L7 proxies can understand the database protocol and protocol routing and can be significantly customized.

Some of this functionality can include the following:

- Health checking and redirection to healthy servers
- Splitting of reads and writes to send reads to replicas
- Query rewriting to optimize queries that cannot be tuned in code

- Caching query results and returning them
- Redirecting traffic to replicas that are not lagged
- Generate metrics on queries
- Perform firewall filtering on query types or hosts

All of this functionality does come at a cost, of course. The trade-off in this case is latency. So, deciding on an L4 proxy versus an L7 will depend on the needs of your team for functionality as well as latency. A proxy can help mitigate the effects of technical debt by fixing things at a different layer. But, this can also cause technical debt to be ignored for a longer amount of time, and it can make your application less portable toward other datastores as things evolve.

Availability

One major function of a proxy server is the ability to redirect traffic during the failure of a node. In the case of a node serving as a replica, a proxy can run a healthcheck and pull a node out of service. In the case of a primary or write failure, if there can be only one writer, the proxy can stop traffic to allow a safe failover to occur. Either way, the use of an effective proxy layer can dramatically reduce the MTTR of a failure. This assumes that you've set up your proxy layer to be tolerant. Otherwise, you've simply added a new failure point.

Data Integrity

If a proxy is simply directing traffic, there will be little impact to the data's integrity. There are some opportunities for improving and affecting this, however. In an asynchronous repliction environment, an L7 proxy can pull any replicas out of service that are lagging behind in replication. This reduces the chance of stale data being returned to an application.

On the other hand, if the proxy is caching data to reduce latency and increase capacity on the database nodes, there can be a chance for stale data to be returned from that cache if it is not effectively invalidated after writes. We will discuss this and other caching issues in the caching section.

Scalability

A good proxy layer can dramatically improve scale. We've already discussed the scaling patterns, which include distributing reads across multiple replicas. Without a proxy, you can perform rudimentary load distribution, but it is not load or lag aware, and thus not as useful. But, using a proxy to distribute reads is a very effective approach for workloads that are heavy on reads. This assumes that the business makes enough money to pay for all of those replicas and that effective automation is put in place to manage them.

Another area for which a proxy layer can improve scalability is by load shedding. Many database servers suffer from a large number of concurrent connections. A proxy layer can act as a connection queue, holding a large number of connections while only allowing a certain number of those to do work in the database. While this might seem counterintuitive because of the increase in latency from concurrency, constraining connections and work can allow greater throughput.

Latency

Latency is a crucial consideration when adding another tier to the transaction flow. An L4 proxy adds minimal latency, but L7 adds significantly more. On the other hand, there are ways in which that can be amortized with latency improvements. These improvements include caching regularly executed queries, avoiding overly loaded servers, and rewriting ineffective queries. The trade-offs will vary dramatically across applications, and it will be up to you, the architects and engineers, to make those decisions. As with most trade-offs, we recommend simplicity over rich features unless they are absolutely needed. Simplicity and lower latency can be incredibly valuable to your organization.

Now that we've looked at the data access and proxy layers—the layers that help get an application to the database—let's talk about the applications that function downstream from the database. These are the systems that consume, process, transform, and generally create value from those frontend datastores.

Event and Message Systems

Data does not exist in isolation. Because transactions occur in a primary datastore, there are any number of actions that must occur after a transaction is registered. In other words, these transactions function as events. Some examples of actions that might need to be taken after a transaction, include the following:

- Data must be put into downstream analytics and warehouses
- Orders must be fulfilled
- Fraud detection must review a transaction
- Data must be uploaded to caches or Content Delivery Networks (CDNs)
- Personalization options must be recalibrated and published

Those were just a few examples of the possible actions that can be triggered after a transaction. Event and message systems are built to consume data from the datastores and publish those events for the downstream processes to act on them. Messaging and event software enables communication sharing between applications via asynchronous messages. These systems produce messages based on what they detect in the datastore. Those messages are then consumed by other applications that are subscribed to them.

There are a diverse group of applications that perform this function. The most popular as of this writing is Apache Kafka, which functions as a distributed log. Kafka allows for significant horizontal scale at the producer, consumer, and topic level. Other systems include RabbitMQ, Amazon Kinesis, and ActiveMQ. At its simplest, this can be an Extract, Transform, and Load (ETL) job or jobs that are constantly or periodically polling for new data in the datastore.

Availability

An event system can positively affect the availability of a datastore. Specifically, by pushing the events and the processing of those events out of the datastore, we are eliminating one mode of activity from the datastore. This reduces resource utilization and concurrency, which could potentially affect availability of core services. It also means that event processing can occur even during peak activity periods because they do not need to worry about disturbing production.

Data integrity

One of the biggest risks when moving data across systems is the risk of data corruption and loss. In a distributed message bus with any number of data sources and consumers of that data, data validation is an incredible challenge. For data that cannot be lost, the consumer must write a copy of some sort or another back into the bus. An audit consumer can then read those messages and compare them to the original one. Just like the data validation pipeline we discussed in the recovery section, this is a lot of work in terms of coding and resources. But, it is absolutely necessary for data that you cannot afford to lose. Of course, this can be sampled for data that can tolerate some loss. If there is detected loss, there needs to be a way to notify downstream processes that they must reprocess a specific message. How that occurs will depend on the consumer.

Similarly, it is important to verify that the storage mechanism for events or messages is durable enough to maintain persistence for the life of the message. If there can be data loss, there is a data integrity issue. The inverse of this is duplication. If data can be duplicated, an event will be reprocessed. If you cannot guarantee that the processing is idempotent and thus can be rerun with the same results if the event is reprocessed, you might be better off using a datastore that can be indexed appropriately to manage duplicates.

Scalability

As just discussed in "Availability" on page 234, by pulling the events and their subsequent processing out of the frontend datastore, we are reducing the overall load on the database. This is workload partitioning, which we have discussed in scaling patterns as a step on the path to scale. By decoupling orthogonal workloads, we eliminate multimodal workload interference.

Latency

Pulling event processing out of the frontend datastores is an obvious win on reducing potential conflicts that can reduce frontend application latency. The time it takes to get the events from the frontend datastore to the event processing system is additional latency for the processing of those events, however. The asynchronous nature of this process means that applications must be built to tolerate a delay in processing.

So, now that we have reviewed how to get to the datastores and the glue to connect data between the frontend datastore and the downstream consumers, let's look at some of those downstream consumers.

Caches and Memory Stores

We have already discussed how incredibly slow disk access is in comparison to memory. This is why we strive to get all datasets of our datastores to fit in memory structures like buffer caches rather than reading them from disk. That being said, for many environments, the budget to keep a dataset in memory just does not exist. For data that that is too large for your datastore's cache, consideration of caching systems and in-memory datastores is worth merit.

Caching systems and in-memory datastores are fairly similar in terms of the basics. They function to store data on RAM rather than disk, providing rapid access for reads. If your data is infrequently changed and you can tolerate the ephemeral nature of in-memory storage, this can prove to be an excellent option. Many in-memory datastores will offer persistence by copying data to disk via background processes that run asynchronously from the transaction. But, that introduces a high risk of data being lost in a crash before it can be saved.

In-memory datastores often have additional features, such as advanced datatypes, replication, and failover. Newer in-memory stores are also optimized for in-memory access, which can prove faster than even a dataset in a relational system that fits fully in the database cache. Database caches still must do validation on the freshness of their stores and manage concurrency and ACID requirements. Thus, an in-memory datastore might prove the best fit for systems requiring the fastest latency.

There are three approaches to populating caches. The first approach is putting data in cache after it has been written to a persistent datastore like a relational database. The second approach is writing to cache and persistence at the same time in a double-write. This approach is fragile due to the opportunity for one of the two writes to fail. Expensive mechanisms for guarantees, including post-write validation or two-phase commit, are required to make this work. The final approach is writing to cache first and then letting that persist to disk asynchronously. This is also called a *write-through approach*. Let's discuss how each of these approaches can affect your database ecosystem.

Availability

Use of a cache can positively affect availability by allowing reads to continue even in the case of a datastore failure. For read-heavy applications, this can be very valuable. On the other hand, if a caching system provides improved capacity and/or latency, or if the caching systems fails, the persistence data behind it might prove to be inadequate for the traffic load sent back to it. Maintaining availability at the caching layer becomes just as critical as availability at the datastore, meaning that you have twice the complexity to manage.

Another major issue is that of the thundering herd. In a thundering herd, all of the cache servers have a very frequently accessed piece of data invalidated due to a write or due to a time-out. When this happens, a large number of servers then simultaneously send requests for reads to the persistence store so that they can refresh their cache. This can cause a concurrency backup that can overload the persistence datastore. When that happens it might prove impossible to serve the reads from the cache or the persistence tier.

You can manage thundering herds with multiple approaches. Ensuring that cache time-outs are offset from one another is a simple, if not very scalable approach. Adding a proxy cache layer that can limit direct access to the datastore is a more manageable approach. At this point, you have a persistence tier, a proxy cache tier, and a cache tier. As you can see, scaling can rapidly become quite complex.

Data integrity

Data integrity can be quite the sticky situation with caching systems. Due to the fact that your cached data is generally a somewhat static copy of potentially ever-changing data, you must make a trade-off between how frequently you allow for the refreshing of data and the inherent impact to your persistence store versus how much of a chance there is that you are showing stale data to anything querying the cache.

When putting data into cache after saving it, you must be prepared for the chance for stale data. This approach is best suited for relatively static data that rarely needs to be invalidated and recached. Examples would include lookup datasets such as geocodes, application metadata, and read-only content, such as news articles or user-generated content.

When putting data into persistence and cache at the same time, you are eliminating the opportunity for stale data. This does not eliminate the need for validation that the data is not stale, however. Directly after a write, and periodically thereafter, you must continue to run validation checks to ensure that you are providing the consumer with the correct data.

Finally, when writing data to your cache first, followed by a write to your persistence store, you must have a means of reconstructing the write in the event that your cache crashes before it can send the write forward to the persistence tier. Logging all writes and treating them as events that can trigger validation code is one approach to doing this. Of course, at this point, you are in many ways reproducing the complexity that many home-built datastores already provide. Thus, you must carefully consider whether the write through approach is worth the complexity required to validate and maintain integrity across datastores.

Scalability

One primary reason for using caches and in-memory databases is because you are scaling the read dimension of your workload. So, yes, by adding a caching tier you can effectively achieve greater degrees of scale at the cost of complexity in your environment. But, as we discussed in the availability section, you are now creating a dependency on this tier to successfully achieve your Service-Level Objectives (SLO). If your cache servers fail, or become invalidated or corrupted, you can no longer rely on your persistence store to maintain reads for your application.

Latency

Outside of scalability, the other reason to use a caching tier is to reduce latency for reads. This is a great use of cache or in-memory technology, but if your cache server fails, you no longer can directly observe what your persistence stores look like without the cache server in existence. It is worth scheduling and performing periodic tests with read traffic bypassing the cache in test environments to see how your persistence tier handles both write and read workloads simultaneously. If failing back to your persistence store is a valid contingency in production, you will want to test these failures in production as well as test.

Caching and in-memory datastores are tried-and-true components of many successful datadriven architectures. They play well with event-driven middleware and can truly level up your application's scalability and performance. That being said, it is an additional tier to manage in terms of operational expense, risk of failures, and risk of data integrity. This cannot be overlooked, which often happens because many cache systems are just so darned easy to implement. It is your job as the DBRE to ensure that your organization takes the availability and integrity responsibilities of this subsystem seriously.

Each of these components plays a vital role in the availability, scalability, and enhanced functionality of your datastores. But, each one of these increases architectural complexity, operational dependencies, and risk of data loss and data integrity issues. Those trade-offs are crucial when making architectural decisions. Now that we have looked at some of the individual components, let's look at some of the architectures used to push data through frontend production through the datastore and into any number of downstream services.

Data Architectures

The data architectures in this chapter are an example set of data-driven systems that are designed to accept, process, and deliver data. In each, we will discuss the basic principles, uses, and tradeoffs. Our goal in this is to give context to how the datastores and associated systems that we have been discussing throughout this book exist in the real world. It goes without saying that these are simply examples. Real-world application will always vary tremendously based on each organization's needs.

Lambda and Kappa

Lambda is a real-time big data architecture that has gained a certain level of ubiquitousness in many organizations. Kappa is a response pattern that seeks to introduce simplicity and take advantage of newer software. Let's go over the original architecture first and then discuss the permutation.

Lambda architecture

The Lambda architecture is designed to handle a significant volume of data that is processed rapidly to serve near-real-time requests, while also supporting long-running computation. Lambda consists of three layers: batch processing, real-time processing, and a query layer, as illustrated in Figure 12-1.

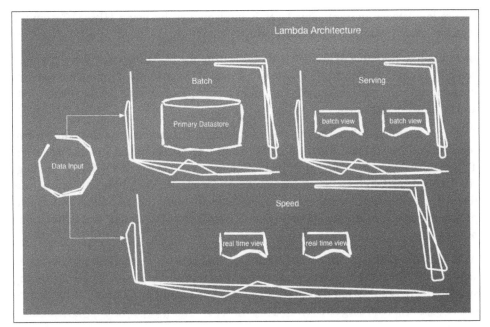

Figure 12-1. Lambda architecture

If data is written to a frontend datastore, you can use a distributed log such as Kafka to create a distributed and immutable log for the Lambda processing layers. Some data is written directly to log services rather than going through a datastore. The processing layers ingest this data.

Lambda has two processing layers, so it can support fast queries with a "good enough" rapid processing while also allowing for more comprehensive and accurate computations. The batch-processing layer is often done via Mapreduce queries, which have a latency that simply cannot be tolerated by real-time or near-real-time queries. A typical datastore for the batch layer is a distributed filesystem such as Apache Hadoop. Mapreduce then creates batch views from the master dataset.

The real-time processing layer processes the data streams as fast as they come in without requiring completeness or 100% accuracy. This is a trade-off on data quality for latency to present recent data to the application. This layer is the delta that fills in data that is lagging from the batch layer. After batch processing completes, the data from the real-time layer is replaced by the batch layer. This is usually accomplished with a streaming technology such as Apache Storm or Spark backed by a low-latency datastore such as Apache Cassandra.

Finally, we have the serving layer. The server layer is the layer that returns data to the application. It includes the batch views created from the batch layer and indexing to ensure low-latency queries. This layer is implemented by using HBase, Cassandra, Apache Druid, or another similar datastore.

In addition to the value of low-latency results from the real-time layer, there are other benefits to this architecture, not least of which is that the input data remains unchanged in the master dataset. This allows for reprocessing of the data when code and business rules change.

The most significant drawback to this architecture is that you need to maintain two separate code bases, one for the real time and one for the batch processing layers. This complexity comes with much higher maintenance costs and a risk of data integrity issues if the two code bases are not always synchronized. There are frameworks that have come about that can compile code to both the real-time and batch-processing layers. Additionally, there is the complexity of operating and maintaining both systems.

Another valid criticism of this architecture is that real-time processing has matured significantly since the Lambda architecture was introduced. With newer streaming systems, there is no reason that semantic guarantees cannot be as strong as batch processes without sacrificing latency.

Kappa architecture

The original concept of the Kappa architecture (Figure 12-2) was first described by Jay Kreps when he was at LinkedIn. In Lambda, you use a relational or NoSQL datastore to persist data. In a Kappa architecture, the datastore is an append-only immutable log such as Kafka. The real-time processing layer streams through a computational system and feeds into auxiliary stores for serving. Kappa architecture eliminates the batch processing system, with the expectation that the streaming system can handle all transformations and computations.

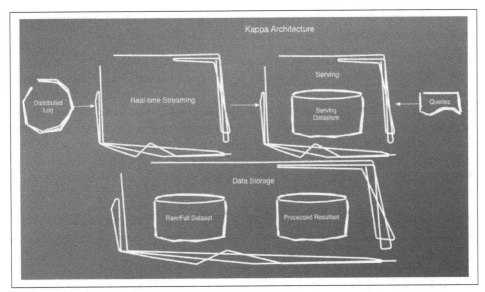

Figure 12-2. Kappa architecture

One of the biggest values to Kappa is the reduction in complexity and operational expense of Lambda by eliminating the batch processing layer. It also aims to reduce the pain of migrations and reorganizations. When you want to reprocess data, you can start a reprocessing, test it, and switch over to it.

Lambda and Kappa are examples of patterns that you can use to process and present large amounts of data in real time. Next, we look at some architectural patterns that are data driven and are built as alternatives to the traditional approach to applications that speak directly to their datastores.

Event Sourcing

Event Sourcing is an architectural pattern that completely changes how you retrieve and insert stored data. In this case, data storage's abstraction layer is taken lower, which creates flexibility in the creation and reconstruction of data views.

In the event-sourcing architectural pattern, changes to entities are saved as a sequence of state changes. When state changes, a new event is appended to the log. In a traditional datastore, changes are destructive, replacing the previous state with the current. In this model, with all mutations recorded, the application can reconstruct current state by replaying the events from the log. This datastore is called an *event store*.

This is more than just a new log for mutations. Event sourcing and distributed logs are a new data modeling pattern. Event sourcing complements traditional storage such as relational or key–value stores by exposing a lower level of data storage that functions as events rather than stateful values that can be overwritten.

The event store also functions not only as a distributed log of events and database of record, but also as a message system, as we reviewed earlier in the chapter. Downstream processes and workflows can subscribe to them. When a service saves an event in the event store, it is delivered to all interested subscribers. You can implement the event store in relational or NoSQL datastores or in a distributed log such as Kafka. There is even an event store called EventStore, an open source project that stores immutable, append-only records. The choice will depend a lot on the rate of change and the length of time in which all events must be stored prior to snapshotting and compaction.

Event sourcing offers a number of benefits. Unlike the world of destructive mutations, it is quite simple to audit the life cycle of an entity. It also makes debugging and testing much easier. With event stores, even if someone accidentally removes a table or a chunk of data, you have the distributed log to recreate tables wholesale or on the fly based on a specific entity that is missing. There are challenges, however. Not least of which is managing schema evolutions of the entities because the change can invalidate previous events that have been stored. External dependencies can also be challenging to recreate when replaying an event stream.

With the benefits of event sourcing, many shops might find use for implementing it even if their many applications still use the more traditional datastores instead of the event store. Over time, giving full historical access via API for auditing, reconstruction, and different transformations can provide significant benefits.

CQRS

There is a natural evolution from using an event store as an ancillary storage abstraction to using an event store as the core data storage layer. This is *command-query-responsibility segregation* (CQRS). The driver for CQRS is the idea that the same data can be represented for consumption using multiple models or views. This need for different models comes from the idea that different domains have different goals, and those goals require different contexts, languages, and ultimately views of the data.

You can accomplish this by using event sourcing. With a distributed log of event state changes, worker processes that subscribe to those events can build effective views to be consumed. CQRS can also enable some other very useful behaviors. Instead of just building new views, you can build views of that data in different datastores that are optimized for the query patterns that consume them. For instance, if the data is text that you want to search, putting it into a search store like ElasticSearch for one view can create an optimized view for the search application. You are also creating independent scaling patterns for each aggregate. By using read optimized data stores for queries and an append-only log that is optimized for writes, you are effectively using CQRS to distribute and optimize your workloads.

There is a great potential for unnecessary complexity in this architecture, however. It is entirely possible to segregate data that needs only one view or over-segregate to more views than are absolutely necessary. Focusing only on the data that actually requires the multimodel approach is important to keep complexity down.

Ensuring that writes or commands return enough data to effectively find the new version numbers of their models can go a long way in helping reduce complexity within the application as well. If commands return success/failure, errors, and a version number that can be used to get the resulting model version will help with this. You can even return data from the affected model as part of a command, which might not be exactly according to the theory of CQRS but can make everyone's life much easier.

You do not need to couple CQRS with event sourcing. Event sourcing as the core data storage mechanism is quite complicated. It is important to make sure that only the data that has functions as a series of state changes is represented in that manner. You can perform CQRS using views, database flags, and external logic or any number of other ways that are less complex than event sourcing itself.

This was just a sampling of data-driven architectures that you might find yourself working with or designing. The key in each is recognizing the life cycle of the data, and finding effective storage and transport to get that data to each component of the system. Data can be presented in any number of ways, and most of today's organizations will eventually need to be able to accomplish multiple presentation models while maintaining the integrity of the core dataset.

Wrapping Up

With this sampler, we hope you see some of the opportunities to create even more functionality, availability, scale, and performance within your datastores. There are plenty of opportunities to lock yourself into complex architectures that cost a tremendous amount to maintain. The worst case, of course, is the loss of data integrity, which should be a real concern throughout your career.

With this chapter, we are coming to the conclusion of our book. In the final chapter, we will bring this all back together with some guidance on how you can continue to develop your own career and the culture of database reliability within your organizations.

CHAPTER 13

Making the Case For DBRE

Throughout this book, we have attempted to show how the landscape of database engineering has shifted over the years. Within the context of that landscape, we have enumerated the operational and developmental disciplines that the database reliability engineer (DBRE) must be involved with and how to begin to do so. Finally, we attempted to lay out the current ecosystems of storage, replication, datastores, and architectures, or at least a reasonable subset, to broaden your minds and knowledge.

The reason we feel there is a real need for an emphasis on reliability in not just the job title of the DBRE but in everything they do is because the database is a place where risk and chaos simply has no place. A lot of what is now commonplace in our day-to-day work—virtualization, infrastructure as code, containers, serverless computing, and distributed systems—all came about from risk at areas of computing where risk could be tolerated. Now that they are ubiquitous, it is up to the stewards of one of the organization's most precious resources, the data, to find paths to bring databases into these paradigms.

A lot of this work is still aspirational. There is only so much risk that can be tolerated within any organization when data comes into play. Thus, how we introduce these concepts to the rest of the organization, or how we respond to others doing so, becomes an actual discipline and job function for us. It is not enough to have the vision and the intent, we must simultaneously find ways to introduce this vision in such a way to be successful.

In this chapter, we show you how to shepherd a culture of database reliability into your organizations, now and into the future. You will get some ideas on ways to become involved in a wide range of functions within the organization while representing and speaking up for database reliability engineering.

A Culture of Database Reliability

What does a culture of database reliability look like and how can you promote it? There are many items that people think of when they think of reliability culture that are not specific to the database world:

- Blameless post-mortems
- Automating away repetitive work
- Structured and rational decision making

This all makes sense, and everyone within an operations or site reliability engineer (SRE) organization should constantly be working toward this. But what should we, as DBREs or people who want to become DBREs, foster in our own environments? Here, we go over some approaches to become involved, to inject reliability culture, and to bring our expertise as DBREs to the rest of the organization.

Breaking-Down Barriers

The DBA who maintains isolation away from the other teams that interact with the datastore will simply not be successful. To be effective, we absolutely need to be active team members and partners at a much higher layer of abstraction than the one in which we have traditionally functioned. There is an inherent challenge in this because the database role is not one that is generally highly populated. Throughout the book, we have stressed that the database role simply cannot scale to the number of developers and operations engineers who will be working with them.

There are areas in which the DBRE can prove to be a highly effective member of cross-functional teams and work. Any time the DBRE becomes involved in cross-functional work, there should be a goal of contributing subject matter expertise, eliminating constraints on DBRE resources, or learning more about other functions to improve our own ability to function within the organization.

The architectural process

It goes without saying that those with deep database expertise should be involved more at all layers of the architectural process, particularly the design phase. The DBRE can provide incredibly valuable data on choosing the right datastore, preferably one that has already been significantly tested and proven in production. As we discussed in Chapters 7 and 11, the DBRE's job is to truly vet the datastores that might be brought into service in their organization.

In larger organizations that require self-service in order to build and deploy services, the DBRE has a particular power in determining which storage services are put into the self-service catalog. By working with the rest of the technical organization, the

DBRE can help support the mandate of using these approved services that have been tested thoroughly for edge cases, scale, reliability, and data integrity. Sometimes, this can also come with the caveat that all organizations can build and deploy services outside of the catalog, or at different tiers in the catalog, but that they must accept different Service-Level Agreements (SLAs) in order to do so. For example:

Tier 1 Storage
> Tested in core services in production. Use of self-service patterns means that Ops and DBRE can provide 15-minute Sev1 response SLAs for escalation, and will guarantee highest SLAs on availability, latency, throughput, and durability.

Tier 2 Storage
> Tested in production on non-critical services. Use of self-service patterns means that Ops and DBRE can provide 30-minute Sev1 response SLAs for escalation, and will guarantee reduced Service Level Objectives (SLOs) on availability, latency, throughput, and durability.

Tier 3 Storage
> Not tested in production. Escalation from Ops and DBRE is on best effort, and no guarantees on SLOs can be guaranteed. Must be fully supported by software engineering (SWE) teams.

If your organization doesn't support such self-service platforms, the DBRE must work harder on ensuring that every team is aware of the methods they use in evaluating datastores and architectures and the value that is provided by doing so. Although premature optimization is always a danger, one of the most important values provided by DBREs is helping to guarantee that architectural datastore decisions do not hamstring a service in the future as they hit scaling inflection points.

In many organizations, this begins as a mandatory checklist on a technical project that includes DB review in any project before it goes into production. However, it is easy for this to wait too far into the life of a project, simply beyond the point for you to change. This is where the art of politics and ambassadorship comes into play. Finding time to evaluate datastores and publish best practices, trade-offs and patterns for the most common or upcoming datastores in the organization is an important way of showing people the value of DBREs. It also is a great chance to work with SWEs and architects to build this data and publish it to build more mindshare. With this coming out regularly, when a new datastore that you have not evaluated comes into an architectural conversation, people will be more encouraged to sponsor an evaluation as part of their project and resources with you as a matrixed mentor and advisor. The key is getting people to see value and not constraint in using the DBRE.

There are metrics that you can use to measure how well DBREs and the organization are doing in this regards. Here are a few examples:

- How many architectural projects used DBREs or their approved templates? (post mortem)

- What storage was used and deployed? (post mortem)

- How many hours of DBRE work occurred during each phase or user story? (post mortem)

- Availability, throughput, and latency metrics grouped by storage tiers and engines to provide proof of reliability.

Database development

Much like architecture, DBREs being involved in database development early in the development cycle can be a force multiplier in the success of a project. We discussed a lot of this opportunity and value in Chapter 8. One of the biggest barriers to this is SWEs forgetting to discuss their designs with DBREs. Other times, SWEs might feel they do not need such guidance. One of the biggest wins in this struggle is to assist the SWE teams in seeing the value in the work that they do with DBREs.

Embedding DBREs, whether full-time or just at certain times in a project's life cycle. Pairing with software engineers is a great opportunity to help those SWEs see the value of DBRE collaboration. Even if the DBRE is not particularly strong with coding, her input on data modeling, database access, and use of features can prove invaluable, while also building relationships between organizations. Pairing SWEs with DBREs who are performing reviews, implementations, or oncall to support data-driven applications can similarly foster relationships, empathy, and cross-team knowledge that will accelerate development.

We also discussed the importance of providing best practices and patterns for the functions that each SWE performs in integration with the data layer. For instance, you can implement checklists for models, queries, or feature usage that require the SWE to indicate whether he used patterns or not. These checklists can raise flags on stories or features that might need review prior to pushing into production.

There are metrics that you can use to measure how well DBREs and the organization are doing in this regard. Here are some examples:

- Development pairing hours between SWEs and DBREs
- User stories that used DBRE
- Feature metrics, such as latency and durability, mapped to use of DBRE or not
- On-call shifts with an SRE paired

Production migrations

Everyone wants more error-free migrations. There is no doubt about that. But often the rate of deployment rapidly outstrips the time DBREs have to support those deployments. Backlogs end up being bundled into large, fragile changesets that can introduce dramatic risk, or migrations are done without significant DBRE review. As we discussed in Chapter 8, an effective way to manage this is to build process and tools to enable SWEs to make better choices about what can be implemented through normal deployment mechanisms, what DBREs should implement, and what should be reviewed by DBREs when ambiguity is present.

The easiest first step is to incrementally create a library of heuristics that can indicate whether the changes are safe or dangerous. Even though the bottleneck is not removed immediately, creating a mandate to build this library together with DBREs will begin to build traction over time. Having a review board periodically going through the most recent changes, the resulting heuristics and guidance and the success or failure of those changes can prove to be an effective watchdog on this process. You can do this as part of regular post-mortems of changes, both successful and unsuccessful ones.

Another way to continue to incrementally enable the SWE organization to be as autonomous as possible is to build a database of migration patterns that can be applied heuristically to upcoming changes. By doing this with SWEs over time as you pair together with changes, you can build a living document that the SWEs not only use, but also feel enabled to build upon themselves over time. Again, doing post-mortems and reviews to validate the success of these patterns is crucial.

You can build further upon this by providing guardrails to implementations that heuristics and migration patterns indicate can be performed by SWEs. These guardrails give confidence to everyone—SWEs, operations staff, DBREs, and leadership. The more you show success and build trust, the further this can go. By enabling the autonomy of SWEs, you can find that your relationships with those teams become much healthier as you prove to be more of value than of hindrance. Continuing to impart the depth of your expertise in database storage and access will continue to optimize their velocity and the relationship. You can do this individually via pairing or via more educational approaches, such as workshops, knowledge shares, and documents.

No amount of enablement will change the fact that there are some migrations that the DBRE must take on. Even at this phase, there are approaches that can be done to educate and enable others. Again, pairing with the engineers during the migration planning and execution can be an excellent approach. Pairing with operations engineers as well can be highly valuable, as the more people who can assist and eventually own complex production implementations, the better.

Even without significant automation, there are plenty of ways for you and the DBRE team to continue to drive more reliable, error-free change in a way that does not cause the development pipeline to stagnate. The addition of technology, tools, and code can take this even further after trust and repeatability of manual processes has been refined.

There are metrics that you can use to measure how well DBREs and the organization are doing in this regard. Here are a few examples:

- Migration pairing hours between SWEs/Ops staff and DBREs
- Count of migrations requiring DBREs versus all migrations
- Failure or success of migrations and impact

Infrastructure design and deployment

In the section on architecture, we discussed working with engineering to choose tested and trustworthy datastores. Similarly, you must work constantly with operations and infrastructure staff to ensure that they have everything necessary not only to host those datastores, but also to deploy and maintain them. In Chapter 5 we discussed the various parts of this function in detail, and in Chapter 6, we discussed the software and tools needed to manage those infrastructures at scale. But, we are still in the early stages of doing this for datastores, particularly distributed ones.

As with production implementations and giving software engineers more autonomy, so much of introducing this into the organization is about building trust through incremental steps. The first steps that can provide significant value to the DBRE team and the organization are using the same code repositories and versioning systems to manage your scripts, configuration files, and documentation. Then, you can work with the operations team to begin configuring and deploying empty datastores via configuration management and orchestration. This will still require you to finalize those datastores with the actual data, but it is an incremental step forward.

Throughout this, by pairing with operations, you can do testing for proper configurations, security testing, load testing, and even more advanced tests for data integrity and replication. The more you familiarize the entire team with how your databases work and how they break, the better. Availability and failure testing is also a critical test to bring in other organizations to work with.

Finally, you can begin to give primary on-calls to operations staff and even senior developers managing their own infrastructures. With you and your team mirroring and pairing with them, they can rapidly gain confidence in working with these infrastructures while minimizing risk. It is only when the team truly feels confident knowing the inside and out of maintaining all of this that you can begin to automate the riskier components, such as data loading, replication reworking, and primary node failovers.

There are metrics that you can use to measure how well DBREs and the organization are doing in this regard:

- Count of infrastructure components that are managed via configuration management
- Count of infrastructure components that are integrated into orchestration platforms
- Count of successful and failed provisioning
- Metrics on resource consumption—all subsystems used by the datastores
- On-all shifts managed by non-DBREs
- Incidents managed by non-DBREs and the Mean Time to Restore (MTTR)
- Escalation counts to DBREs

So much of the success of this work is in relationships, empathy, trust, and shared knowledge. We know that many DBAs are used to functioning in isolation, but with these steps, you and your team can bring database work into the sunshine. No longer should it be a murky, scary function that only the bravest or most foolish engineers are willing to tackle. The key to this is repetitive exposure, constant incremental trust building, and pairing with others.

Data-Driven Decision Making

Trust cannot be built without excellent data on the impacts of changes. The Deming Cycle of plan, do, check, and act requires the observability we reviewed in Chapter 4. Remembering to define clear appropriate metrics for determining success before gathering baselines with every change and then finally taking the time to analyze the results with a skeptical eye is key.

Using your knowledge of the organizations SLOs as discussed in Chapter 2 and Chapter 3 is crucial to understanding the changes you must make and the metrics and results you need to prove to the rest of the organization the potential value that will drive the change and the resulting value of the effort to take them there.

Hopefully you find yourself in an organization that has already seen the value of data-driven decision making and thus has already implemented the platform for observing, the processes for analyzing, and the discipline to consistently execute. Similarly, we hope that you are in an organization that has already defined clear, useful SLOs to drive your decision making. But, if not, you will need to begin with these practices to be able to drive deeper and more potentially far-reaching changes.

Data Integrity and Recoverability

We discussed the criticality of data integrity and the ability to recover from loss or corruption in Chapter 7. Too often organizations view this as the responsibility of the DBRE, but we know that that is an impossible task for the DBRE organization alone. Being the champion of a data integrity program will often fall upon the DBRE organization. Convincing the SWE organization of the importance of allocating resources for data validation pipelines and recovery APIs is a constant responsibility. Serendipitously, if you are breaking down the barriers between architecture, software development, and the lack of DBRE involvement in early phases of work, you will find yourself with the relationships and the trust to incrementally build the shared code and the knowledge required to implement an effective data integrity pipeline.

This is not an easy sell. Our experience with this is that most SWEs feel data integrity is the domain of the DBRE only. And constrained organizations will balk at the development of validation pipelines and recovery APIs. Thus, you will find yourself having to make the case while implementing "poor man's" solutions that can gather the data around data-integrity issues. Similarly, tracking the efforts taken for manual recovery of data can go a long way toward convincing leadership to commit resources for recovery APIs and validatoin pipelines.

As you can see, the successful evolution of database reliability requires incremental, and comprehensive organizational shifts. Choosing the areas that consume the most of your time, and that create the largest constraints on other organizations is a skill you would be smart to practice. Then, building incremental points of change to build trust and create improvements will build momentum. But this all takes time, trust, and a lot of experimentation regarding what works for your organization's risk levels, and what doesn't.

Wrapping Up

We'd like to thank you for taking the time to read through this book. Both of us are so passionate about evolving one of the most burdensome and byzantine of technical careers. Although a good portion of this book is aspirational, or still being proven in the wild, we believe that the DBRE movement is one that can drive so much value to data-driven services and organizations.

Our hope is that you are inspired to explore these shifts in your organization and that you are eager to learn more. We have tried to give further reading and exploration options throughout, as this framework is flexible. But, most important, we hope we've helped you see that there is opportunity to bring the time-honored role of DBA into the modern world and into the future. The role of DBA isn't going away, and whether you are new to this career or a tried-and-scarred veteran, we want you to have a long career ahead of you as you drive value to every organization you are a part of.

Index

A

abstraction and encapsulation, 142
acceptance testing and compliance, 109
access control, network and host access, 163
ACID transactions, 216
    atomicity, 216
    consistency, 217
    durability, 220
    isolation, 217-220
administrative connections to databases, 170
administrative traffic, 86
AES (Advanced Encryption Standard), 172, 173
affected users (security exploits), 162
agile methodology, 134
alerts, 60
Amazon machine images (AMIs), 104
Amazon Web Services (AWS), 93
Amazon's Relational Database Service (RDS), 95
analytics, user-facing datastores used for, 230
ANSI/ISO SQL standard, transaction isolation levels, 218
Ansible, 101
anti-entropy, 208
Apache Kafka, 234
APIs and web services, 142
AppDynamics, 57
append-only write schemas, 89
application errors, 119, 129, 131
    detection and recovery from, 123
application instrumentation, 66-68
    distributed tracing, 66
application layer instrumentation, 158

application performance management solutions, 66
application traffic, 86
application-level security, 175
architectural pipeline, adding to risk management process, 47
architecture
    architectural process, DBRE and, 246
    data architecture sampler, 229-243
        caches and memory stores, 235-238
        command-query-responsibility-segregation (CQRS), 242
        data access layer, 230
        database proxies, 231-233
        event and message systems, 233-235
        event sourcing, 241
        frontend datastores, 229
        lambda and kappa, 238
    domain-specific knowledge on, 135
    keeping simple, 55
asserts (database), monitoring, 79
asynchronous replication models, 191
atomicity, 216
    durability and, 220
attackers, categories of, 174
audits and compliance, 130, 155
    repudiation and, 161
authentication
    security vulnerabilities in authentication protocols, 168
    testing authentication layer for common flaws, 158
automation
    as an output of monitoring, 61

automated deployment, 151
database build, 140
elimination of toil through, 4
opportunities for, 99
availability, 16, 226
    availability metrics and customer experience, 14
    considerations for recovery, 115
    database proxies and, 232
    five 9's as shorthand for, 15
    impacts of caches and memory stores, 236
    impacts of event and message systems, 234
    impacts of SST merges and compaction, 186
    in CAP theorem, 224
    indicators, 20
        designing for downtime, 22
        resiliency versus robustness in availability, 21
    monitoring, 25, 64
    multi-leader replication and, 203
    replication, 200
    single-leader replication and, 194
    storage, 90
averages
    for latency, 18
    storing actual values instead of, 19

B

B-tree structures, 188
    attributes and benefits of, 184
    permutations of B-tree indexes, 188
    writes to, 184
backups, 7, 113-115
    damaging, 154
    data to use for testing restores, 118
    failures of, in datastores, 44
    full and incremental
        online, fast storage with, 128
        online, slow storage with, 129
    full and incremental logical backups, 127
    full and incremental physical backups, 129
    full physical backups, 126
    full, incremental, and differential backups, 115
    in data safety monitoring, 63
    incremental physical backups, 126
    issues in Database as a Service (DBaaS), 96
    online versus offline, 114
    physical versus logical, 114

replication and, 126
    size of, 117
baking, 103
BASE (basically available, soft state, and eventual consistency), 221
best practices and standards, 136
BigTable, 185
bitmap indexes, 188
blackbox monitoring, 57
blackbox testing
    and queueing theory, 57
block-level encryption systems, 178
blocks, 182
    aligned versus nonaligned block/stripe configurations, 182
    block-level replication, 193
bloom filters, 187
Bouncy Castle, 175
Brewer, Eric, 223
buffer overflows, 158, 166
build testing, 143
bus, SSDs and, 89
business continuity, 130
business data, confidential/sensitive, encryption of, 170
business intelligence (BI) systems, treating operational visibility systems as, 52

C

caches
    and memory stores, 235-238
    database, monitoring, 76
CAP theorem, 223-225
    availability, 224
    consistency, 224
    partition tolerance, 224
capacity, 61, 65, 72
    monitoring in cloud and virtualized systems, 71
    replication availability and, 200
    utilization and, 56
capacity planning
    DDL operations creating enough I/O to affect latency, 149
    need to add more nodes, 128
    USE data and, 68
cardinality of data, 78
    high cardinality, 188
Cassandra, 63, 74

connections, use of resources on operating system, 72
  full backups, 126
  last write wins, 205
  memory allocation, 83
  monitoring replication state, 76
  non-uniform memory access (NUMA) and, 86
  seed nodes, 110
  SSTables, 89
  THP defragmentation and, 84
  use of bloom filters, 187
  use of JVMs to manage memory, 77
cattle versus pets metaphor, 5
certificates, 172, 173
CFEngine, 101
change data capture (CDC), 193
change-sets
  Etsy's guardrails for application of, 9
  making sure all changes are safe as possible, 123
  versioning, 146
Chaos Monkey, 117
checkpointing, flushing, and compaction operations in databases, 75, 92
checksums on data
  checking replicas for replication drift, 76
  checksumming filesystems to detect bad data, 120
  using in testing restores, 118
Chef, 101
churn, 76
cipher suites, 171, 173
Circonus, 79
client-side throttling, 165
cloud computing, 93
  advantages for database infrastructure, 94
  data integrity and, 120
  monitoring in cloud and virtualized systems, 70
  public cloud providers offering DBaaS platforms, 95
clusters
  building new production clusters, 117
  cluster-wide scope for recovery, 121
  multiple cluster scope for recovery, 121
  rolling migrations in, 150
collaboration in release management, 137

command-query-responsibility-segregation (CQRS), 242
commits, redo, and journaling, monitoring, 75
commodity service components, 5
common vulnerabilities and exposures (CVEs), 156
communications encryption
  communication within the network, 172
  communications outside the network, 173
  evaluating needs of, 172
compliance and auditing standards, 155
component redeploys to eliminate configuration differences, 105
concurrency
  databases running within hypervisors, 94
  monitoring for database memory structures, 77
  monitoring locking and concurrency, 77
concurrency control, 217
  multiversion concurrency control (MVCC), 219
configuration management applications, 101
configurations
  building from configuration, 103
  configuration definition, 101
  maintaining, 104-105
    enforcement of configuration definitions, 105
    precautions against security vulnerabilities and exploits, 162
conflict resolution in multi-leader replication, 204
  conflict-free replicated datatypes, 206
  custom resolution options, 206
  eliminating conflicts, 204
conflict-free replicated datatypes (CRDTs), 206
connection layer
  memory usage limits, 84
  monitoring for datastores, 71-74
    errors, 73
    saturation, 72
    troubleshooting connection speeds for PostgreSQL, 73
    utilization, 71
connections
  basic encryption of, 173
  establishing secure data connections, 173
consistency
  eventual consistency, 76, 207

in CAP theorem, 224
in transactions, 217
replication consistency, 201
single-leader replication guarantee on, 190
trade-offs with latency, 225-226
Consul.io, 110
containers, 95
continuous delivery (CD), 138
continuous integration (CI), 138
establishing CI at the database level, prerequisites, 139
CI server and test framework, 141
database build automation, 140
database migrations and packaging, 140
test data, 140
version control system, 139
controls to mitigate or eliminate risks, 45
cost and efficiency, 16
cloud and virtualized systems, 70
indicators, 23
monitoring, 28
counters, metrics storage by, 59
critical data
audit data on, 158
monitoring distribution of, 78
culture of database reliability, 246-252
breaking down barriers, 246
architectural process, 246
database development, 248
infrastructure design and deployment, 250
production migrations, 249
data-driven decision making, 251
customer experience
availability metrics and, 15
monitoring anything that disrupts, 65
CVEs (common vulnerabilities and exposures), 156

D

damage potential, 161
data access layer, 230
data access objects (DAOs), 142, 231
data corruption
detection of, 122
repair of, 129, 131
resulting from OS and hardware errors, 119
example of silent corruption at Netflix, 120

data definition language (DDL)
applying the latest DDL scripts, 140
operations creating enough I/O to affect latency, 149
data encryption (see encryption of data)
data governance, 215
data in the database, encryption of, 174-177
application-level security, 175
database plug-in encryption, 175
query performance considerations, 176
transparent database encryption, 176
data in the filesystem, encryption of (see filesystems)
data in transit, encryption of, 171-174
basic connection encryption, 173
cipher suites, 171
communication within the network, 172
communications outside the network, 173
dynamically built database users, 174
establishing secure data connections, 173
securely stored secrets, 174
data integrity, 252
database proxies and, 232
impacts of caches and memory stores, 236
impacts of event and message systems, 234
issues with, in database deployment, 147
data loss, 14, 45, 122
detection of, 122
single-leader replication and, 194
data models, 212-215
document model, 214
domain-specific knowledge on, 136
key-value model, 214
navigational model, 215
relational model, 212
data structure storage (see storage)
data validation, 129, 131
key to eary detection of application errors, 123
using input validation to mitigate against SQL injection, 167
data-driven decision making, 251
database access and workloads, continual improvement of, 166
database administration (DBA), 6
database administrators (DBAs), isolated from other teams, 246
Database as a Service (DBaaS), 95-97
challenges of, 96

database reliability engineers and, 96
database clients, building your own, 157
database development, 248
database layer instrumentation, 159
database management systems (DBMSs), 82
database metadata scope for recovery, 121
database objects, 78
database proxies, 231-233
    availability, 232
    data integrity and, 232
    impacts on latency, 233
    improving scalability with, 232
database security as a function, 155-160
    education and collaboration, 155
    integration and testing, 157
    operational visibility, 158-160
    self-service approaches, 156
databases
    build automation, 140
    enumerating moving parts of, 62
    internal visibility, 74-78
        commits, redos, and journaling, 75
        locking and concurrency, 77
        memory structures, 76
        replication state, 75
        throughput and latency metrics, 74
    logs and, 189
    monitoring, 62, 71
        tying application monitoring to, 67
    monitoring database asserts and events, 79
    monitoring database queries, 79
    relational, 213
    sample availability monitors, 65
    transport layer, 87
datacenters
    datacenter scope for recovery, 121
    failures of, 120, 204
        early detection, 124
dataset scope (recovery), 121
datasets
    for database integration testing, 140
        full dataset testing, 144
    large, problems with, 196
    partitioning or sharding, 197
datastores, 62, 211-228
    (see also databases)
    choosing the right datastore, 2, 181
    common failure points in, 44
    conceptual attributes of, 212-222

BASE, 221
    data model, 212-215
    summary, 221
    transactions, 216-221
frontend, 229
instrumenting, 71
internal attributes of, 222-228
    availability, 226
    CAP theorem, 223-225
    consistency latency trade-offs, 225-226
    storage, 222
    summary, 227
monitoring connection layer, 71-74
treating as pets versus cattle, 5
datatypes, optimizations on, for databases, 79
days, 205
DBRE (database reliability engineering)
    DBREs and the DBaaS, 96
    guiding principles of, 2-6
        databases are not special snowflakes, 5
        eliminating barriers between software
            and operations, 5
        elimination of toil, 4
        protecting the data, 2
        self-service for scale, 3
    making the case for, 245-252
        culture of database reliability, 246-252
deadline scheduler (I/O), 83
deadlocks, 77, 219
debuggability, 9
decaying function, 26
decryption of data, 175
defaults, security dangers of, 163
degrading results, 165
delete operations
    on data stored in SSTs, 186
    soft deletes, 149
DELETE statement without a WHERE clause,
    119
denial of service (DoS) attacks, 154, 161
    impacts of DB-DoS attacks to mitigate, 164
    mitigation, 165
        continual improvement of database
            access and workloads, 166
        logging and monitoring, 166
        resource management and load shed-
            ding, 165
deployment, 146-151

component redeploys in configuration management, 105
impact analysis, 147
    data integrity issues, 147
    locking of objects, 147
    replication stalls, 147
    saturation of resources, 147
manual or automated, 151
migration patterns, 148-151
    high resource utilization operations, 149
    locking operations, 148
    migration testing, 150
    rollback testing, 150
    rolling migrations, 150
migrations and versioning, 146
design documents, 135
detection of potential data loss or corruption, 122
deterministic transactions, 192
development environments, 107
    testing infrastructure locally, 111
development practices, test friendly
    abstraction and encapsulation, 142
    being efficient, 142
device-level encryption (storage media), 179
DevOps cultures, 134
devops needs, 8
differential backups, 115
dirty reads, 218
disaster recovery, 75
    (see also recovery)
    using multi-leader replication for, 204
discoverability (security threats), 162
diskchecker.pl, 92
Distributed Replicated Block Device (DRBD) for Linux, 193
distributed tracing for applications, 66
distributions, visualizing, 60
Docker, 95
document model, 214
domain-specific knowledge, 135-137
    architecture, 135
    best practices and standards, 136
    data model, 136
    tools, 137
downstream tests, 145
downtime, 21
    (see also failures)
    designing for, 22

DRBD (Distributed Replicated Block Device) for Linux, 193
DREAD algorithm, 161
DSA or DSS algorithm, 171
durability, 16, 91
    considerations for recovery, 115
    in transactions, 220
    issues in Database as a Service (DBaaS), 96
dynamically built database users, 174
Dynamo-based datastores, 208, 214

E
education and collaboration
    in database security, 155
    in release management, 133-138
        collaboration, 137
        DBRE becoming a funnel, 134
        domain-specific knowledge, 135-137
        fostering conversations with software engineers, 134
efficiency (see cost and efficiency)
ElasticSearch, 57
    master and replica roles, 74
    non-uniform memory access (NUMA) and, 86
    security exploits against databases listening on Public IPs, 163
elevation of privilege (see privilege escalation)
elevator algorithm, 82
elimination of toil, 4
elliptic curve version of key exchange, 171
encapsulation, 142
encryption cyphers for SSL protocols, 171
encryption of data, 168-179
    checklist for, 179
    confidential/sensitive business data, 170
    data in the database, 174-177
        application-level security, 175
        plug-in encryption, 175
        query performance considerations, 176
        transparent database encryption, 176
    data in the filesystem, 177-179
        data ecryption above the filesystem, 178
        device-level encryption, 179
        filesystem encryption, 178
    data in transit, 171-174
        basic connection encryption, 173
        cipher suites, 171

communications outside the network, 173

communications within the network, 172

dynamically built database users, 174

securely stored secrets, 174

financial data, 169

military or government data, 170

personal health data, 169

private individual data, 170

environments, different, building, 117

ephemeral environmennts, distributed, trending to the norm, 52

ephemeral key exchanges, 171

ephemeral storage, 94, 183

production datastores on, 3

ephemeral user accounts, 174

error rates, 65

errors, 68

(see also utilization, saturation, and errors)

database and client logs, information on asserts and errors, 79

error correction code (ECC), 120

monitoring for datastore connection layer, 73

esteem (for databases), 9

Etcd, 110

event routers/processors, 57

event stores, 241

events, 60

event and message systems, 233-235

availability and, 234

data integrity and, 234

latency and, 235

scalability and, 235

event sourcing architectural pattern, 241

CQRS and, 242

in application monitoring, 68

logging for database hosts, 70

monitoring database asserts and events, 79

eventual consistency, 76, 126, 207

(see also consistency)

maintaining using anti-entropy, 208

exploitability, 162

exposure of data, protecting against, 155

information disclosure, 161

extract, transform, and load (ETL), 116, 194

processes for downstream datastores, 118

query-based ETL, 195

F

failovers, 7, 45

automated failover for MySQL, 45

database failovers, using service catalogs, 110

single leader, 197

failures

emphasizing resiliency over elimination of failure, 44

key questions about in evaluating a SLO for availability, 21

treated as normal scenario in resilient systems, 21

filesystems

checksumming to detect bad data, 120

encryption of data in, 177-179

data encryption above the file system, 178

device-level encryption, 179

filesystem encryption, 178

operations causing corruption and inconsistency, 92

financial data, encryption of, 169

five 9's, 15

fragmentation, memory allocation and, 83

framing, 42

frontend datastores, 229

frying, 103

fsync function call (OS), 91

hypervisors and, 94

full backups, 115, 129

full logical backups, 127

full physical backups, 126, 129

functional partitioning, 8, 196

functions (mathematical) applied to metrics, 59

G

Galois/Counter mode (GCM), 172

garbage collection, 20

downtime from, 25

gauges, metrics from, 59

globc's malloc, 83

government data, encryption of, 170

Graphite, 57

graphs

graph data model, 215

output from operational visualization platforms, 61

Gregg, Brendan, 68

group factors affecting risk assessment, 34
guardrails, building, 8
    Etsy's guardrails, 9
guest machine, 93

H

Hadoop, 40, 63
    THP defragmentation and, 84
hard disk drives (HDDs), 184
    failure rates, Google study on, 90
    I/O latency and, 90
    IOPs, 89
hardware
    errors from, 119
        early detection of, 124
    failures of, 120
        early detection, 124
harvest, 226
hash maps, 188
hashed MAC (HMAC), 172, 176
health checks
    excessive, 64
    in off-premises monitoring, 64
Health Insurance Portability and Accountability Act of 1996 (HIPAA), 170
hello bug (CAN-2002-1123), 168
hierarchy of needs, 7-11
    esteem, 9
    love and belonging, 8
    self-actualization, 10
    survival and safety, 7
high and low bounds, means, and cardinality of data, 78
high cardinality, 188
high resolution for key metrics, 54
hinted hand-offs, 208
histograms, 59
hit ratios for cached/uncached data in databases, 77
HMAC (hashed MAC), 172, 176
Honeycomb, 57
horizontal scaling, 8
horizontally separated infrastructure definitions, 108
host machine, 93
hosts, 81-92
    access to, 163
    operating a system and kernel, 82
        durability, 91

I/O scheduler, 82
    memory allocation and fragmentation, 83
    networks, 86
    non-uniform memory access, 85
    storage, 87
    storage availability, 90
    storage capacity, 88
    storage latency, 90
    storage throughput, 89
    swapping, 84
    user resource limits, 82
    physical servers, 81
        benefits of, 92
        cons of, 92
    shared OS/host model in containers, 95
    storage area networks (SANs), 92
human error and root cause of incidents, 50
human factors affecting risk assessment, 33
hypervisors, 93

I

I/O operations, storage latency and, 90
I/O schedulers (for database hosts), 82
idempotent actions, 102
identification of key failure points in a service, 44
identity spoofing, 160
images, 104
    creating multiple images from same configuration, using Packer, 112
    infrastructure images, detecting problems with, 124
    infrastructure images, testing, 109
immutable infrastructures, 104
impact analysis
    in deployment, 147
        data integrity issues, 147
        locking of objects, 147
        replication stalls, 147
        saturation of resources, 147
    in post-commit testing, 143
implementation of risk controls, 45
in-memory datastores, 235-238
incident management, 47
incremental backups, 115, 124, 129
    incremental logical backups, 127
    incremental physical backups, 126, 129
indexing, 78, 188

bitmap indexes, 188
hash indexes, 188
permutations of B-trees, 188
using B-tree structures, 183-185
indicators, 15
(see also service-level indicators)
InfluxDB, 57
information disclosure, 161
information secuity (IS) teams, 155
infrastructure as code, 100
infrastructure design and deployment, 250
infrastructure engineering, 81-97
containers, 95
Database as a Service (DBaaS), 95-97
hosts, 81-92
operating a system and kernel, 82
physical servers, 81
security, 156
virtualization, 93-95
concurrency, 94
hypervisors, 93
storage, 94
use cases, 94
infrastructure management, 99-112
acceptance testing and compliance, 109
building from configuration, 103
configuration definition, 101
development environments, 111
infrastructure definition and orchestration, 105-109
monolithic infrastructure definitions, 106
separated tiers (horizontal definitions), 108
separating vertically, 107
maintaining configuration, 104-105
service catalog, 109
using the concepts for MySQL, 110
version control, 100
infrastructure services
damages from, 119
detection and recovery from, 124
InnoDB storage engine, 75
(see also MySQL)
using mutexes/semaphores to monitor, 77
input validation, 167
instrumentation, 9
integration, 138-141
catching security vulnerabilities, 157

prerequisites for establishing CI at database level, 139
CI server and test framework, 141
database build automation, 140
database migrations and packaging, 140
test data, 140
version control system, 139
integration testing, 129
internode communications, 86
introspection, 9
inventory, systems and environment, 40
IOPS (input and output operations per second), 89
high IOPS with SSDs, 90
isolation (transactions), 217-220

J
Java Database Connectivity (JDBC), 231
Java Virtual Machines (JVMs), 20
use in databases for managing memory, 77
JBOD, 88, 91
jemalloc, 83
Jepsen testing framework, 141
journaling fileysystems, 92
journaling, monitoring for databases, 75

K
Kafka, 234
kappa architecture, 240
kernel, operating for database hosts, 82-86
key exchange algorithms, 171
key management infrastructure secure services, 174
key-value model, 214
keys for filesystem encryption, 178
killing long-running queries, 165

L
lambda architecture, 238
last write wins algorithm, 205
latency, 15
critical nature of, 18
impacts of caches and in-memory data-stores, 237
impacts of database proxies on, 233
impacts of event and message systems, 235
increases due to swapping, 84
indicators, 17-20

latency distributions, 18

low latency with single-leader replication, 194

minimizing, using single-leader replication for locality, 195

monitoring, 28, 65

monitoring for databases, 74

replication, 75

replication lag and, 199

SLO, sharers in, 24

storage, 90

throughput and, 16, 23

trade-offs with consistency, 225-226

versus response time, 16

laws, bodies, and standards regulating financial data in the U.S., 169

layers (OSI model), 231

leaders (in replication), 189

leap seconds, 205

LevelDB, 185

Linux systems

Distributed Replicated Block Device (DRBD), 193

filesystem encryption, 178

I/O scheduler, 82

nodes, 85

page cache, storage latency and, 90

resources to monitor, 69

storage stack, 87

swapping, 84

Transparent Huge Pages memory management system, 83

understanding, importance of, 69

load shedding, 233

local or single-node scope, recovery in, 121

local storage in virtualized environments, 94

locality

use of single-leader replication for, 195

using multi-leader replication for, 203

locking (database), 22

2-phase locking (2PL), 219

locking of objects in database migrations, 147

locking operations during migrations, 148

monitoring locking and concurrency, 77

log-structured merge (LSM) trees with SSTables, 185-187

datastores that utilize as storage engines, 187

logical backups, 114

full and incremental, 127

logical replication, 193

logs, 60, 189

application, 68

capturing errors for datastore connection layer, 73

for database hosts, 70

replication log formats in single-leader replication, 191

statement-based logs, 191

write-ahead logs, 192

using to mitigate DoS attacks, 166

love and belonging needs, 8

M

MAC (see message authentication code; HMAC)

major impact risks (imminent SLO violation), 42

malloc libraries, 83

manual database changes, 4

Maslow, Abraham, 7

master/replica setup for databases, 52, 74

mathematical functions applied to metrics, 59

mean time between failures (MBTF), 21

mean time to recover (MTTR), 21

emphasizing over MTBF, 44

reducing with immutable infrastructure, 105

replication and, 194

memory

caches and memory stores, 235-238

memory allocation and fragmentation, 83

non-uniform memory access, 85

swapping and, 84

memory contexts (PostgreSQL), 83

memory structures (in datastores), 76

memtables, 75, 185, 186

Merkle trees, 209

message authentication code (MAC), 172

HMAC, 176

message systems, 233-235

metadata

for data blocks, 182

testing in database integration, 140

metrics, 59

central collector for, 57

collecting too many, 55

DBRE and the architectural process, 247
focusing, 56
from application monitoring, 66
monitoring between database, system, storage, and application layers, 62
throughput and latency, for datastores, 74
MHA-managed MySQL cluster, 110
migrations, 249
    and versioning, 146
    impact analysis on production service, 147
    patterns in, 148-151
        allowing for automatic deployment, 151
        high resource utilization operations, 149
        locking operations, 148
        migration testing, 150
        rollback testing, 150
        rolling migrations, 150
military data, encryption of, 170
minimum viable monitoring set, 62
minor impact risks, 42
mission-critical data, replication of, 63
moderate impact risks, 42
MongoDB, 63
    connections, use of resources on operating system, 72
    master and replica roles, 74
    memory allocation libraries, 83
    non-uniform memory access (NUMA) and, 86
    security exploits against databases listening on Public IPs, 163
monitoring
    alerts on reaching threshold of downtime, 25
    bootstrapping, 61-66
        availability monitors, 64
        common progression, 62
        customer experience, anything that disrupts, 65
        data safety, 63
    characteristics of traditional monitoring systems, 51
    Database as a Service (DBaaS) and, 96
    for node or component failure requiring recovery to new nodes, 128
    for SQL injection attacks, 168
    of availability, 25
    of cost and efficiency, 28
    of latency, 28

of single-leader replication, 198
    operational processes, 202
    replication availability and capacity, 200
    replication consistency, 201
    replication lag and latency, 199
of throughput, 28
testing, using Chaos Monkey, 117
to identify DoS attacks, 166
top goal for service-level management, 25
monitoring services, third-party, 63
monolithic infrastructure definitions, 106
multi-leader replication, 203-209
    conflict resolution in, 204
        custom options for, 206
        last write wins, 205
    use cases, 203
        availability, 203
        disaster recovery, 204
        locality, 203
    write-anywhere replication, 206
multiple object scope for recovery, 121
multiversion concurrency control (MVCC), 219
mutexes, 77
MySQL, 63
    connections, use of resources on operating system, 72
    frying up a Galera Cluster, 103
    InnoDB storage engine
        block overhead, 183
        memory allocation library, 83
    master and replica roles, 74
    NUMA and, resolving at Twitter, 85
    statement-based replication, 192
    THP defragmentation and, 84
    using infrastructure concepts for, 110
    using mutexes/semaphores to monitor InnoDB storage engine, 77

N

Nagios, 57
navigational model, 215
network interface cards (NICs), 87
Network Time Protocol (NTP), 101, 199
    Database as a Service (DBaaS) and, 96
    timestamps and, 205
networks
    access to, 163
    communications outside, encryption of, 173

communications within, encryption of, 172
database performance and availability and, 86
security vulnerabilities in network and authentication protocols, 168
New Relic, 57
nodes
    in Linux systems, 85
    new production nodes, building, 117
    replacing failed nodes and introducing new nodes, 128
non-uniform memory access (NUMA), 85
    solving NUMA and MySQL at Twitter, 85
nondeterministic statements, 192
nonrepeatable reads, 218
noop scheduler (Linux), 82
normalization, 213
NoSQL datastores, 207
notifications
    from operational visibility platforms, 61
    testing, using Chaos Monkey, 117
NTP (see Network Time Protocol)
NUMA (see non-uniforrm memory access)

O

object storage, 125, 131
object stores, 127
object-relational mappers (ORMs), 213, 231
    SQL dynamically generated for, 66
object-relational mapping (ORM), 213
objects, locking, 147
observability, 9
off-premises monitoring, 64
offline storage, 125, 130
OnLine Analytics Processing (OLAP), 230
OnLine Transactional Processing (OLTP) systems, 230
online versus offline backups, 114
online, fast storage with full and incremental backups (recovery strategy), 128
online, high performance storage, 124
online, low-performance storage, 125
online, slow storage with full and incremental backups (recovery strategy), 129
Open Systems Interconnection (OSI) model, 231
OpenSSL, 175
operating systems

datastore connections opening resources on, 72
errors from, 119
    early detection of, 124
instrumentation of, 159
shared OS/host model in containers, 95
understanding, importance of, 69
operational processes, monitoring for single-leader replication, 202
operational tests, 145
    in planned recovery scenario, 118
operational visibility, 49-80
    bootstrapping your monitoring process, 61-66
    data in, 57-60
        events, 60
        logs, 60
        telemetry/metrics, 59
    data out, 60
    Database as a Service (DBaaS) and, 96
    database asserts and events, 79
    database objects, 78
    database queries, 79
    framework for, 56
    in database security, 158-160
        application layer instrumentation, 158
        database layer instrumentation, 159
        OS instrumentation, 159
    instrumenting the application, 66-68
    instrumenting the datastore, 71
    instrumenting the server or instance, 68-71
    internal database visibility, 74-78
        commits, redos, and journaling, 75
        locking and concurrency, 77
        memory structures, 76
        replication state, 75
        throughput and latency metrics, 74
    new rules, 51-56
        distributed ephemeral environments trending to the norm, 52
        keep your architecture simple, 55
        store at high resolutions for key metrics, 54
        treating OpViz systes like BI systems, 52
    planned recovery operations, 116
operations
    and software development, eliminating barriers between, 5
    core overview, 6

optimistic replication, 206
OpViz (see operational visibility)
Oracle
    storage of data in data blocks, 182
    THP defragmentation and, 84
ordering-latency trade-off, 226
outputs from operational visibility platform, 57, 60

P

Packer, 104, 112
page table entries, 83
page tables, 83
pager fatigue, 34
pages (memory allocation), 83, 182
    Transparent Huge Pages (THPs) in Linux, 83
parameterized statements, 167
partition tolerance (CAP theorem), 224
patching
    of database binaries to reduce exploitable bugs, 167
    security patches, keeping up to date, 163
PCIe bus flash solutions, 89
perfect forward secrecy (PFS), 171
persistent block storage in virtualized environments, 94
personally identifiable information (PII)
    audit data on, 158
    encryption of, 170
Pester for Windows, 141
pets versus cattle metaphor, 5
phantom reads, 218
physical backups, 114
    full, 126
    incremental physical backups, 126
physical servers
    as database hosts, 81
    benefits of, 92
pipeline processes for downstream datastores, 118
planned recovery scenarios, 116
    building different environments, 117
    ETL and pipeline processes for downstream datastores, 118
    new production nodes and clusters, 117
    operational tests, 118
plug-in encryption, 175
portability

use of single-leader replication for, 195
    with large datasets, 196
POSIX days, 205
post-build testing, 143
post-commit testing, 143
PostgreSQL
    connections, use of resources on operating system, 72
    master and replica roles, 74
    memory allocation library, 83
    non-uniform memory access (NUMA) and, 86
    troubleshooting connection speeds for, 73
pre-build testing, 143
predictive analytics
    for availability data, 26
    for latency data, 28
preferred node, 85
prepared statements, 167
primary timeout retry trade-off, 226
prioritization of risks, 41
Privacy Act of 1974, 170
private individual data, encryption of, 170
privilege escalation, 161, 166, 168
product development, workload shifts due to, 26
production migrations, 249
production nodes and clusters, building new, 117
protecting the data, 2
    new approach to, 3
proxies (see database proxies)
Puppet, 101

Q

quality of service quotas, making DoS attacks more difficult, 165
queries
    monitoring database queries, 79
    perfomance considerations querying encrypted data, 176
query killers and heavy-handed approaches to reducing DoS attacks, 165
queueing theory, 57
quorums, 207
    sloppy, 208

R

RAID 0, 88

RAID levels, 91
random IOPs, 89
read and write quorums, 207
    sloppy quorums, 208
read committed isolation level, 218
read failures (datastores), 44
read repair, 208
read uncommitted isolation level, 218
reader timeout retry trade-off, 226
reads
    dirty, 218
    nonrepeatable, 218
    phantom, 218
real user monitoring (RUM), 26
recovery, 115-132
    advantages of an immutable infrastructure,
        105
    anatomy of a recovery strategy, 122-128
        building block 1, detection, 122
        building block 2, tiered storage, 124
        building block 3, varied toolbox, 125
        building block 4, testing, 127
    considerations for, 115
    data integrity and recoverability, 252
    defined recovery strategy, 128
        object storage, 131
        offline storage, 130
        online, fast storage with full and incre-
            mental backups, 128
        online, slow storage with full and incre-
            mental backups, 129
    disaster recovery, using multi-leader replica-
        tion, 204
    scenarios for, 116-122
        planned recovery, 116
        scenario impact, 121
        scenario scope, 121
        unplanned scenarios, 118
    testing success of restores, 118
Redis
    memory allocation library, 83
    non-uniform memory access (NUMA) and,
        86
    SSL and, 173
redo logs, 192
redos, monitoring for databases, 75
reductive bias, 32
relational model, 212
    object relational mapping (ORM) layer, 213

release management, 133-152
    deployment, 146-151
        impact analysis, 147
        manual or automated, 151
        migration patterns, 148-151
        migrations and versioning, 146
    education and collaboration, 133-138
    integration, 138-141
    testing, 141-146
        downstream tests, 145
        full dataset testing, 144
        operational tests, 145
        post-commit testing, 143
        test-friendly development practices, 142
reliability engineers, 1
remote desk protocol (RDP), 170
repeatable reads isolation level, 218
replica lag, 196
replicas
    building, in single-leader replication, 196
    keeping synchronized, in single-leader rep-
        lication, 196
replication, 7, 189-209, 225
    backups and, 126
    failures of, in datastores, 44
    for mission-critical data, 63
    issues in Database as a Service (DBaaS), 96
    monitoring replication state in databases, 75
    multi leader, 203-209
        conflict resolution in, 204
        use cases, 203
        write-anywhere replication, 206
    replication stalls caused by database
        changes, 147
    row-based versus statement-based, 114
    safety checks in monitoring, 64
    single leader, 190-203
        block-level replication, 193
        challenges in, 195
        monitoring, 198-203
        replication log formats, 191
        replication models, 190
        row-based replication, 193
        statement-based logs, 191
        uses of, 194
        write-ahead logs, 192
reproducibility (exploits), 161
repudiation, 161
resiliency

robusness versus, in availability, 21

striving for resilience in handling risks, 35

traits of resilient systems, 21

resource management and load shedding to mitigate DoS attacks, 165

response time versus latency, 16

Riak, 74

last write wins, 205

risk analysis and prioritization (DREAD), 161

risk assessment

considerations, 32

availability of resources, 33

group factors, 34

human factors, 33

unknown factors and complexity, 32

risk elimination, 45

risk management, 31-48

bootstrapping a working process, 37-46

architectural inventory, 40

control and decision making, 43

prioritization of risks, 41

service risk evaluation, 38

ongoing iterations of the process, 46

what not to do, 35

risk mitigation, 45

Robot for Linux, 141

robustness versus resiliency (in availability), 21

RocksDB, 185

rollbacks

failure of migrations/deploys, 150

monitoring, 77

rolling migrations, 150

rolling upgrades, 22, 150

rows

database row storage, 182-185

row-based replication, 193

RSA algorithm, 171

RUM (real user monitoring), 26

S

safety of data, monitoring, 63

SaltStack, 101

SANs (see storage area networks)

saturation (see utilization, saturation, and errors)

scalability, 8

impacts of caches and in-memory data-stores, 237

impacts of event and message systems, 235

improving with database proxies, 232

single-leader replication and, 195

scaling

patterns of, 8

premature, 8

scaling out (see horizontal scaling)

scaling up (see vertical scaling)

secret management services, 174

security, 153-180

database security as a function, 155-160

education and collaboration, 155

integration and testing, 157

operational visibility, 158-160

self-service approaches, 156

encryption of data, 168-179

confidential/sensitive business data, 170

data in the database, 174-177

data in the filesystem, 177-179

data in transit, 171-174

financial data, 169

military or government data, 170

personal health data, 169

private individual data, 170

new attack vectors, 153

purpose of, 153-155

compliance and auditing standards, 155

protecting data from exposure, 155

protecting data from theft, 154

protecting from accidental damage, 154

protecting from purposeful damage, 154

safety of data, 7

vulnerabilities and exploits, 160-168

basic precautions against, 162

denial of service (DoS), 163-166

DREAD algorithm, 161

network and authentication protocols, 168

SQL injection, 166-168

STRIDE classification for known threats, 160

self-actualization (for databases), 10

self-service for scale, 3

semantic names, 109

semaphores, 77

semi-synchronous availability-latency trade-off, 226

semi-synchronous replication, 191

Sensu, 57

sequential IOPs, 89

serial snapshot isolation (SSI), 219
serializable isolation level, 219
    variability in implementations of, 220
serverless computing models
    data integrity and, 120
    operational expertise and, 7
servers
    instrumenting the server or instance, 68-71
    physical servers as database hosts, 81
        (see also hosts)
ServerSpec, 109
service catalog, 109
service delivery reviews, 47
service discovery, 109
service discovery tools, 109
service issues, 17
service risk evaluation, 38
service-level agreements (see SLAs)
service-level indicators, 15
    availability, 16
    cost or efficiency, 16
    durability, 16
    latency, 15
    throughput, 16
service-level management, 13-29
    defining service objectives, 17-24
    monitoring and reporting on SLOs, 25-29
    need for SLOs, 13
service-level objectives (see SLOs)
severe impact risks (immediate SLO violation),
    41
SHA-256, 172
sharding, 8, 79, 196, 196
    using infrastructure management concepts
        for, 110
    using service catalog for, 110
signal from noise, sorting, 58
single-leader replication, 190-203
    block-level replication, 193
    challenges in, 195
        building replicas, 196
        keeping replicas synchronized, 196
        single leader failovers, 197
    monitoring, 198
        operational processes, 202
        replication availability and capacity, 200
        replication consistency, 201
        replication lag and latency, 199
    other methods, 194

replication models, 190
    row-based replication, 193
    statement-based logs, 191
    uses of, 194
        availability, 194
        locality, 195
        portability, 195
        scalability, 195
    write-ahead logs, 192
single-object scope for recovery, 121
site reliability engineers (SREs), 3
size (backups), compressed and uncompressed,
    117
SLAs (service-level agreements), 13
    calibrating recovery processes to meet, 127
sloppy quorums, 208
SLOs (service-level objectives), 13
    considerations for recovery, 115
    defining, 17-24
        additional considerations, 24
        availability indicators, 20
        latency indicators, 17-20
        throughput indicators, 23
    defining for cost or efficiency, 17
    focusing on metrics directly related to, 56
    monitoring and reporting on, 25-29
        availability, 25
        cost and efficiency, 28
        latency, 28
        throughput, 28
    recovery scenario impacts on, 122
snapshot isolation, 219
    serial snapshot isolation (SSI), 219
soft deletes, 149
software and operations, eliminating barriers
    between, 5
software engineering, 6
    making your data a first-class citizen in, 8
software engineers
    collaboration with DBREs in release man-
        agement, 137
    creating active dialogue and interactions
        with, 134
    educating about datastores, 133
    educating and collaborating with in data-
        base security, 156
    necessity of learning operations, 6
solid-state drives (SSDs), 184
    I/O latency and, 90

I/O scheduling, 82
IOPs, 89
sorted string tables (SSTs) and log-structured
    merge trees, 185-187
    datastores using as storage engine, 187
Speed Matters, 18
spike erosion, 18
spoofing identity, 160
SQL (Structured Query Language)
    tracking SQL calls, 66
    traditional SQL analysis, 67
SQL injection attacks, 166-168
    identifying, 158
    mitigation, 167
        harm reduction, 167
        using input validation, 167
        using prepared statements, 167
    monitoring for, 168
    vulnerability to, 158
SSH2, 170
SSL (Secure Sockets Layer), 170
    evaluating database implementation of, 172
SSL/TLS
    for communications outside the network,
        173
    OpenSSL, 175
    support by modern database systems, 173
SSTables, 75, 185
standardization, 56
    and use of physical servers as database
        hosts, 92
    databases as commodity service compo-
        nents, 5
    elimination of toil through, 4
statement-based logs, 191
steal time, monitoring, 70
storage, 87, 181, 222
    data structure storage, 181-189
        database row storage, 182-185
        indexing, 188
        logs and databases, 189
        sorted-string tables and log-structured
            merge trees, 185-187
    in tiers, 247
    in virtualized environments, 94
    major demands or objectives for, 88
    object storage recovery strategy, 131
    object stores, 127
    storage availability, 90

storage capacity, 88
storage latency, 90
storage throughput, 89
tiered storage in a recovery strategy, 124
    object storage, 125
    offline storage, 125, 130
    online, fast storage, 128
    online, high performance storage, 124
    online, low-performance storage, 125
    online, slow storage, 129
storage area networks (SANs), 92
storage engines, 222
    datastores utilizing LSM structure with
        SSTables as, 187
stored code, attack vector using SQL injection,
    166
stored procedures, 142
STRIDE, 160
Structured Query Language (see SQL; SQL
    injection attacks)
summaries, metrics stored in, 59
survival and safety needs (databases), 7
swapping, 84
    disabling, 85
symmetric multiprocessing (SMP), 85
synchronization of configuration, 105
synchronous replication models, 191
synchronous replication-latency trade-off, 226
synthetic monitoring, 27
system engineering, 6

T
tampering with data, 161
tcmalloc, 83
TCP/IP, tuning for databases, 87
telemetry/metrics, 59
Terraform, 107
    using with MySQL, 110
test-driven development (TDD), 109
testing
    acceptance testing and compliance for infra-
        structure, 109
    building test environments for feature inte-
        gration and operations testing, 128
    building test environments for operations
        testing, 129
    configurations, 103
    in a recovery strategy, 127
    in object storage recovery strategy, 131

in release management, 142-146
   downstream tests, 145
   full dataset testing, 144
   operational tests, 145
   post-commit testing, 143
   test-friendly development practices, 142
integration and testing, catching security
   vulnerabilities, 157
migration, 150
operational tests in planned recovery scenario, 118
rollbacks of partial or full changesets, 150
test data for database integration, 140
testing frameworks, 141
theft of data, protecting against, 154
throughput
   assessing in planned recovery scenario, 117
   defined, 16
   indicators, 23
   monitoring, 28
   monitoring for databases, 74
   storage, 89
tickets and tasks, 61
time (for planned recovery processes), 117
timeouts, 226
timestamps
   in last write wins, 205
   issues with, 205
TLS (Transport Layer Security), 170
toil, 4
tombstones, 186
tools
   giving to software engineers for develop-
      ment process, 137
   varied toolbox for recovery, 125
tracing, distributed tracing of performance, 66
transactions, 216-221
   ACID, 216
      atomicity, 216
      consistency, 217
      durability, 220
      isolation, 217-220
   functioning as events, 233
translation lookaside buffers (TLBs), 83
Transparent Huge Pages (THP), 83
Transport Layer Security (TLS), 170
triggers
   causing a statement to be nondeterministic,
      192

use for replication, 194, 195
2-phase locking (2PL), 219

U
unplanned recovery scenarios, 118
   resulting from application errors, 119
   resulting from datacenter failures, 120
   resulting from hardware failures, 120
   resulting from OS and hardware errors, 119
   resulting from user error, 119
UPDATE statement without a WHERE clause,
   119
user errors, 119, 129, 131
   detection and recovery from, 123
user resource limits (for database hosts), 82
user-centric approach to SLOs, 24
users
   dynamically built database users, 174
   removing unnecessary users, 163
utilization, saturation, and errors, 68
   for aggregate hosts on a distributed system,
      69
   high resource utilization operations during
      migrations, 149
   monitoring for datastore connection layer,
      71
      saturation, 72
   saturation of resources during database
      deployment, 147
   USE page for Linux, 70
   utilization for database memory structures,
      76

V
version control, 100
version control systems (VCS), 100
   prerequisite for continuous integration of
      databases, 139
versioning, migrations and, 146
vertical scaling, 8
vertically separated infrastructure definitions,
   107
virtual infrastructures, database instance lifecy-
   cles and, 52
virtual machine monitors (VMMs) (see hypervisors)
virtual machines (VMs), 93
   containers versus, 95

images for, downloading and building with
    Vagrant, 112
virtualization, 93-95
    concurrency, 94
    database clusters, configuration standards,
        93
    hypervisors, 93
    storage in virtualized environments, 94
    use cases for database infrastructure, 94
virtualized systems, 3
    monitoring, 70
    testing in a defined recovery strategy, 129
visibility (see operational visibility)
visualizations, output from OpViz, 59, 61
Vivid Cortex, 79
vulnerabilities, 160-168
    basic precautions against, 162
    common vulnerabilities and exposures
        (CVEs), 156
    denial of service (DoS) attacks, 163-166
    DREAD classification algorithm, 161
    in network and authentication protocols,
        168
    SQL injection, 166-168
    STRIDE classification for known threats,
        160

W

WHERE clause (DELETE and UPDATE state-
    ments), absence of, 119

whitebox monitoring, 57
whitebox testing, 57
write-ahead logs, 192, 220
write-anywhere replication, 206
    anti-entropy, 208
    eventual consistency, 207
    read and write quorums, 207
    sloppy quorums, 208
write-through approach, 236
writes
    conflict resolution in multidirectional repli-
        cation, 204
    conflict-free replicated datatypes, 206
    custom options for, 206
    eliminating conflicts, 204
    last write wins, 205
    write failures, evaluation of, 45

Y

yield, 226

Z

Zipkin, 66
Zookeeper, 110

About the Authors

Laine Campbell works as Senior Director of Production Engineering at Fastly. She was also founder and CEO of PalominoDB/Blackbird, a consultancy servicing the database needs of a number of companies, including Obama for America, Activision Call of Duty, Adobe Echosign, Technorati, Livejournal, and Zendesk. She has 18 years of production experience, running databases and distributed systems at scale.

Charity Majors works as the CEO/cofounder of honeycomb.io. Honeycomb combines the raw accuracy of log aggregators, the speed of time series metrics, and the flexibility of APM (application performance metrics) to provide the world's first truly next-generation analytics service. She previously ran operations at Parse/Facebook, managing a massive fleet of MongoDB replica sets as well as Redis, Cassandra, and MySQL. She also worked closely with the RocksDB team at Facebook to develop and roll out the world's first Mongo+Rocks deployment using the pluggable storage engine API.

Colophon

The animal on the cover of *Database Reliability Engineering* is a Suffolk punch, also known as a Suffolk horse or Suffolk sorrel. This English breed of draught horse is always chestnut in color and has an energetic gait.

The Suffolk punch was developed in the 16th century for farm work. Though the breed gained popularity in the early 20th century, it fell out of favor in the middle part of the century because of the mechanization of agriculture. Suffolk punches are around 65 to 70 inches tall and weigh around 2,000 pounds; they are shorter but more massive than other British draught breeds such as Clydesdales or Shires.

Many of the animals on O'Reilly covers are endangered; all of them are important to the world. To learn more about how you can help, go to *animals.oreilly.com*.

The cover image is from the Museum of British Quadrapeds. The cover fonts are URW Typewriter and Guardian Sans. The text font is Adobe Minion Pro; the heading font is Adobe Myriad Condensed; and the code font is Dalton Maag's Ubuntu Mono.

Learn from experts.
Find the answers you need.

Sign up for a **10-day free trial** to get **unlimited access** to all of the content on Safari, including Learning Paths, interactive tutorials, and curated playlists that draw from thousands of ebooks and training videos on a wide range of topics, including data, design, DevOps, management, business—and much more.

Start your free trial at:

oreilly.com/safari

(No credit card required.)

Milton Keynes UK
Ingram Content Group UK Ltd.
UKHW010906050924
447865UK00004BA/9

9 781491 925942